Iconoclastic Controversies

A photographic inquiry into antagonistic nationalism

First published in the UK in 2021 by Intellect, The Mill, Parnall Road, Fishponds, Bristol, BS16 3JG, UK

First published in the USA in 2021 by Intellect, The University of Chicago Press, 1427 E. 60th Street, Chicago, IL 60637, USA

A catalogue record for this book is available from the British Library.

Cover image: Nico Carpentier, 2014

Copy editor: Newgen KnowledgeWorks
Cover designer: Aleksandra Szumlas
Production managers: Jelena Stanovnik, Mareike Wehner
Typesetter: Newgen KnowledgeWorks

Print ISBN 978-1-78938-455-0
ePDF ISBN 978-1-78938-456-7
ePub ISBN 978-1-78938-457-4

Printed and bound by Gomer, UK.

To find out about all our publications, please visit www.intellectbooks.com.
There you can subscribe to our e-newsletter, browse or download our current catalogue, and buy any titles that are in print.

Iconoclastic Controversies

A photographic inquiry into antagonistic nationalism

Nico Carpentier

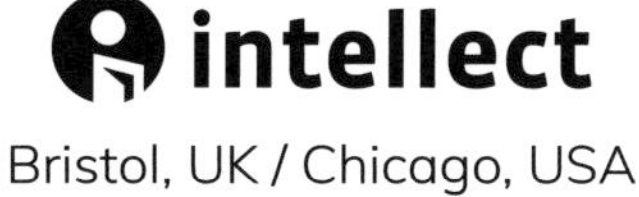

Bristol, UK / Chicago, USA

Earlier Publications

This book republishes material from the following earlier publications:

Carpentier, Nico (2017), *The Discursive-Material Knot: Cyprus in Conflict and Community Media Participation* (a selection of chapter 3), New York: Peter Lang.
Carpentier, Nico (2018a), "Deconstructing nationalist assemblages: A visual essay on the Greek Cypriot memorials related to two violent conflicts in 20th century Cyprus," *Comunicazioni sociali*, 1, pp. 33–49.
Carpentier, Nico (2018b), "Iconoclastic Controversy in Cyprus: The problematic rethinking of a conflicted past," in Vaia Doudaki and Nico Carpentier (eds), *Cyprus and Its Conflicts: Representations, Materialities and Cultures*, New York: Berghahn, pp. 25–54.
Carpentier, Nico (2020), "Communicating academic knowledge beyond the written academic text: An autoethnographic analysis of the mirror palace of democracy installation experiment," *International Journal of Communication*, 14, pp. 2120–43.
Carpentier, Nico, Doudaki, Vaia, Christidis, Yiannis, Köksal and Fatma Nazli (2018), "De-naturalizing antagonistic nationalism through an academic intervention: The reception of two photography exhibitions on the memorialization of the Cyprus Problem," *Comunicazioni Sociali*, 1, pp. 50–67.

Moreover, this book also contains transcripts of interviews by Eva Giannoukou (for the IC website), Yiannis Christidis (for CUT-Radio) and Fernando Paulino (for UnBTV); of the film *Nico Carpentier: The Art and Science of Peace* by Fernando Molina; and of the lyrics of songs by Monsieur Doumani and Julio (feat. Stelios Pellaras). It also features a traditional Cypriot song. Some of the photographs documenting the events were made by Yiannis Christidis, Vaia Doudaki, Jairo Faria and Yiannis Colakides. The *Iconoclastic Controversies* posters were designed by, or in collaboration with, AHDR & Eva Giannoukou, NeMe and the Faculty of Communication of the University of Brasilia.

Every effort has been made to trace the copyright holders and obtain permission to reproduce this material. I wish to thank all publishers, authors and interviewers for their kind permission to reproduce this material in this book. Please do get in touch with the author for any enquiries or any information relating to the material in this book.

Contents

Illustrations

Chapter 1: An Introduction to Iconoclastic Controversies

ICONOCLASTIC CONTROVERSIES AND ITS MULTIPLE AIMS

The Iconoclastic Controversies project is a research project with multiple aims and focal points. First, as a research project, Iconoclastic Controversies enquires into the relationship of memorials and commemoration sites with antagonistic nationalism. Memorials and commemoration sites are material structures that invoke a particular past, and invite to remember it, in evenly particular ways. They are interventions located on the intersection of the spatial and the political, which use space to articulate what is deemed important to be remembered by collectivities (and what not) and how it should be remembered (and how not). Memorials and commemoration sites aim to impact on what has been termed "collective memory" (see, e.g. Halbwachs 1980, 1992), which implies that they are deeply implicated with the discursive, by invoking discourses, condensing them into matter, communicating them and (potentially) contributing to their hegemonic ambitions.

Of course, memorials and commemoration sites relate to an immense variety of persons, events and processes, as existing overviews and typologies (e.g. Ragsdale and Brandau-Brown 2011) abundantly demonstrate, which also implies that these memorials and commemoration sites are aligned with a variety of discourses. The Iconoclastic Controversies project was interested in one particular discourse, namely the discourse of antagonistic nationalism, as it was articulated in the context of the armed conflicts of twentieth-century Cyprus. By analysing the Cypriot war memorials and commemoration sites, in particular those located in the south of the island, I want to show the role that these material objects play in sustaining a particular discursive hegemony, which revolves around the nationalist definition of the Greek Cypriot community as a unified community, through its heroism, sacrifice and victimhood.

Public art, and the visibility that is attached to it, gives this discourse a material presence in the southern Cypriot landscape – through what Abousnnouga and Machin (2013: 218) call the mobilization of particular "material semiotic resources" – so that these statues are permanently and literally waiting to support, advocate and reinforce this hegemonic discourse. But no discourse is safe from internal contradictions, and from possible reinterpretations and resistances, and the Iconoclastic Controversies project has been evenly interested in studying how the hegemonic ambitions of memorials were dislocated, by material and/or signifying practices, but also how memorials with counter-hegemonic ambitions existed, challenging the nationalist hegemonies. It is this struggle that inspired the name of the entire project, Iconoclastic Controversies.

Even if the Iconoclastic Controversies research project is located in Cyprus (and a significant part of the written texts deal with the Cyprus Problem), its relevance is not restricted to Cyprus. Even if this book does not wish to discredit all forms of nationalism, the analysis of the violent conflicts in Cyprus that have been driven by *antagonist* nationalism demonstrates the harm that nationalism – which is a global phenomenon – can do. Moreover, the Iconoclastic Controversies research project reflects on how a hegemonic nationalist discourse also has a material component, where the celebration of a heroic national identity is encoded in stone or bronze. Simultaneously, it shows the limits of this hegemonic force, how resistance (and counter-hegemony) emerges from the ways these memorials are ignored in everyday life and how some memorials that question this nationalist hegemony have been erected.

This brings us to the second aim of Iconoclastic Controversies, which is to contribute to the more general discussions about the relationship between the discursive and the material, as theorized in an earlier publication, the *Discursive-Material Knot* (Carpentier 2017). Discourses are the structures of our minds and are needed to think our world. Used here in a macro-(con)textual definition (see Carpentier 2017: 15ff), discourse is defined as a framework of intelligibility. Discourses are thus more than language: they are the vital structures of meaning behind language. As two key authors in the field of discourse theory, Ernesto Laclau and Chantal Mouffe, wrote in their 1985 book *Hegemony and Socialist Struggle*, whether an earthquake is seen as the wrath of god, or as a natural phenomenon, depends on the integration of this event within a particular discursive framework. The necessity of discourse to make sense of our worlds does not imply that these discourses are stable, though. On the contrary, discourses are always debated, contested and resisted. But sometimes discourses become dominant – or hegemonic – which means that it has become difficult to think outside the horizon they create.

However fascinating this discourse-theoretical perspective is, questions are still to be raised about the role of the material. Is the material a mere object of the meaning-making capacities of the discursive, or does the materiality of the material also play a role? The discursive-material knot approach used in the Iconoclastic Controversies research project (which has reciprocally assisted in the development of this theory of entanglement) argues for a non-hierarchical ontology of the discursive and the material, where the discursive has the capacity to signify but the material has the agency to invite – through its materiality – for particular meanings to be allocated, and where the material also has the agency to dislocate existing discourses through events that escape signification and thus disrupt discourses that promise to provide for that signification. These discursive-material elements intersect and interact continuously, in assemblages that are always particular articulations of signifying practices and materials. For instance, the statue of a Greek Cypriot independence fighter that is featured in one of the photos in this book is an assemblage that combines a brass figure that resembles a particular human body and that is seen holding a machine gun. The pose invites for discourses on heroism, masculinity and leadership to be articulated into the assemblage. The central position of the statue, in one of the main squares of the city of Limassol, invites to think of the person that is represented, Grigoris Afxentiou, as important. The text on the front of the soccle, "ΜΟΛΩΝ ΛΑΒΕ" and "1955–1959," invokes a historical discourse that articulates the defiance of the Spartan king Leonidas before the battle of Thermopylae in 480 BC, who (according to Plutarch) was asked by the Persian king Xerxes I to surrender his weapons and replied, "Come and take [them]," with the last stand of Afxentiou, who had quoted Leonidas before being burned alive by British soldiers in his own last stand in 1957, as part of the *Ethniki Organosis Kyprion Agoniston*, or the National Organization of Cypriot Fighters (EOKA) uprising.

The third aim of the Iconoclastic Controversies project is to bring a more critical and interventionist approach to the analysis, by deconstructing and de-naturalizing the Greek Cypriot hegemonic antagonistic-nationalist discourse and the material support that is provided by the majority of the memorials and commemoration sites in the south of Cyprus. Three de-naturalization strategies were used through the Iconoclastic Controversies photographs. The first strategy was to place the (photographs of) the memorials that are spatially dispersed (all over the south of Cyprus), in one and the same location (and now in one publication), which allowed/allows to demonstrate their strong similarities. This, in turn, made it clear that they were particular in inviting identification with a particular discourse, namely antagonistic nationalism. In some cases, humour was used to magnify the repetitive nature of particular tropes. Second, the photographs also represented the contradictions between the memorials' invitations and their everyday life usages, contrasting the demand for respect with the obliviousness they are subjected to. And third, the exhibition also included a series of photographs of memorials that extended alternative or counter-hegemonic invitations, demonstrating the discursive-material struggle that was going on in Cyprus and the diversity of positions that could be taken.

Finally, the Iconoclastic Controversies research project also aims to rethink the ways that academics communicate their research outcomes, moving away from an exclusive emphasis on the written text. Moreover, the research project demonstrates how academic communicational practices – written and non-written – are not outside knowledge production processes and cannot be confined to a second, disconnected stage. In contrast, academic communicational practices can be seen to form an integrated part of knowledge production.

Without neglecting (the importance of) the written text, the Iconoclastic Controversies project strongly depended on the use of two other communicative modes, namely photography and exhibition. This book, with a combination of written texts and photographs that featured in the three exhibitions that were organized between 2015 and 2018, is very much part of this endeavour, together with a series of visual essays[1] that were published earlier (Carpentier 2014, 2018a, 2018b). It is important to emphasize that Iconoclastic Controversies remains an academic research project, driven by the basic principles of academic research, for example, paradigmatic and theoretical embeddedness, methodological rigour and systematicity, radical ethical sensitivity, integrity and independence. But at the same time, inspired by visual sociology, arts-based research and multimodal academic communication, the Iconoclastic Controversies research project proudly uses less traditional narrative structures to convey academic research outcomes (and to produce new ones).

These multiple project aims turn this book into a hybrid signifying practice in its own right. This book aims to first argue and then demonstrate the capacity of arts-based research to convey and produce academic knowledge. This is why it can be read as an invitation to scholars in the field of Communication and Media Studies and beyond, to experiment more with these non-written academic communicational practices. The book's affiliation with arts-based research also brings out an emphasis on aesthetics, through the book's photography and design, which foregrounds the affective dimension of knowledge. In other words, this book not only aims to provide an understanding of – and critique on – the workings of antagonistic nationalism but simultaneously offers an opportunity to experience and to feel this analysis and this critique. The book is thus driven by the integration of rational and affective argumentation and by the articulation of analysis, contextualization and critique.

THREE ICONOCLASTIC CONTROVERSIES PHOTOGRAPHY EXHIBITIONS

The book is centred around a series of photographs that have been displayed at three exhibitions. These *Iconoclastic Controversies* photography exhibitions, which played a significant role in the analysis of Cypriot nationalism and in the creation of this book, were organized in November 2015, in January/February 2016 and in September/October 2018. All three exhibitions were curated by me, and the organizing teams included Vaia Doudaki, Yiannis Christidis, Fatma Nazli Köksal, Eva Giannoukou, Stella Theocharous, Helene Black, Yiannis Colakides, Marina Simon, Jairo Faria, Fernando Oliveira Paulino, Liziane Guazina and Rose May Carneiro.

The first exhibition was organized in collaboration with the Association for Historical Dialogue and Research (AHDR) and took place from 13 to 21 November 2015 in the Home for Cooperation (H4C), which is located in the Nicosia[2] Buffer Zone. This space was very much defined through its role as an NGO meeting location and a centre for bi-communal cooperation and activism. As one of the renovated buildings in the Buffer Zone, visitors were required to go through one of the checkpoints (either the Greek Cypriot or the Turkish Cypriot one), but not both. The exhibition, with its twenty photographs and ten text panels, opened with a reception on 13 November 2015. A first seminar, on "Monuments and Memories. A Debate on the Relevance of Remembering the Past through Memorials," was organized by AHDR on 18 November, while the second one, entitled "Covering the Cyprus Conflict" and organized by the Cyprus Community Media Centre (CCMC), took place on 19 November. The collaboration with CCMC allowed for a series of interviews, but also the recordings of

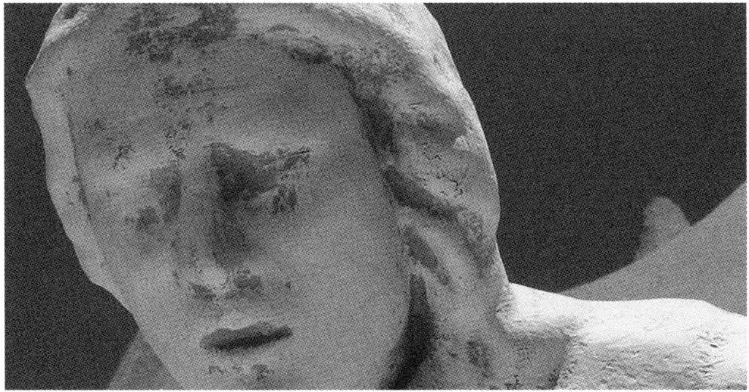

Figure 1: The first exhibition poster. By AHDR, Eva Giannoukou and Nico Carpentier.

the seminars, to be broadcast on CCMC's web radio station, MYCYradio (see Appendix 1).

The second exhibition ran in the NeMe Arts Centre (NAC) in Limassol, a coastal city in the south of Cyprus, in close collaboration with the cultural NGO NeMe. The exhibition started with a seminar on 23 January 2016 – entitled "Monuments and Memorials as Rhetoric/Objectivity as Male," which was followed by a reception at the NAC. The exhibition was originally scheduled to run until 6 February, but it was

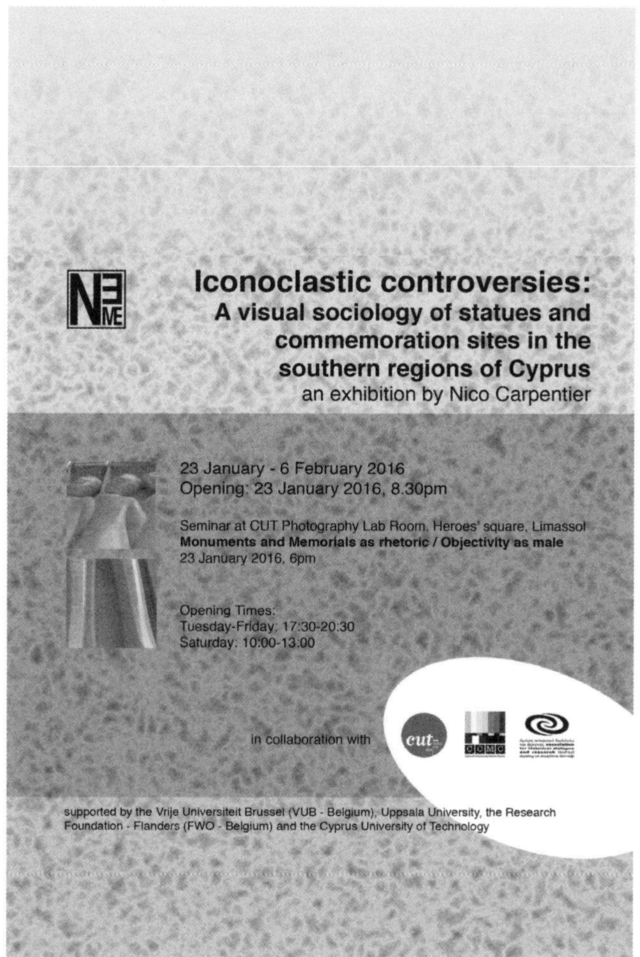

Figure 2: The second exhibition poster. By NeMe.

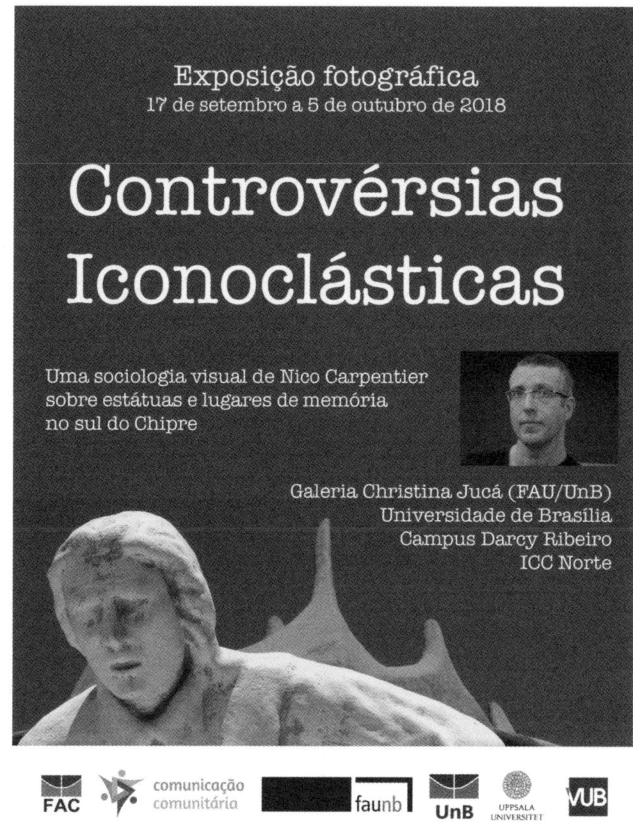

Figure 3: The third exhibition poster. By UnB Faculty of Communication and Nico Carpentier.

extended for one week, until 13 February 2016. As the NAC had two floors, more space was available. The main exhibition, with again twenty photographs and fifteen text panels, was constructed on the ground floor, and a 1 m × 1.5 m print of one of the photographs – "The Louroujina Salient," showing a beautiful Cyprus sky with a fragment of the Buffer Zone fortifications in the lower right corner – was positioned at the very end of the rectangular space. The basement floor was used to construct a series of listening posts, where visitors could listen to the recordings from the first exhibition and to a series of new recordings. These audio files could also be downloaded via a QR code on display.

The third exhibition took place at the end of 2018, in Brazil. It ran from 17 September to 5 October 2018 at the Galeria Christina Jucá of the University of Brasilia. This gallery was large, with one 100 m² and one 170 m² room, located at the very middle of the 700 m long *Instituto Central de Ciências* (ICC) building, designed by architect Oscar Niemeyer. In order to deal with the space, and to break up the two large rectangles, a wooden construction was built in the middle of the largest room, with barbed wire on top of it, as a reminder of the Cypriot Buffer Zone. This construction was also used for hanging four large (75 cm by 50 cm) photographs, while the other nineteen photographs were placed on the walls of the two rooms. To maximize the visual impact of the photographs, and separate the photography from the written texts (which provided contextual information), the written texts were placed horizontally, on top of large black boxes and covered by glass plates (or, in a few cases, by small rocks, painted white[3]). As the Brazilian visitors were unlikely to know much about the Cypriot history, an additional exhibition was produced and placed in the large room. This exhibition-within-the-exhibition displayed historical material related to the Cyprus Problem. Two main boxes displayed objects from the 1950s and from the 1960s and 1970s, respectively. A third box contained a series of maps, and above a fourth box a globe was hanging from a wire, inviting visitors to look for the island of Cyprus on the globe. Moreover, one of the CCMC producers, Orestis Tringides, selected a series of Cypriot songs,[4] which were played at the gallery. In collaboration with the Faculty of Communication of the University of Brasilia, three lectures were organized during the exhibition period: "Antagonistic Nationalism and Constructions of the Enemy" (on 19 September 2018), "Political Struggles over Conflict and Memory" (on 20 September) and "Beyond the Written Text: Visual Sociology as a Method to Communicate Research" (on 26 September).

Iconoclastic Controversies 1

Home for Cooperation, at Ledra Palace, Nicosia, Cyprus
from 13 November to 21 November 2015

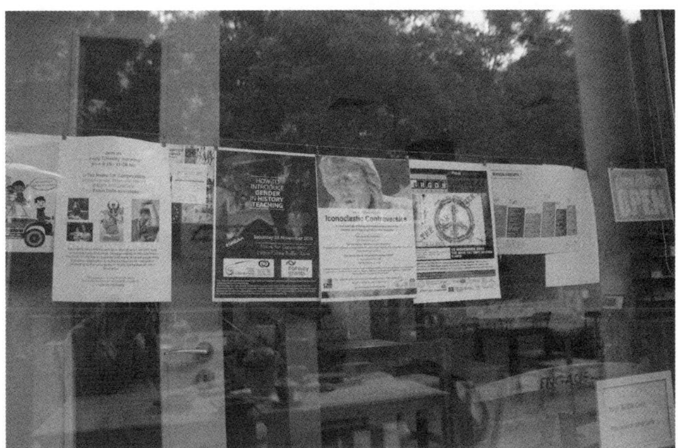

by Nico Carpentier

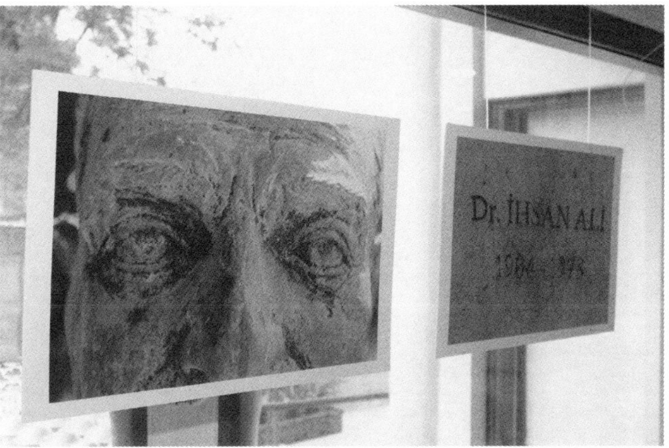

by Nico Carpentier

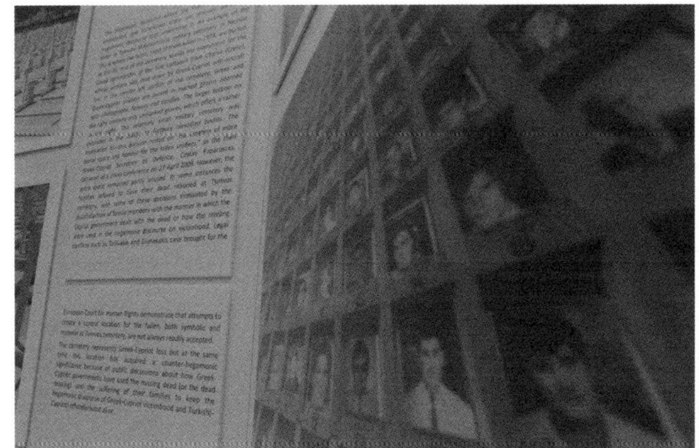

by Yiannis Christidis

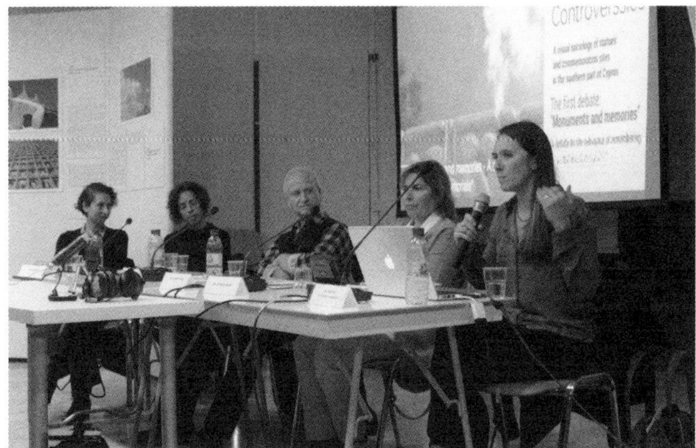

by Nico Carpentier

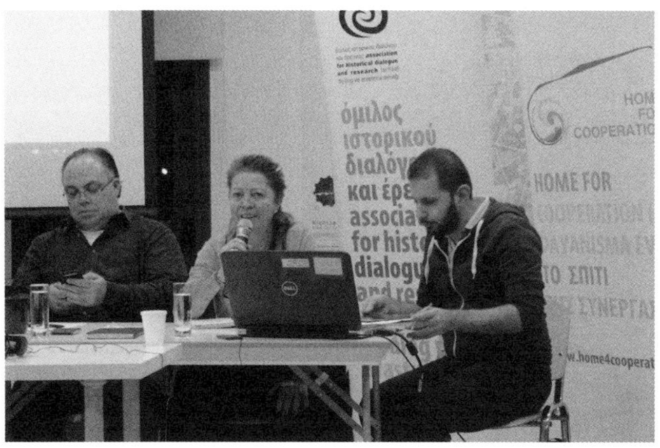

by Nico Carpentier

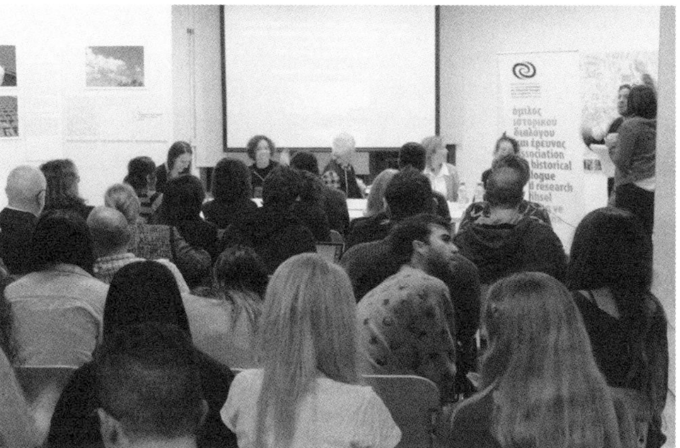

by Nico Carpentier

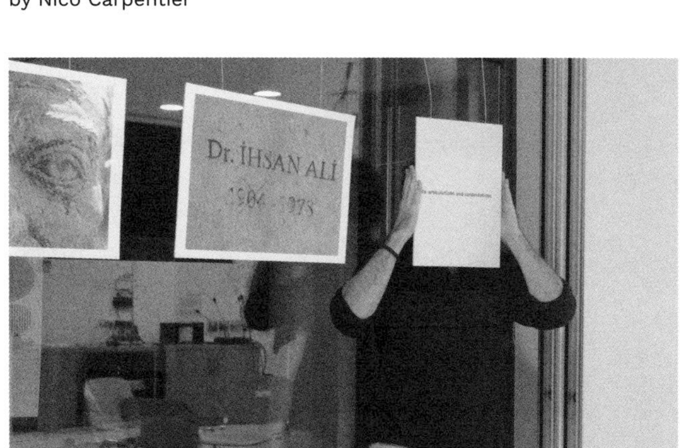

by Vaia Doudaki

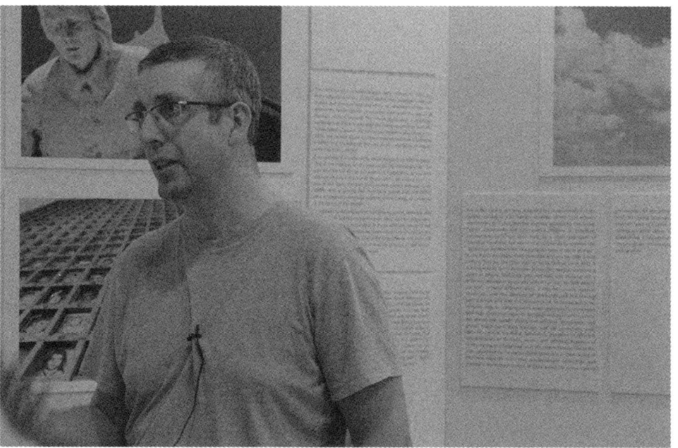

by Vaia Doudaki

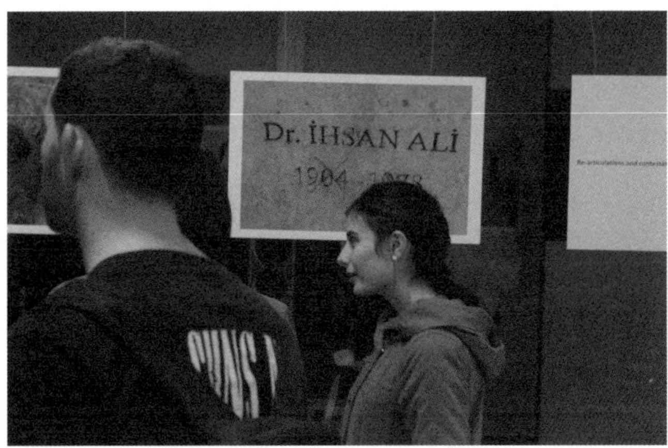

by Yiannis Christidis

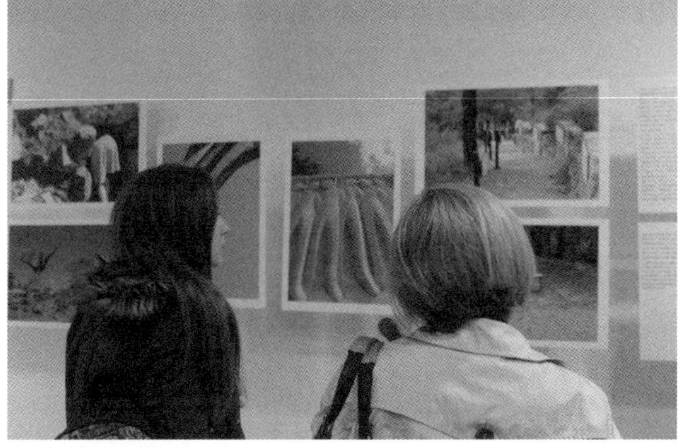

by Vaia Doudaki

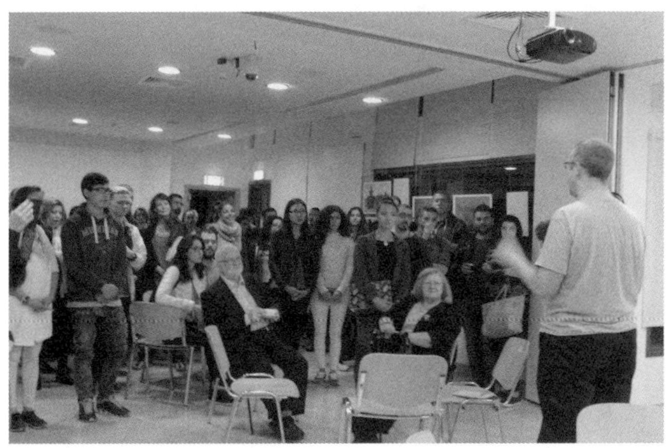

by Vaia Doudaki

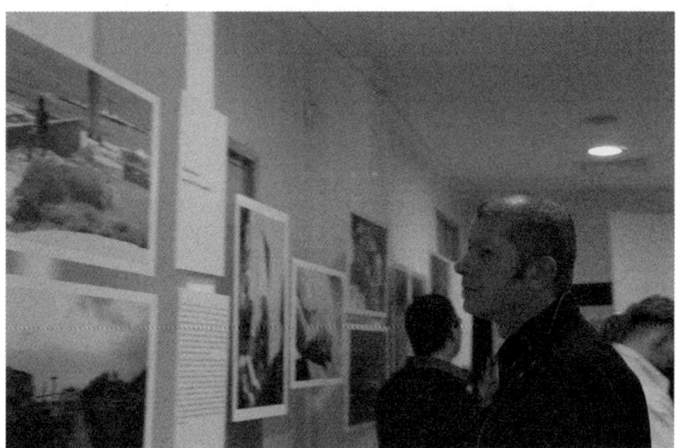

by Vaia Doudaki

Iconoclastic Controversies 2

NeMe Arts Centre, Limassol, Cyprus
from 23 January to 6 February 2016

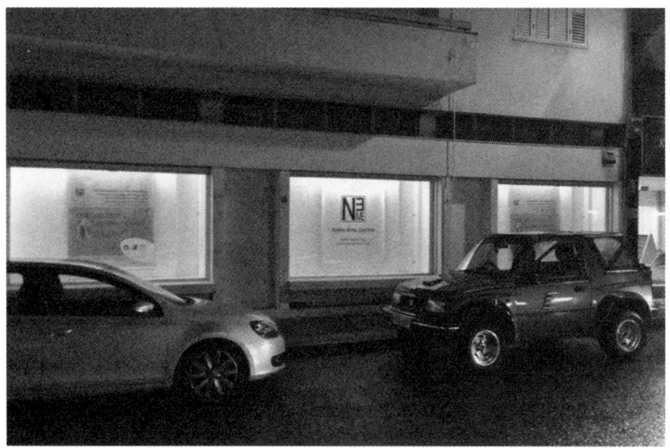

by Yiannis Colakides

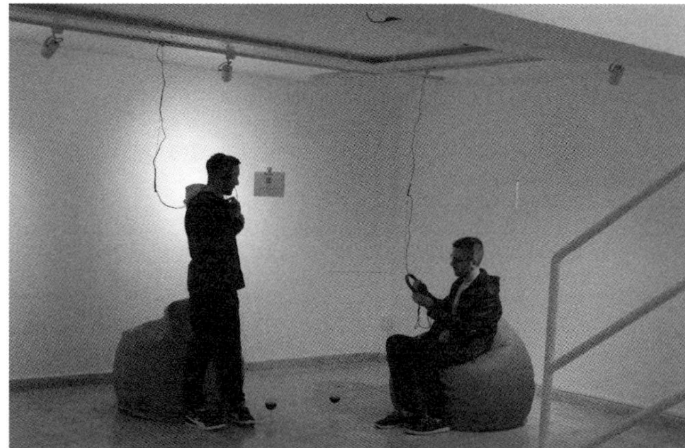

by Vaia Doudaki

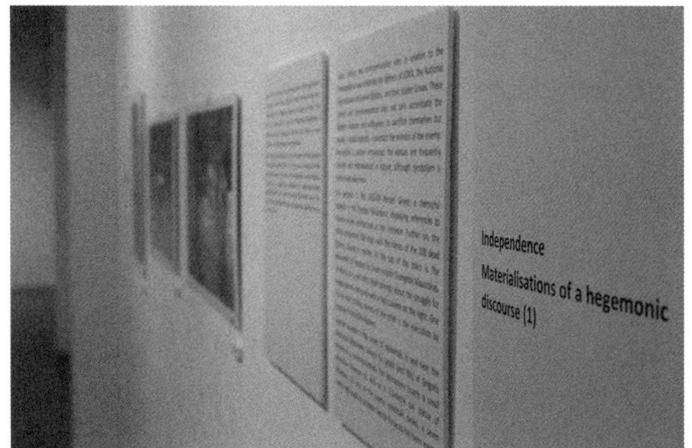

by Nico Carpentier

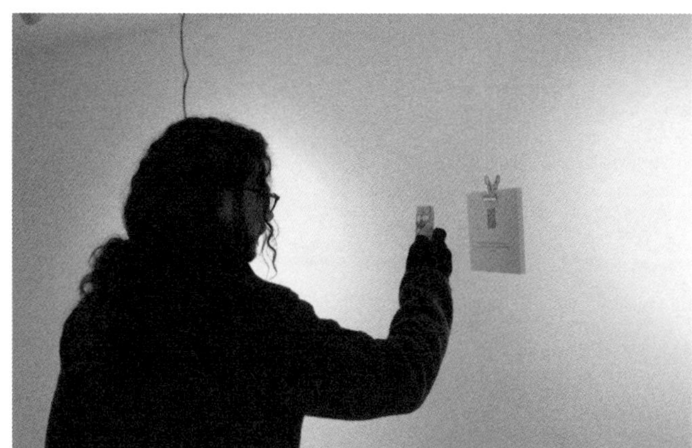

by Yiannis Christidis

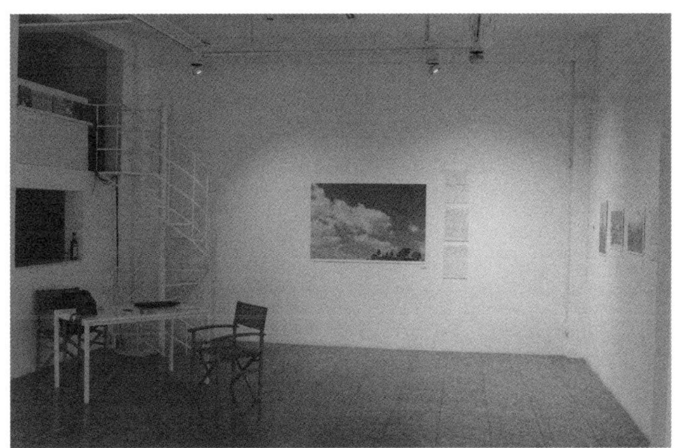

by Nico Carpentier

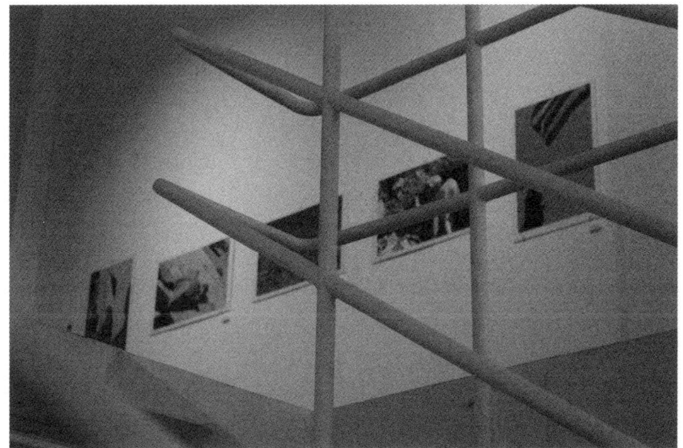

by Nico Carpentier

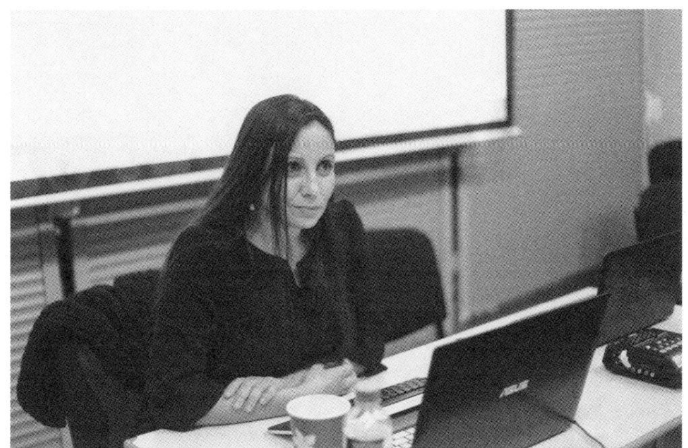

by Yiannis Christidis

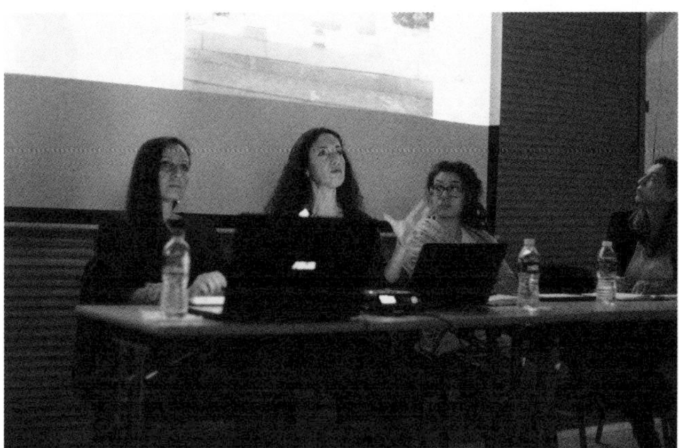

by Yiannis Christidis

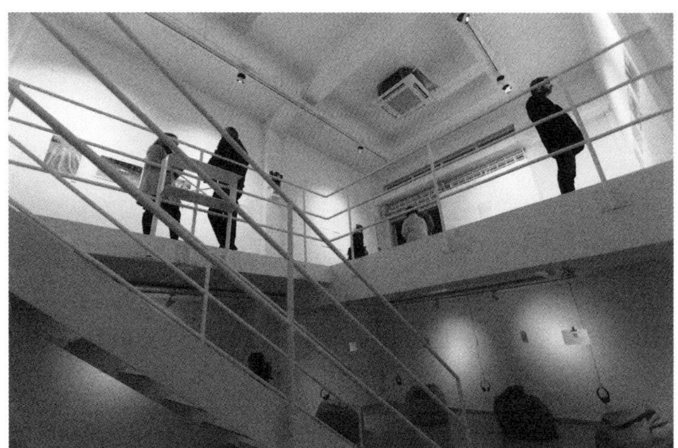

by Yiannis Christidis

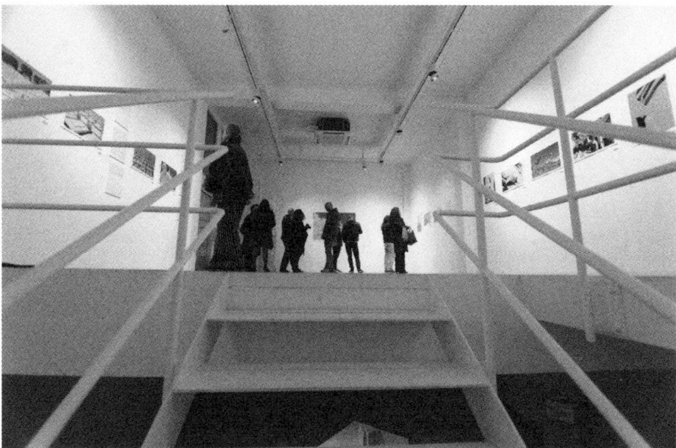

by Yiannis Christidis

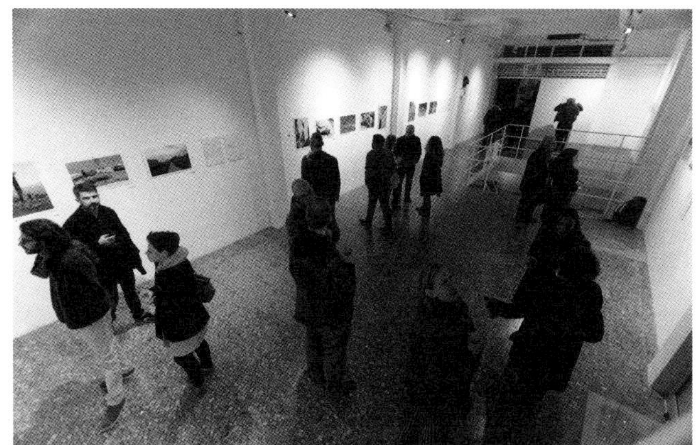

by Yiannis Christidis

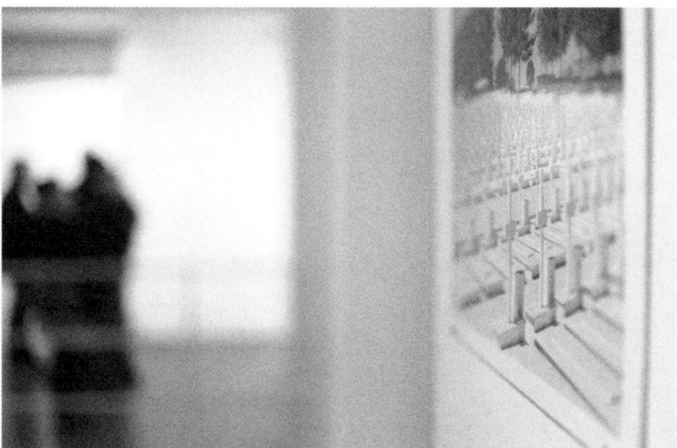

by Yiannis Christidis

Iconoclastic Controversies 3

Galeria Christina Jucá, University of Brasilia, Brasilia, Brazil
from 17 September to 5 October 2018

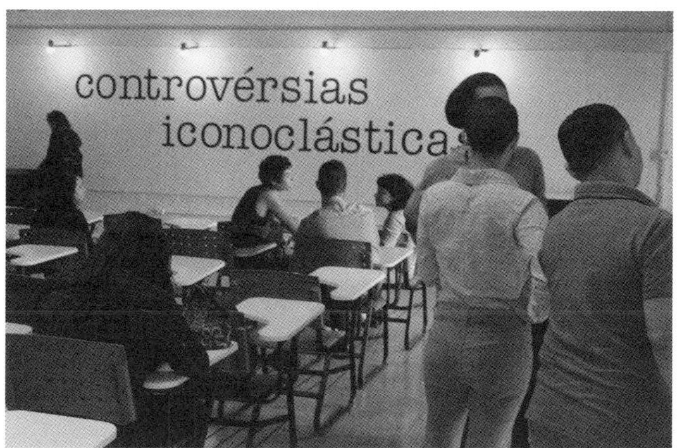

by Jairo Faria

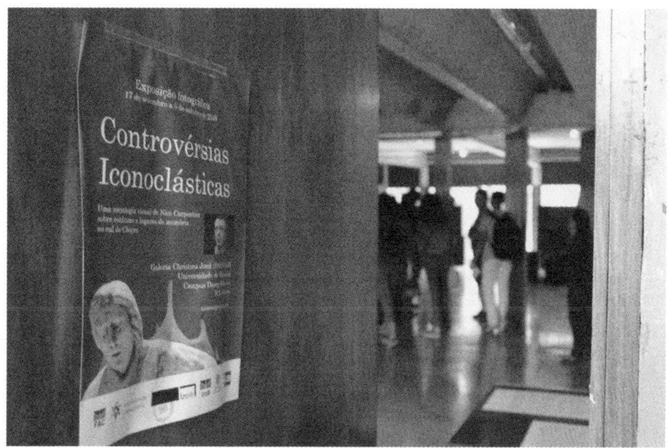

by Jairo Faria

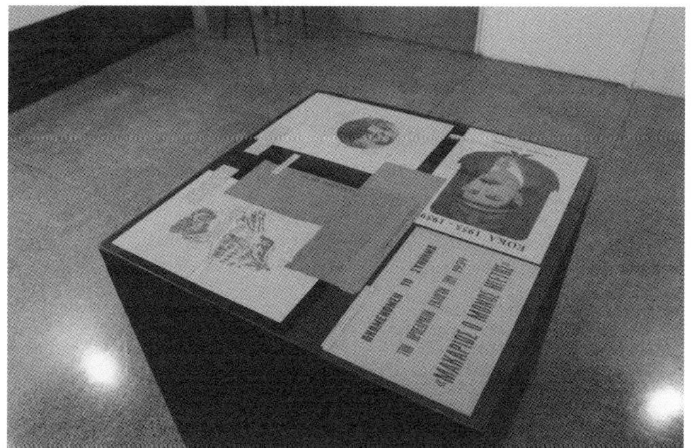

by Nico Carpentier

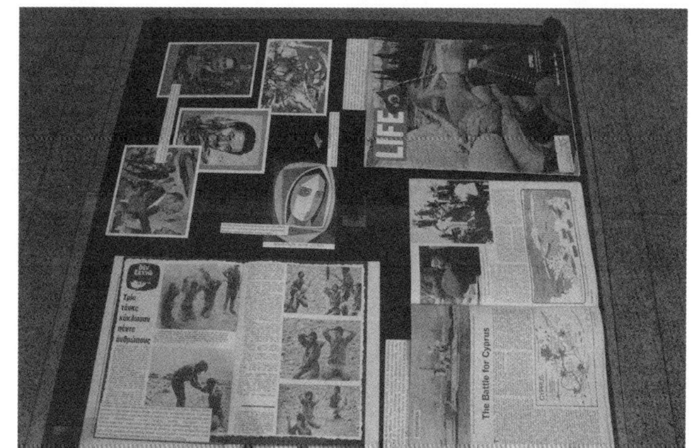

by Nico Carpentier

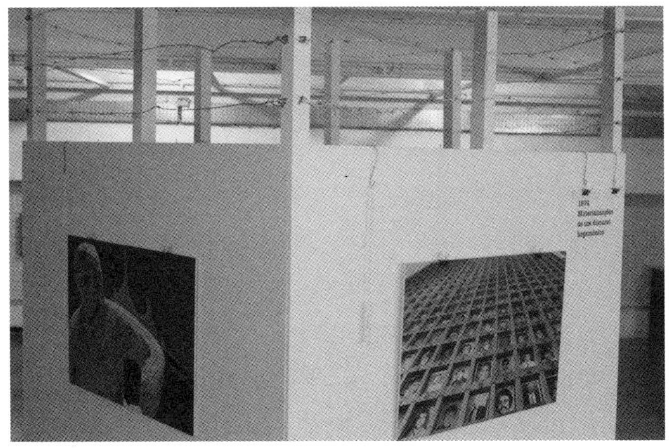

by Nico Carpentier

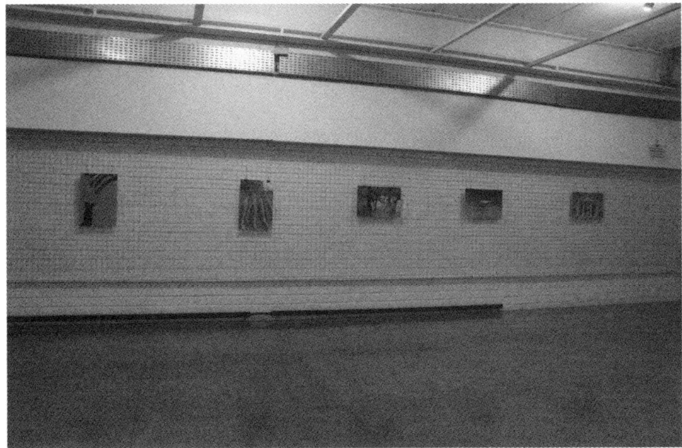

by Nico Carpentier

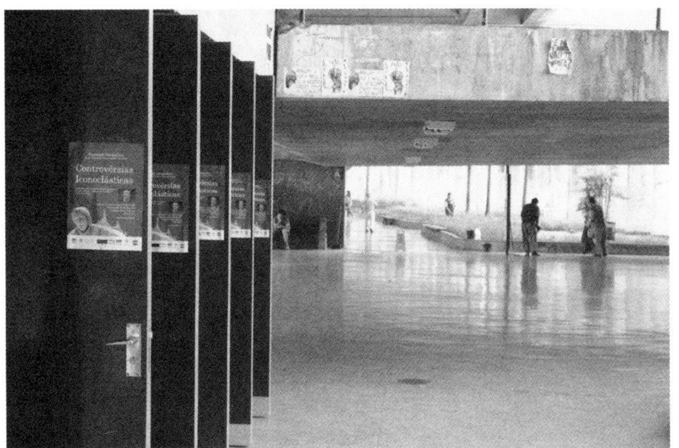

by Nico Carpentier

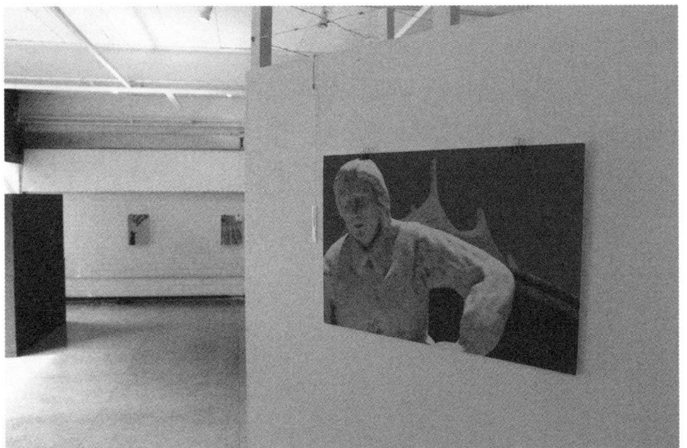

by Nico Carpentier

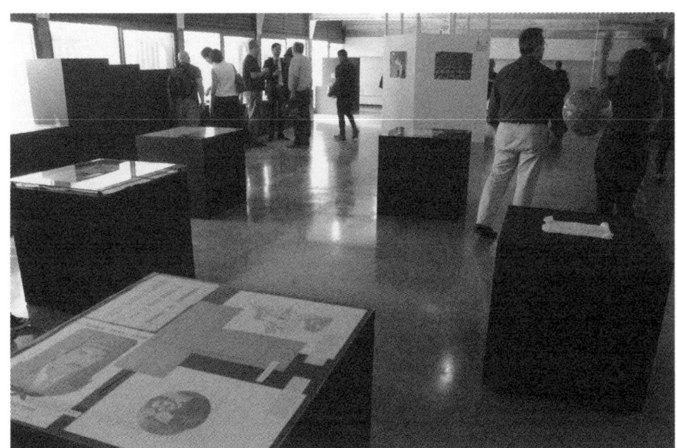

by Jairo Faria

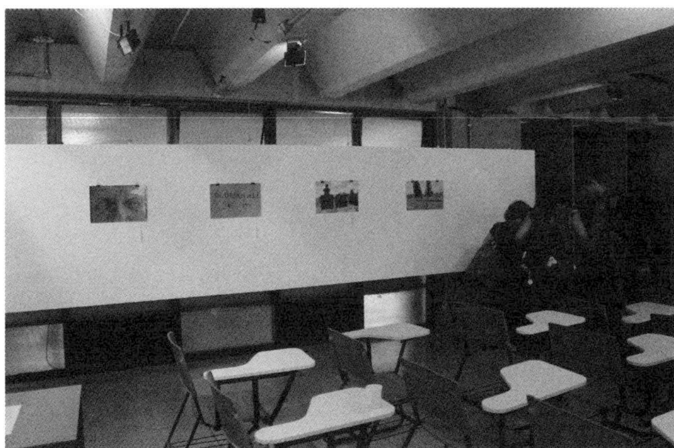

by Jairo Faria

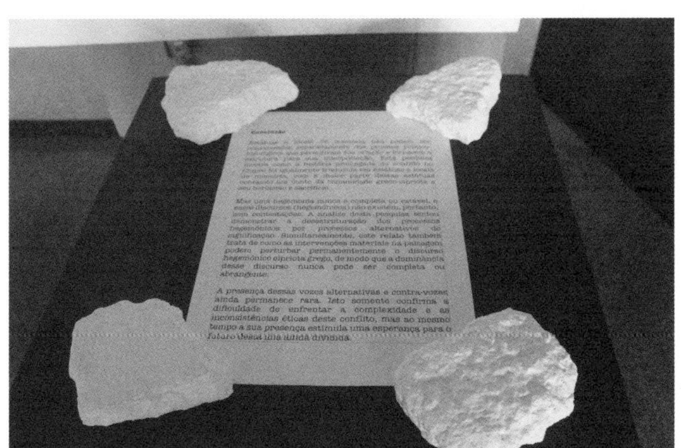

by Nico Carpentier

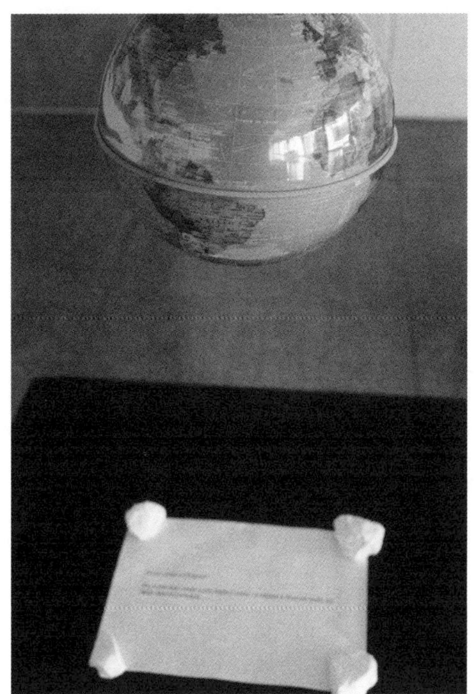

by Nico Carpentier

Monsieur Doumani – Μεθύσιν τζαι φιλίν (Drinking and kissing) (original title: Petrakkouros)

Music played at the *Iconoclastic Controversies* Exhibition 3 in Brasilia
English translation by Nicoletta Demetriou; selection by Orestis Tringides[5]

Να πιάσω το σιπέττον μου που 'ζώστηκα με (το) ζόριν
Ούχχου τζ' ούχχου, μάνα μου, ψυσή μου, μαντζουράνα μου
Τζαι να τον σύρω του κρεμμού, θα σπάσει, εν ιμπόρει
Ου, που να λαώννεται, με την ψυσήν καμώννεται
Τζ' εδάκκασεν με μια κουφή τζ' εψόφησεν της ώρας
Γιατ' είχα γαίμαν της φωθκιάς, της αστραπής, της μπόρας
Τ' αστέρκα ούλλα τ' ουρανού, τα χόρτα μες τα δάση
Εννά μου βοηθήσουσιν, που 'χουν γερήν την κράσην
Σε τούν' τον κόσμον τον καλόν πο' 'πνίηκεν χαζίριν
Να 'ρτει μεθύσιν τζαι φιλίν, τζ' όμορφον παναΰριν

I'm grabbing my shotgun, given to me despite my will
Oh and oh, my dear, my soul, my sweet flower
Throwing it down the cliff will certainly break it
Oh, let it suffer, my soul is blossoming
A snake bit me and died within the hour
Because my blood was filled with fire, with lightning, with storm
All the stars in the sky, all the greens in the forests
Will help me with their might
In this good world that has been almost drowned
May there be drinking, may there be kissing, may there be a beautiful feast

Julio, Feat. Στέλιος Πελλάρας – Συρματοπλέγματα (Julio, Feat. Stelios Pellaras – Barbed wires)

From *Iconoclastic Controversies* Exhibition 3 in Brasilia
Selection and English translation[6] by Orestis Tringides

ΕΣΥ ΠΟΤΖΕΙ ΕΓΩ ΠΟΔΑ ΤΖΑΙ ΜΕΣ'ΤΗ ΜΕΣΗ ΣΥΡΜΑΤΟΠΛΕΓΜΑ
Η ΑΛΗΘΚΕΙΑ ΜΑΣ ΧΩΣΜΕΝΗ ΤΖΑΙ ΠΝΙΜΕΝΗ ΜΕΣΤΟ ΟΙΝΟΠΝΕΥΜΑ
ΕΤΣΙ ΜΑΣ ΘΕΛΟΥΝ ΧΩΡΙΣΤΑ ΤΖΑΙ ΠΑΝΤΑ ΞΕΝΟΙ
ΕΝ ΣΥΜΦΕΡΕΙ ΤΟΥ ΜΑΣΤΟΡΟΥ ΟΙ ΔΟΥΛΟΙ ΝΑΝ ΑΓΑΠΗΜΕΝΟΙ ΤΖΑΙ ΕΝΩΜΕΝΟΙ...
ΕΝ ΤΟΥΣ ΣΥΜΦΕΡΕΙ Η ΑΔΕΛΦΟΣΥΝΗ
ΕΧΟΥΝ ΔΥΝΑΜΗ ΤΑ ΖΩΑ ΑΜΑΝ ΜΕΤΑΞΥ ΤΟΥΣ ΦΙΛΟΙ
ΤΖΑΙ ΘΕΛΟΥΝ ΠΑΝΤΑ... ΝΑ ΜΑΣ ΧΩΡΙΖΟΥΝ
ΟΥΛΛΟΙ ΤΟΥΤΟΙ ΠΟΥ ΤΟΝ ΝΟΥ ΣΟΥ ΦΑΝΑΤΙΖΟΥΝ
ΠΕ ΜΟΥ ΑΞΙΖΟΥΝ...? 400 ΕΥΡΩ ΤΟΝ ΜΗΝΑ
ΓΙΑ ΝΑ ΓΙΝΕΣΑΙ ΕΜΠΑΘΗΣ, ΡΑΤΣΙΣΤΗΣ ΤΖΑΙ ΦΑΣΙΣΤΑΣ
ΕΝ ΦΤΕΝ ΟΙ ΞΕΝΟΙ ΓΙΑ ΤΗΝ ΚΑΤΑΝΤΙΑ ΜΑΣ...

YOU, ON THAT SIDE, AND ME, ON THIS SIDE, AND BARBED WIRE, IN-BETWEEN
OUR TRUTH CRAMMED AND DROWNED IN ALCOHOL
THAT'S HOW THEY WANT US TO BE, SEPARATED AND ALWAYS STRANGERS
IT IS NOT IN THE INTERESTS OF THE MASTER, FOR THE SLAVES TO BE LOVED AND UNITED...
BROTHERHOOD IS NOT IN THEIR INTERESTS
THE ANIMALS HAVE POWER WHEN THEY ARE FRIENDS AMONGST THEM
AND THEY ALWAYS WANT... TO DIVIDE US
ALL THOSE WHO FANATISIZE YOUR MIND
TELL ME, ARE THEY WORTH IT...? 400 EUROS PER MONTH
SO YOU BECOME SPITEFUL, RACIST AND FASCIST
IT'S NOT THE FAULT OF THE FOREIGNERS FOR OUR ABJECTION...

ΕΒΑΛΑΜΕ ΤΑ ΣΙΕΡΚΑ ΜΑΣ ΤΖΑΙ ΕΦΚΑΛΑΜΕΝ ΤΑ ΜΑΘΚΙΑ ΜΑΣ
ΑΡΦΕ ΜΟΥ... ΔΕ ΠΟΥ ΤΑ ΜΑΘΚΙΑ ΜΟΥ ΤΖΑΙ ΠΕ ΜΟΥ
ΕΝΝΕΝ ΜΟΝΟΙ ΜΑΣ ΠΟΥ ΕΜΑΘΑΜΕ ΤΗΝ ΑΠΛΗΣΤΙΑ ΓΙΕ ΜΟΥ?
ΕΝΝΕΝ ΜΟΝΟΙ ΜΑΣ ΠΟΥ ΕΒΑΛΑΜΕ ΤΑ ΠΑΝΤΑ ΥΠΟΘΗΚΗ
ΤΖΑΙ ΕΚΑΜΑΜΕ ΤΟ ΜΕΣΑ ΜΑΣ ΑΠΥΘΜΕΝΟ ΚΑΘΙΚΙ
ΓΙΑ ΛΛΙΕΣ ΑΝΕΣΕΙΣ ΠΑΡΑΠΑΝΩ?
ΠΑΡΕΑ ΜΟΥ ΑΛΗΘΚΕΙΑ ΑΜΑΝ ΤΑ ΣΚΕΦΤΟΥΜΕ ΚΟΝΤΕΥΚΩ ΝΑ ΠΕΛΛΑΝΩ!
ΤΙ ΤΟ ΗΘΕΛΕΣ ΤΟ ΔΕΥΤΕΡΟ ΤΟ ΣΠΙΤΙ ΤΖΑΙ ΤΟ ΚΑΠΡΙΟ?
ΕΝ ΣΕ ΕΚΑΝΕΝ ΤΟ ΣΗΜΕΡΑ ΗΘΕΛΕΣ ΤΖΑΙ ΤΟ ΑΥΡΙΟ ?
ΤΟ ΔΑΝΕΙΟ ΤΙ ΤΟ 'ΘΕΛΕΣ ΚΥΠΡΑΙΟ?
ΤΩΡΑ ΜΕΣ'ΤΑ ΜΝΗΜΟΝΙΑ ΠΕΖΕ ΤΟΝ ΕΥΡΩΠΑΙΟ
ΤΖΑΙ ΚΑΜΕ ΤΗ ΘΑΛΑΣΣΑ ΣΟΥ ΛΑΝΤΑ
ΕΙΣΙΕΣ ΠΟΛΛΑ ΕΘΕΛΕΣ ΤΖ ΑΛΛΑ ΤΖ ΕΤΣΙ ΕΧΑΣΕΣ ΤΑ ΠΑΝΤΑ...
ΕΜ'ΕΝ ΟΙ ΡΙΖΕΣ ΜΟΥ ΒΑΘΚΙΕΣ, ΑΠ' ΑΚΡΗ Σ' ΑΚΡΗ ΤΟΥ ΝΗΣΙΟΥ
ΤΖΙΑΙ ΦΟΡΤΩΜΕΝΟΣ ΤΗ ΚΑΤΑΡΑ ΚΑΠΟΙΟΥ ΑΓΝΩΣΤΟΥ ΘΕΟΥ
ΝΑ ΕΙΜΑΙ ΠΡΟΣΦΥΓΑΣ, ΜΕΣ' ΣΤΑ ΔΙΚΑ ΜΟΥ ΤΑ ΧΩΡΑΦΚΙΑ
ΝΑ ΓΥΡΕΥΚΩ ΜΙΑ ΠΑΤΡΙΔΑ ΣΕ ΑΠΥΘΜΕΝΑ ΠΗΓΑΘΚΙΑ
ΤΖ' Η ΓΕΝΙΑ ΜΟΥ ΚΑΤΑΚΑΘΙ, ΝΑ ΠΟΤΙΖΕΙ ΤΖΕΙΝ' ΤΑ ΛΑΘΗ
ΠΟΥ ΦΥΤΡΩΝΟΥΝ ΜΕΣ'ΤΟ ΝΟΥ ΜΑΣ ΣΑΝ Τ' ΑΓΚΑΘΙ...

WE THREW OUR HANDS AND TORE OUR EYES OUT
MY BROTHER... TAKE A LOOK FROM MY EYES AND TELL ME
ISN'T BY OUR OWN SELVES THAT WE CONFORMED IN GREEDINESS, MY SON?
ISN'T IT BY OUR OWN SELVES THAT WE PUT EVERYTHING ON MORTGAGE
AND MADE OUR INSIDE A BOTTOMLESS POTTY CHAIR
FOR A FEW COMFORTS MORE?
MY BUDDY, TRULY, WHEN I THINK ABOUT ALL THESE I AM NEARLY GOING CRAZY!
WHAT DID YOU NEED THAT SECOND HOUSE AND THAT CABRIO FOR?
WASN'T TODAY GOOD ENOUGH FOR YOU, DID YOU ALSO WANT TOMORROW AS WELL?
WHAT DID YOU NEED THAT LOAN FOR, OH CYPRIOT?
PRETEND NOW YOU ARE A EUROPEAN WHILE BEING STUCK IN THE MEMORANDA
AND MAKE YOUR SEA A MIRE
YOU HAD A LOT AND YOU WANTED MORE, BUT IN THAT WAY, YOU LOST EVERYTHING...
AS OF ME, MY ROOTS ARE DEEP, FROM SIDE TO SIDE OF THIS ISLAND
AND BURDENED WITH THE CURSE OF SOME UNKNOWN GOD
TO BE A REFUGEE, IN MY OWN LAND
LEFT SEEKING FOR A COUNTRY IN BOTTOMLESS WELLS
AND MY GENERATION, A DREG, WATERING THOSE MISTAKES
THAT GROW IN OUR MIND LIKE A THORN...

ΠΡΩΤΟ ΤΟ ΜΙΣΟΣ... ΠΑΛΙΑ ΣΠΟΡΑ ΘΚΙΑΟΛΟΥ
ΔΙΕΡΕΙ ΤΖΙΑΙ ΒΑΣΙΛΕΥΚΕ ΜΕΤΑ ΕΠΙ ΣΥΝΟΛΟΥ,
ΤΟ ΤΡΙΤΟ ΤΖΙΑΙ ΚΑΛΛΗΤΕΡΟ, ΤΟΥ ΕΘΝΟΥΣ ΤΟ ΣΥΜΦΕΡΟΝ
ΔΗΧΑ ΝΑ 'ΧΟΥΜΕΝ ΙΔΕΑ – ΠΟΙΟΣ Ο ΑΓΩΝ, ΠΟΙΟΣ Ο ΦΕΡΩΝ
ΕΒΑΛΑΝ ΜΑΣ ΜΕΤΑ ΣΤΩΝ ΜΑΣΤΟΡΩΝ ΤΟΝ ΑΓΩΝΑ
ΤΖΙΑΙ ΕΚΑΜΑΝ ΤΟΝ ΛΑΟ ΤΟΥ ΒΑΣΙΛΙΑ ΤΟΝ ΠΡΟΜΑΧΩΝΑ...
ΕΤΣΙ ΤΟ ΠΡΩΤΟ ΣΥΡΜΑΤΟΜΠΛΕΓΜΑ ΗΡΤΕΝ ΠΟΥ ΤΗΝ ΑΓΓΛΙΑ,
ΤΟ ΔΕΥΤΕΡΟΝ ΕΦΥΤΡΩΣΕΝ ΒΑΘΚΙΑ ΜΕΣ ΤΗΝ ΠΑΙΔΕΙΑ,
ΤΟ ΠΡΩΤΟΝ ΕΜΑΣΙΕΡΩΣΕΝ ΤΗΝ ΚΥΠΡΟ ΠΟΥ ΤΗΝ ΜΕΣΗ,
ΣΤΟ ΔΕΥΤΕΡΟΝ ΓΥΡΕΥΚΟΥΜΕΝ 'ΚΟΜΑ ΠΟΙΟΣ ΕΝ ΝΑ ΦΤΕΞΕΙ...
ΠΟΥ ΤΗΝ ΜΙΑ ΚΛΥΩΜΕΝΟΙ ΣΤΑ ΜΙΣΑ ΤΟΥ ΝΗΣΙΟΥ ΜΑΣ
ΠΟΥ ΤΗΝ ΑΛΛΗ ΤΤΕΛΙΑΣΜΕΝΟΙ ΜΕΣ ΤΑ ΣΥΝΟΡΑ ΤΟΥ ΝΟΥ ΜΑΣ
ΤΖ' Η ΓΕΝΙΑ ΜΟΥ ΚΑΤΑΚΑΘΙ ΝΑ ΠΟΤΙΖΕΙ ΤΖΕΙΝ' ΤΑ ΛΑΘΗ
ΠΟΥ ΦΥΤΡΩΝΟΥΝ ΜΕΣ ΤΟΥ ΝΟΥ ΜΑΣ ΣΑΝ Τ' ΑΓΚΑΘΙ...

FIRST IS THE HATE... DEVIL'S OLD SEED
THEN, DIVIDE AND CONQUER ABOVE ALL,
THE THIRD AND THE BEST, THE INTEREST OF THE NATION
WITHOUT US HAVING ANY IDEA – WHAT CREATES THE PROBLEM AND WHAT SOLVES IT
AFTER THAT, THEY HAVE PUT US IN THE WAR OF THE MASTERS
AND THEY MADE THE PEOPLE THE KING'S BASTION...
THUS THE FIRST BARBED WIRE CAME FROM ENGLAND,
THE SECOND ONE GREW DEEP INTO THE EDUCATION,
THE FIRST ONE CUT CYPRUS THROUGH THE MIDDLE,
IN SECOND ONE WE ARE STILL FIGURING OUT WHO WILL TAKE THE BLAME
ON THE ONE HAND WE ARE LOCKED IN THE HALVES OF OUR ISLAND
ON THE OTHER HAND WE ARE FENCED WITHIN THE BORDERS OF OUR MIND
AND MY GENERATION, A DREG, WATERING THOSE MISTAKES
THAT GROW IN OUR MIND LIKE A THORN...

ΕΤΣΙ ΕΒΑΛΑΝ ΣΥΡΜΑΤΟΜΠΛΕΓΜΑ ΤΖΙΑΙ ΠΑΝΩ ΣΤΑ ΟΝΕΙΡΑ ΜΑΣ
ΤΖΙΑΙ ΕΓΗΝΕΙΝ Η ΑΛΗΘΚΕΙΑ ΜΑΣ ΑΚΟΜΑ ΠΙΟ ΠΙΚΡΗ
ΝΑ ΔΟΥΜΕΝ ΤΖΙΑΙ ΣΤΟ ΑΥΡΙΟ ΠΟΣΑ ΕΝ' ΝΑΝ ΔΙΚΑ ΜΑΣ,
Η ΠΡΙΝ ΝΑ ΞΗΜΕΡΩΣΕΙ ΑΝ ΘΑ 'ΜΑΣΤΕΝ ΝΕΚΡΟΙ...
ΘΥΜΟΥΜΕ ΠΟΥ ΤΟ ΣΥΡΜΑΤΟΠΛΕΓΜΑ ΗΤΑΝ ΜΕΣ'ΤΗΝ ΝΕΚΡΑ ΜΟΝΟ
ΤΩΡΑ ΕΝ ΤΖΑΙ ΣΤΗΝ ΨΥΣΙΗ ΜΑΣ ΤΖΑΙ ΕΧΩ ΠΙΟ ΠΟΛΛΥ ΠΑΡΑΠΟΝΟ
ΠΑΡΑΦΩΝΟ ΑΚΟΥΕΤΕ ΜΟΥ ΚΑΘΕ ΚΑΛΗΜΕΡΑ
ΤΖΑΙ ΦΑΙΝΕΤΑΙ ΜΟΥ ΠΙΟ ΨΕΜΑ ΜΕΡΑ ΜΕ ΤΗΝ ΜΕΡΑ...
ΕΚΟΥΡΑΣΤΗΚΑ ΝΑ ΚΑΘΟΥΜΕ ΣΕ ΚΥΚΛΟΥΣ ΞΕΝΟΦΟΒΙΚΟΥΣ
ΝΑ ΑΚΟΥΩ ΤΟΥΣ ΜΙΚΡΟΑΣΤΟΥΣ ΝΑ ΕΧΟΥΝ ΑΓΝΩΣΤΟΥΣ ΕΧΘΡΟΥΣ!
ΤΖΑΙ ΠΑΝΤΑ ΝΑ ΦΤΕΣΕΙΝ ΟΙ ΑΛΛΟΙ...
ΕΝ ΘΩΡΕΙΣ ΟΤΙ ΔΑΜΕ ΕΧΟΥΜΕ ΓΙΑ ΠΑΝΤΑ ΚΑΡΝΑΒΑΛΛΙ?
ΕΝ ΘΩΡΕΙΣ ΠΩΣ ΤΟΥΣ ΦΑΣΙΣΤΕΣ ΕΜΕΙΣ ΚΑΜΝΟΥΜΕΝ ΤΟΥΣ ΠΡΟΕΔΡΟΥΣ
ΤΖΑΙ ΥΣΤΕΡΑ ΓΥΡΕΥΚΟΥΜΕ ΝΑ ΕΒΡΟΥΜΕ ΤΟΥΣ ΦΤΑΙΧΤΕΣ?
ΔΑΜΕ Ο ΜΑΣΤΡΟΣ ΗΤΑΝ ΤΟ ΤΣΙΡΑΚΚΙ ΤΗΣ ΕΟΚΑ ΒΟΥ

THUS THEY PUT A BARBED WIRE ALSO ON OUR DREAMS
AND OUR TRUTH BECAME EVEN MORE BITTER
WE'LL SEE HOW MUCH OF THESE WILL STILL BE OURS TOMORROW,
OR WHETHER WE WILL BE DEAD BEFORE DAWN...
I REMEMBER WHEN THE BARBED WIRE WAS ONLY IN THE BUFFER ZONE
NOW IT IS ALSO IN OUR SOUL AND FOR THIS I HAVE EVEN MORE GRIEVANCE
EVERY "GOOD MORNING" SOUNDS DISSONANT TO ME
AND DAY BY DAY IT SEEMS MORE OF A LIE TO ME...
I AM TIRED OF SITTING IN XENOPHOBIC CIRCLES
LISTENING TO ALL THOSE PETTY BOURGEOIS HAVING UNKNOWN ENEMIES!
AND ALWAYS BLAME THE OTHERS...
CAN'T YOU SEE THAT OVER HERE WE PERPETUALLY HAVE CARNIVAL?
CAN'T YOU SEE THAT WE MAKE PRESIDENTS OF THE FASCISTS
AND THEN WE ARE SEARCHING FOR WHO TO BLAME?
HERE, THE BOSS WAS THE MINION OF EOKA B

ΤΖΑΙ ΕΣΕΙΣ ΑΚΟΜΑ ΘΕΛΕΤΕ ΔΙΑΥΓΕΙΑ ΜΟΥΤΣΟΠΑΙΧΤΕΣ;
ΟΪ ΕΝ ΠΛΑΣΑΡΩ ΚΟΜΜΑ... ΟΪ ΕΝ ΕΙΜΑΙ ΤΡΑΜΠΟΥΚΟΣ!
ΜΑΛΑΚΑ ΕΝ ΟΥΛΛΟΙ ΟΙ ΙΔΙΟΙ ΑΜΑΝ ΛΥΨΕΙ Ο ΣΟΥΣΟΥΚΟΣ
ΤΡΩΟΥΝΤΑΙ ΝΑ ΔΟΥΝ ΠΟΙΟΣ ΕΝΝΑ ΦΑΕΙ ΤΟ ΣΙΗΝΟΥΙ
ΤΖΑΙ ΕΝ ΚΟΛΛΗΤΙΚΗ Η ΛΥΣΣΑ ΓΙ ΑΥΤΟ ΠΡΟΣΕΧΕ ΑΡΦΟΥΙ ΜΟΥ.
ΕΜΥΑΛΗΝΑΜΕΝ ΤΖΑΙ ΑΦΗΣΑΜΕ ΤΑ ΟΜΟΡΦΑ ΠΟΥ ΕΖΗΣΑΜΕ
ΟΤΙ ΟΝΕΙΡΕΥΤΗΚΑΜΕ ΑΛΛΑΞΕ ΧΡΩΜΑ ΤΖΑΙ ΗΡΤΑΜΕ
ΣΤΟ ΤΕΛΟΣ ΝΑ ΖΗΤΗΣΟΥΜΕ ΤΑ ΡΕΣΤΑ ΠΟΥ ΟΠΟΙΟΝ ΝΑΝΕ
ΣΥΝΕΧΕΙΑ ΡΩΤΟΥΜΕ ΠΟΥ ΜΑΣ ΠΕΡΝΟΥΝ ΟΙ ΠΟΥ ΠΑΜΕ...

AND YOU STILL WANT CLARITY, YOU WANKERS?
NO, I AM NOT PROMOTING A PARTY, AND NO, I AM NOT A BULLY!
MALAKA[7], EVERYONE'S THE SAME WHEN THE SHOUSHOUKOS[8] RUNS OUT
THEY KILL EACH OTHER FOR WHO'S GOING TO EAT THE REMAINING HANGING STRING
AND THAT MADNESS IS CONTAGIOUS, SO LOOK OUT, MY BROTHER.
WE GREW UP AND WE LEFT BEHIND ALL THE BEAUTIFUL THINGS WE LIVED
ALL THE THINGS WE DREAMED OF HAVE CHANGED COLOUR AND IN THE END
WE CAME TO ADD INSULT TO INJURY FROM GOD KNOWS WHO
WE KEEP ASKING WHERE ARE THEY TAKING US INSTEAD OF WHERE ARE WE GOING...

Αχερόμπασμαν (Haystacking)

Traditional Cypriot song
From *Iconoclastic Controversies* Exhibition 3 in Brasilia
Selection and English translation[9] by Orestis Tringides

Ἀχέρομπάζω κ̌ι' ἔρκουμαι
αὐκήν στήν γειτονιάν σου
νά δῶ τά μαῦρα μμάθκια σου
ν' ἀκούσω τήν λαλιάν σου.

Ἔχω κοντά σου μιάν ριτζάν
κ̌αί θέλω νά περάσει
ν' ἀφήκεις τό κορμάκ̌ιν μου
στ' ἀγκάλια σου νά πνάσει.

Ξύπνα δκιαμαντοπούλλα μου
κ̌ι' ἤρτα στήν γειτονιάν σου
νά δῶ εἶντα ἐννά μοῦ κάμουσιν
τά γειτονόπουλλά σου.

I stack the hay and I come
to your neighbourhood in the dawn
Oh, to see your black eyes
to hear your voice.

When I'm close to you I feel a desire
and I want it to pass
Oh, let my little body
rest in your embrace.

Wake up my diamond girl
and I came to your neighbourhood
to see what they're going to do to me
your neighbours' children.

The chapters of this book

The book consists of six chapters, in addition to this introduction (Chapter 1), which all add a particular perspective on the Iconoclastic Controversies project. Chapter 2 contains a reflection on the non-written academic text and the five approaches that – each in its own way – have attempted to capture the shift away from the exclusive focus on the written academic text and that were key sources of inspiration for this book. These five approaches are: (1) the cluster of science communication, science popularization and knowledge dissemination; (2) the cluster of knowledge exchange and participatory, transformative and interventionist (action) research; (3) multimodal academic communication; (4) the cluster of visual anthropology and visual sociology; and (5) arts-based research. In the second part of this chapter, the *Iconoclastic Controversies* exhibitions are analysed, demonstrating the integrated and iterative nature of knowledge production and communication, the hybridization of academic–artistic identities and the potential diversification of publics.

As a research project, Iconoclastic Controversies had a particular focus, which was to study antagonistic nationalism and the way it is condensed in memorials and commemoration sites in the south of Cyprus. Chapter 3 provides the theoretical backbone for the study of nationalism, deploying a discursive-material knot perspective (Carpentier 2017). This perspective allows combining an emphasis on the discursive-ideological nature of nationalism, with attention for its materialist dimensions. In the second part of the chapter, the focus is placed on one particular kind of nationalism, namely antagonistic nationalism, which is constructed through the articulation of the other as enemy. Following Mouffe's (2005, 2013a) work on agonism, we can also distinguish different others (e.g. the other-adversary or the other-neighbour), which

also allows us to generate space for the agonization of violent conflict or the transformation of antagonistic nationalism into an agonistic variation, an objective to which the Iconoclastic Controversies project also aims to contribute.

Chapter 4 then brings this discussion on antagonistic nationalism to the Cypriot context, even though the Iconoclastic Controversies project also has the ambition to transcend the specificities of the Cyprus Problem and reflect about the articulation of antagonism, nationalism and memorialization, more in general. Nevertheless, given the specificity of each antagonistic-nationalist hegemonic project, and despite the complexities of the Cyprus Problem, it remains very necessary to provide a basic outline of the role of the two nationalisms (Greek and Turkish nationalism), intertwined with the decades-long history of the different violent conflicts that together make up what we call the Cyprus Problem.

The 23 photographs that form the core of the Iconoclastic Controversies project are rendered in Chapter 5, together with the (slightly updated) texts that were on display at the third *Iconoclastic Controversies* exhibition in Brazil, in 2018. These written texts are not detailed descriptions of what the photographs communicate but provide gentle nudges towards the analytical meanings of the 23 photographs. Further contextualization is offered by Chapter 4, which narrates more in detail the different events that the photographed memorials and commemoration sites refer to. Two main stages of the Cyprus Problem are featured, namely the independence war of 1955–59 and the Turkish invasion of 1974. For both stages, we find photographs that dissect the memorials and commemoration sites that invite to support the hegemonic antagonistic-nationalist project, combined with photographs that show how these invitations fails (for instance through the practices of everyday life) and with photographs of those rare memorials that invite to identify with counter-hegemonic projects (e.g. discourses of peace and collaboration).

Chapter 6 then reports on a reception study of the first two exhibitions, which took place in Cyprus in 2015 and 2016. This collaboration with Vaia Doudaki, Yiannis Christidis and Fatma Nazli Köksal resulted in a (self-)critical analysis of how visitors looked at these exhibitions and how media reported about them. Even though there were many problematizations, which are precious to reflect about, at the same time, many other voices argued for the relevance of the project, and some indications that the Iconoclastic Controversies project triggered further reflection and action were present.

Finally, Chapter 7 also brings in other voices (and yet another format). This chapter includes a series of interviews with me, providing more details about the objectives of the Iconoclastic Controversies project but also about the different production phases, including the photographic work and the exhibition construction work. The inclusion of these interviews is important, because they contribute to the comprehensibility of the analysis (as they use another genre that is quite accessible and immediate) and embed this book in the chain of multimodal communicational practices that the Iconoclastic Controversies project desires to be. The interviews also matter because they introduce multi-vocality into the book, through the questions the interviewers raise and the dialogue they initiate. Moreover, these interviews also show some of the contingencies that are an integral part of research and unhide how some of the ideas (for instance the role of arts-based research and the integrated nature of knowledge) have grown and developed over time. The first interview included in Chapter 7, by Eva Giannoukou, is also the very first interview about Iconoclastic Controversies, dating from October 2015. The second interview, by Yiannis Christidis, took place in January 2016 and was broadcast on the Cypriot community radio station, CUT-Radio, when the second exhibition opened. The third interview, by Fernando Oliveira Paulino, was broadcast on 16 October 2018 at UnBTV, the television station of the University of Brasilia. In addition, Chapter 7 also contains links and transcripts of two films on the Brazilian version of *Iconoclastic Controversies*, namely *Nico Carpentier: The Art and Science of Peace* by Fernando Molina and *Controvérsias Iconoclásticas em Brasília* by me.

NOTES

1. For a discussion on this genre, see Grady (1991).
2. The English names (and Latin spelling) of the Cypriot cities is preferred. This was done mainly for the comfort of the author and the reader. See, for an overview of the Greek Cypriot and Turkish Cypriot names, https://www.wikiwand.com/en/List_of_cities,_towns_and_villages_in_Cyprus.
3. The use of these rocks was inspired by the battlefield of Isandlwana in South Africa, where small white rocks mark the places where the bodies of British soldiers were found, after their defeat against a Zulu army. This was an inconspicuous reminder of the global dimension of antagonism.
4. The translated lyrics of a selection of these songs have been included in this book.
5. This is the band's official translation (by Nicoletta Demetriou), as well how they choose to write up the Cypriot Greek text. The Cypriot Greek notation and English translation can be found, as Monsieur Doumani published it, at https://monsieurdoumani.bandcamp.com/track/drinking-and-kissing.
6. The Cypriot Greek lyrics are provided here verbatim, as the artist has posted them online (as a comment to his own YouTube video) and how he has included them in the album's mp3 download pack (on hiphop.com.cy). This implies that I respect the choices made by the artist in the way of writing the Cypriot Greek text, its capitalization and its punctuation. The English translation, provided by Orestis Tringides, is based on the original lyrics as they were posted online and copies

the original's use of all capital letters. The artist was consulted about the choices taken and the final result.

7. "Malaka(s)" (and its derivatives) is a commonly used and rather ambiguous word in (most cases of) everyday spoken Greek (and in casual written communication, albeit less often). The word is more frequently used in Greece than in Cyprus. Although, when it is taken on its own and used without context, "malaka" is a rather rude word, which can be translated as "wanker," "arsehole," "idiot," etc. However, in this case, the word "malaka" is used to address people who have a mutual affinity with the speaker, as in "listen to me, my friend," "my buddy" etc.

8. "Shoushoukos" is a traditional regional and Cypriot sweet, made by gradually and vertically dipping a thin string in grape must and then extracting it again. Sometimes the string is passed through an array of almonds or walnuts. This process forms the sweet's layers around the string, resulting in a hanging stick.

9. This is a traditional Cypriot song that has many different versions. This form of writing of the Cypriot Greek text was taken from the album *Πού Δύσην ὡς Ἀνατολλήν, Τραγούδια τῆς Κύπρου* ("From West to East, Songs of Cyprus"), by Alkinoos Ioannidis and Miltiadis Papastamou, which includes their interpretation of this song. The English translation provided here is by Orestis Tringides, who took into consideration existing unofficial translations of this specific rendition of the song, as well as English translations of other renditions of the song, with different lyrical variations.

Chapter 2: Communicating Academic Knowledge beyond the Written Academic Text

The Iconoclastic Controversies project explicitly aimed to transcend the written academic text[1] and to complement this particular mode of communication with the use of the photographic and exhibition modes to communicate and produce academic knowledge. This objective is not a complete novelty, even though Communication and Media Studies scholars – the academic field which I consider to be my home – have not used the existing opportunities to their full potential. This makes it necessary to discuss the different approaches that share this objective more in detail here: a number of fields have made considerable headway in deploying these still novel modes, and they offer good reasons to at least engage more in experiments with the use of non-written academic communication, to critically evaluate these practices and learn from them and to then consider including these alternative modes in our "regular" communicative repertoires.

The preference for the written text in academic communication is partially explained by the hegemonic position it has achieved. As Kara (2015: 121) formulates it: "Writing is the one art form with which all researchers must engage." Or in Bazerman's (1988: 18) words: "Knowledge produced by the academy is cast primarily in written language." Although academic writing is omnipresent in academia and crucial to the performance of academic identity (Ivanič 1998), we should keep in mind that academic writing is also a specific genre:

Writers find in existing models the solution to the recurring rhetorical problems of writing science. As these solutions become familiar, accepted, and molded through repeated use, they gain institutional force. Thus though genre emerges out of contexts, it becomes part of the context for future works. (Bazerman 1988: 8)

This (acknowledgement of the) particularity of academic writing has a series of implications. Crucial is that academic writing cannot absorb and represent all knowledge: "Scientific formulations are a human construction and thus are heir to all the limitations of humanity," as Bazerman (1988: 294) writes. This then opens the door for the argument that, as no hegemony is ever total (Mouffe 2005: 18), other forms (or modes) of communicating academic knowledge remain possible and even desirable.[2] The particularity of each mode also produces opportunities for the communication of knowledge, as each particular form has its own affordances (Gibson 1979; Norman 1988) and their combination can enrich academia because of, as Literat and colleagues (2018: 569) wrote about multimodal scholarship, "its potential for more comprehensive and inclusive inquiries, analyses, and representations that can be socially, culturally and politically transformative."

Beyond these theoretical reflections about the non-written academic text, the Iconoclastic Controversies project and this book are also driven by a warm plea to consider using non-written academic texts more in Communication and Media Studies, where it is – as mentioned in the opening lines of this chapter – still rare. Of course, several other academics have argued before in favour of multi-modal and/or arts-based research (Communication and Media Studies) scholarship (see, e.g. McPherson, 2009, in the context of Digital Humanities). And some practice it.[3] Sometimes, this is done in more modest ways, for instance at TED and TEDx talks[4] or when engaging in knowledge exchange activities (see Freeman 2016). In other cases, these examples are more structural, as, for instance, the work of the multidisciplinary Collective for Advancing Multimodal Research Arts[5] or scholars at the Communication Studies Department of Concordia University (Chapman and Sawchuk 2015). Communication and Media Studies scholars also publish their non-written texts in such specialized journals as the *Journal of Video Ethnography*; *Tecmerin: Journal of Audiovisual Essays*; the audiovisual essay track of *NECSUS* and (the now closed) *Audiovisual Thinking, the Journal of Academic Videos*.

Moreover, both the International Communication Association and the International Association for Media and Communication Research have featured exhibitions at some of their recent conferences, the former with the 2017 Making & Doing exhibition[6] and the latter with 2018 Ecomedia Arts Festival,[7] taking gentle steps towards (the acknowledgement of) non-written academic texts. But more could be done in our field at the level of theorizing these practices and deploying them. This book is thus also meant as an informed and informing appetizer.

Even if the written text is the hegemonic mode for communicating academic knowledge, there are various approaches that challenge these "hegemonic conceptions regarding legitimate modes of schol-arly inquiry, analysis and representation" (Literat et al. 2018: 566). These aim to transcend, comple-ment or overturn this hegemony. On the basis of an extensive narrative literature review, I identified five approaches. The first two – the clusters of (1) science communication, science popularization and knowl-edge dissemination and (2) knowledge exchange and participatory, transformative and interventionist (action) research – are relatively autonomous. Some have argued (e.g. Trench and Bucchi 2010) that they are actually (emerging) disciplines in their own right. The three other approaches are more embedded in particular disciplines – namely writing studies, anthropology, sociology and the arts – even though they have moved into other disciplinary arenas as well.

APPROACH 1: SCIENCE COMMUNICATION, SCIENCE POPULARIZATION AND KNOWLEDGE DISSEMINATION

The first approach is the cluster of science commu-nication, science popularization and knowledge dissemination, which not so much tries to provide alternative academic tools for communication, but aims to translate existing academic work (and publi-cations) in other texts that use linguistic repertoires adjusted to a non-academic readership in order to democratize the reception of academic knowledge. Simultaneously, this approach is concerned with the understanding and awareness of science as a whole (Burns, O'Connor and Stocklmayer 2003). Bryant's (2003: 357) definition of science communication as "the processes by which the scientific culture and its knowledge become incorporated into the common culture" is illustrative of this focus on the academic field as a whole, even though the examples he mentions in his article – referring to, for instance, the moment when "ABC television was filming a news item" about Bryant's (2003: 357) research – are indicative of the importance of the micro level, with communication about the work of individual scholars.

Bryant's (2003) example also indicates the impor-tance of (mass) media within this approach in acting as mediators and communicators, or "knowledge brokers" (see Meyer 2010), which brings us back to the original "deficit model,"[8] where science journalists aimed to bridge the gap between science and society (Schiele, Claessens and Shi 2012: xxiii), even if contemporary science communication has moved beyond this model. Still, media continue to be seen as vital, in translating and distributing academic knowledge. One example here is UNESCO's web page on "Science Popularization,"[9] which includes this introductory sentence: "Quality communication of science to the public demands rigorous reporting by science journalists." Also, Kara's (2015: 161ff) overview of knowledge dissemination strategies, which have the "ultimate aim" of allowing "your research and its findings to take on a life of their own and be disseminated further by other people and talking and writing about your work" (2015: 177), explicitly and extensively addresses the role of mainstream media in combination with blogs, podcasts and social media (see also Müllerleile 2014). One of the consequences of this emphasis on the role of external brokers is that the identity of the academic – or, in Laclau and Mouffe's (1985: 115) terminology, the academic's subject position(s) – remains articulated in more traditional ways. Moreover, even if the production of non-written texts, or differently written texts, is a significant component of this approach, these texts tend to be seen as second-stage or post-ante publications that are proceeded by written academic texts and are then translated into new (and more "accessible") texts for publics that nevertheless remain disconnected from the process of knowledge production itself.

APPROACH 2: KNOWLEDGE EXCHANGE AND PARTICIPATORY, TRANSFORMATIVE AND INTERVENTIONIST (ACTION) RESEARCH

A second approach, which responds to the first and is thus still related to it, is the cluster of knowledge exchange and participatory, transformative and interventionist (action) research. Kara (2015: 176) defines knowledge exchange as "a more egalitarian approach that implies a two-way process of sharing knowledge among researchers, practitioners, service users and other interested people." Also more interventionist approaches (e.g. participatory action research; see Fals-Borda and Rahman 1991; Reason and Bradbury 2001), which have the more explicit objective of impacting particular social realities and contributing to social change, place significant emphasis on knowledge exchange and sharing with the aim of democratizing knowledge production itself.

As Gagnon (2011: 28) argues, this type of "collaborative" or "participatory" research implies the development of a "shared perspective" and "common language," which renders it "potentially more time consuming, demanding, and resource intensive than other strategies because it requires both researchers and knowledge users to develop new skills, knowledge, and perspectives" (see also Cvitanovic et al. 2015: 27ff). Nevertheless, this more exchange/collaborative/participatory (cluster of) approach(es) remains significant in the context of this analysis for two reasons, even if they do not always (advocate the) use (of) non-written academic texts. First, they are characterized by an altered power balance between academics and non-academics, which redefines the subject position of the academic, whose voice is no longer seen as privileged. This approach counters the idea that knowledge linearly flows from academia to other fields (Blundell 2017: 308), something that this approach shares with others, for instance, with multi-voiced and polyphonic ethnography (Tyler 1986) and with (some parts of) arts-based research, to which I return later. Here, the emphasis on social change produces more hybrid academic subject positions, for instance through the integration of academic and activist subject positions (Routledge 1996: 405). Second, the collaborative/participatory dimension necessitates the development and implementation of communicational tools and formats that support these dialogues, enabling these more dialogical forms of knowledge creation (Matschke, Moskaliuk and Cress 2012; Mitchell 2006; Murdock, Shariff and Wilding 2013; UNICEF 2015). Moncaster and colleagues' (2010: 170) article, which contains a survey on industry knowledge acquisition tools, is one of the few publications in this field that also refers to audio-visual tools (namely television programs and films). Most of these publications emphasize the importance of communicative tools for knowledge exchange but often restrict themselves to written texts in combination with oral (informal) communication.

APPROACH 3: MULTIMODAL ACADEMIC COMMUNICATION

The other three approaches are embedded in particular disciplines and focus more explicitly on countering the hegemony of the written academic text by providing space for non-written texts and for acknowledging the iterative nature of knowledge production. They also share the objective of expanding their disciplinary boundaries, at the level of both their communicative practices and the (potential) publics they (can) reach. The third approach is multimodal academic communication, which is particularly present in the field of composition[10] (situated in the broader field of writing studies), with, for instance, books such as *Multimodal Composition: Resources for Teachers* (Selfe 2007), *Toward a Composition Made Whole* (Shipka 2011), *Multimodal Composition* (Lutkewitte 2013) and *Bridging the Multimodal Gap* (Khadka and Lee 2019). The conceptual inspiration for this approach comes from multimodal theory, which (obviously) does not explicitly focus on academic communication. *Multimodality*, in this broad sense, refers to "the use of several semiotic modes in the design of a semiotic product or event, together with the particular way in which

these modes are combined" (Kress and van Leeuwen 2001: 20) or, to cite Borgman (2019: 45), "the use of multiple modes of delivery in order to create one cohesive meaning." But this broad conceptualization is then deployed to theorize multimodal academic communication.

This multimodal approach to academic communication explicitly argues, in the words of Murray (2009: 8), that the challenge is "not one of substitution, rather one of addition." She defends the written text "with its sequential structures, disciplinary expectations, and, ultimately, nonaffective tone" but also argues for the need to complement it with what she calls "nondiscursive texts," "with its layers, images, and, without a doubt, pervasive affectivity" (Murray 2009: 8). Part of the argumentation used by this approach relies on the idea that academic communication has never been, and cannot be, restricted to written texts. Lemke (1998: 87; emphasis in original) formulates this argument as follows:

> Science is not done, is not communicated, through verbal language alone. It *cannot* be. The "concepts" of science are not solely verbal concepts, though they have verbal components. They are semiotic hybrids, simultaneously and essentially verbal, mathematical, visual-graphical, and actional-operational. The actional, conversational, and written textual genres are historically and presently, fundamentally and irreducibly, *multimedia genres*.

At the same time, the multimodal academic communication approach still suggests explicating the importance of non-written texts and expanding their use in academic communication, thus also expanding the academic subject position beyond that of the academic writer. Still, even though the non-written text can be "visual, haptic, aural, olfactory, and gustatory" (Murray 2009: 8), in practice, we often find in this approach a strong focus on "texts that incorporate words, images, video, and sound" (Takayoshi and Selfe 2007: 3; see Thorndike-Breeze, Block and Brown (2019) for the use of comics) driven and enabled by the affordances of the online. One example is Lauer's (2012) article "What's in a name? The anatomy of defining new/multi/modal/digital/media texts," a web text that is partially about multimodality and that combines written text, images, hyperlinks and sound. In her introduction, Lauer (2012) has also included a more self-reflexive part, which describes the complexity of multimodal academic production, the resources and skills needed, and the impact on the (self-)identity of the author.

> Because of the complexity of multimodal texts, it takes a village to compose them, and this fundamentally changes how it feels to be an author. I was responsible for orchestrating and composing the elements you see and read here; however, because I had to attend to so many layers of meaning, I needed to rely on people and already-developed content in ways that I would have never had to were I composing an alphabetic print text.

APPROACH 4: VISUAL ANTHROPOLOGY AND VISUAL SOCIOLOGY

A fourth approach, which also tackles the hegemony of the written text, can be found in the cluster of visual anthropology and visual sociology,[11] which have a long tradition in expanding their academic communicative practices by articulating written text, photography and film. But we should also keep in mind that before the label *visual* was combined with anthropology, key anthropologists such as Margaret Mead had already integrated photography and written text, grounded in a critique on anthropology as a "discipline of words" (Mead 1995). One example is Mead's collaboration with Bateson, which resulted in the 1942 book *Balinese Character: A Photographic Analysis*

(Bateson and Mead 1942), which consisted of a joint essay and an essay by Mead, followed by 100 pages of photographs (and 100 pages of captions) by Bateson. Moreover, also the integration of literary elements in anthropological writing was used and advocated, among others by Geertz. As Barone (2008: 107) summarizes it, Geertz "described and advocated for the storytelling and poetic qualities of ethnography." Moreover, Geertz also analysed how academic writing more in general was characterized by blurred genres, in an article with the same title. There, Geertz (1980: 166), for instance, points out how some authors "made their theories rhyme" and places the increase of this phenomenon in the broader context of changes in the object of knowledge.

When focusing more on visual anthropology, we can find, for instance, in Hockings's (1995a) *Principles of Visual Anthropology* – originally published in 1975 – the record of the importance (and long history) of ethnographic films. Even if Hockings is still careful about the capacity of film to communicate academic knowledge,[12] later work in visual anthropology more clearly acknowledges the use of photography and film for "conveying research results" (Holm 2008: 326), arguing that these communicative modes can "be engaged in the processes through which ethnographic knowledge is created and represented" (Pink 2004: 1). These practices also translated into the establishment of specialized journals, such as the *Journal of Video Ethnography*, which aims to "advance the social scientific use of video/film as a method for exploring human society, systems, and cultures and as a medium for presenting the findings of those explorations."[13]

Although visual sociology is still more geared towards the analysis of the visual (Holm 2008: 327), a number of authors have argued for using the visual to communicate academic knowledge. In his article "The scope of visual sociology," Grady (1996: 10) argues[14] that the proliferation of new technologies has "created new modes of representing information as well as entirely new media for communicating research findings." Chaplin (1994: 3) makes a similar argument in her book *Sociology and Visual Representation*, critiquing that "we tend to take for granted the pre-eminence of the written text in almost all areas of knowledge, and to regard any accompanying visual material as subsidiary to it." She argues not only that "social analysis is beginning to make more use of visual representation" but also that it "*should* make more use of visual depictions, unconventional typography and page layout in its analysis" (Chaplin 1994: 2; emphasis in original).

APPROACH 5: ARTS-BASED RESEARCH

The fifth and last approach discussed here is arts-based research.[15] Arts-based research is different from artistic research (Klein 2017), even though it is related. As Leavy (2015: ix; original emphasis removed) writes, arts-based research[16] is "a set of methodological tools used by researchers across the disciplines during all phases of social research, including data generation, analysis, interpretation, and representation." A similar emphasis can be found with Finley (2008: 72), who lists a number of "salient features," where arts-based research

(1) makes use of emotive, affective experiences, senses, and bodies, and imagination and emotion as well as intellect, as ways of knowing and responding to the world [...] (2) gives interpretive license to the researcher to create meaning from experience [...] (3) attends to the role of form in shaping meaning (and) (4) exists in the tensions of blurred boundaries.

Still rooted in academia, arts-based research consists of a search for different communicational modes to communicate academic knowledge, or, to use Leavy's (2015: 11) words, it "advances critical conversations about the nature of social scientific practice and expands the borders of our methods repository." Leavy's (2015: 11, 19, 294) claim, that arts-based research is an "alternative" paradigm, distinct from the quantitative and qualitative paradigms, might be slightly excessive, but at the same time, it should be acknowledged that the focus on resonance and evocation (Leavy 2015: 294) makes arts-based research particular. Moreover, its emphasis on doing (making) brings in the idea that knowledge is or, expressed more modestly, can be embodied and produced through the creation of the artistic practice itself. To use Cooperman's (2018: 22) more poetic formulation, "Arts-based research is a research of the flesh where our source material originates from the closeness and collaboration of the bodies and voices of one another."

Arts-based research's use of artistic communicational repertoires partially still implies the use of written texts to communicate (academic) knowledge, however. One seminal example is Leavy's (2011) novel *Low-Fat Love*, which uses a fictional format to communicate (interview-based) research about women's relationships with partners and relatives and with their own body. In addition, the wealth of artistic communicational repertoires allows using a variety of very distinct non-written communicational tools. Leavy's (2015: ix) overview gives a first idea of the possibilities:

Representational forms include but are not limited to short stories, novels, experimental writing forms, graphic novels, comics, poems, parables, collages, paintings, drawings, sculpture, 3-D art, quilts and needlework, performance scripts, theatrical performances, dances, films, and songs and musical scores.

There are many examples possible, ranging from ethnodrama and ethnotheatre (Saldaña 2005, 2011), which respectively translate research findings into a dramatic script and generate a live performance on the basis of such a script, to installation art (Bischop 2005; Lapum 2018).

AN OVERVIEW

The five approaches can be summarized as in Table 1, but it should be immediately noted that this overview is bound to be limited, not only because of the impossibility of doing justice to the complexity of (and contradictions within) each of these five approaches but also because of the overlap among them. For instance, Kara (2015), who focuses on knowledge dissemination, has an extensive discussion on the use of artistic repertoires for academic dissemination. She lists many examples, many of which could be just as well discussed as examples of arts-based research. One other example is the renaming of the visual anthropology section in *American Anthropologist*. The new name *multimodal anthropology* was motivated by the section editors through the "changes in the media ecologies we engage as anthropologists, changes that have broadened our perspective to include other forms of media

practice, while remaining inclusive of visual anthropology" (Collins, Durington and Gill 2017: 142).

One of the more interesting areas where the overlap becomes very tangible is related to participatory practices. In this chapter, participatory research has already been discussed as part of the knowledge exchange approach, but some authors writing about arts-based research argue that participation is key to the latter approach as well, emphasizing the opportunities for joint knowledge production: "At the heart of arts-based inquiry is a radical, politically grounded statement about social justice and control over the production and dissemination of knowledge" (Finley 2008: 72). Others consider (visual) arts-based participatory methods, with "research participants creating art that ultimately serves both *as* data, and may also *represent* data" (Leavy, 2015: 232; emphasis in original) as a subset of arts-based research or consider them as two separate traditions that can be combined (Gutberlet, Jayme de Oliveira and Tremblay 2017). In this sense, it is, for instance, remarkable how the photovoice genre/method – "the combination of participant created photographs and narratives" (Jarldorn 2019: 1) – features in many of the approaches that were discussed here.

TABLE 1: AN OVERVIEW OF THE FIVE APPROACHES						
APPROACH	OBJECTIVE	RELATION TO ACADEMIC DISCIPLINE(S)	DOMINANT MODE(S)	RELATION TO PUBLIC(S)	SUBJECT POSITION(S)	KNOWLEDGE PRODUCTION
Science communication, science popularization and knowledge dissemination	Democratize knowledge reception	Post ante	(Mass) media	Disconnected target group	Traditional academics working with knowledge brokers	Two linear stages
Knowledge exchange and participatory, transformative and interventionist (action) research	Democratize knowledge production	In multiple disciplines	Dialogical formats (dominance of oral and written)	Joint knowledge production	Hybridizing academic subject position	Dialogical
Multimodal academic communication	Expand writing	In writing studies (and beyond)	Audiovisual and online	Expanding publics	Postwriting academic subject position	Iterative
Visual anthropology and visual sociology	Expand anthropological writing	In anthropology and sociology	Film and photography	Expanding publics	Postwriting academic subject position	Iterative
Arts-based research	Expand knowledge production and communication	Combining arts with multiple disciplines	Artistic repertoires	Expanding publics	Hybridizing academic subject position	Iterative

These five approaches – all in their own way calling for textual diversity when communicating academic knowledge – have played an instrumental role in the *Iconoclastic Controversies* exhibitions, even if (originally) these exhibitions were called "visual sociologies" (linking them [too] exclusively to approach 4) and even if the first approach, focussed on science communication, science popularization and knowledge dissemination, served more as negative inspiration source.

THE ITERATIVE NATURE OF KNOWLEDGE PRODUCTION

What the *Iconoclastic Controversies* exhibitions[17] first demonstrated is the integrated and iterative nature of the different components of knowledge production, in which the communicative dimension cannot be segregated from the entire process of knowledge production. The *Iconoclastic Controversies* exhibition was not a phase *after* the knowledge production phase but was integrated into the knowledge production itself. Murray (2009: 8) already made this kind of argument in her book *Non-Discursive Rhetoric*, in the following words:

> Similarly, inventing, composing, and designing need no longer sound like completely separate, stand-alone processes. One of the consequences of acknowledging the efficacy and rhetorical power of non-discursive text is the knowledge that not only are these elements iterative, they are consubstantial: they exist at once in body, and though their production could be broken down into these elements, they are happening simultaneously even while the text is being read.

This is not a new argument, though, and has been made in relation to academic writing as well (see, e.g. Bazerman 1988), where the written text, as a communicative tool, also impacts on knowledge and how exactly ideas are articulated, communicated and remembered. Moreover, the acknowledgement of the knowledge-generative capacity of communicative tools and the deep implementation of the communication of knowledge in the process of knowledge production has not remained restricted to written text. For instance, Mitchell's (1994) discussion on metapictures[18] in his book *Picture Theory*, where he articulates pictures-as-theory, also implies the recognition that pictures are not mere illustrations – added only at the end of a linear (writing) process – but integrated into the process of knowledge production itself.

In this context, iterability gains a meaning that is very much in line with its (qualitative) methodological meaning (Aspers and Corte 2019). In their manifesto on multimodality, Wysocki and colleagues (2019: 19) argue that the "practice of making" is not disconnected from "critical activity" or, in the particular case of the Iconoclastic Controversies project, that the production of the photographs and the construction of an exhibition itself also (iteratively) contributes to theory formation. They write, "Furthermore, practices of making and critical activity must be rendered mutually supportive. Such a perspective does not privilege one or another paradigm but sees them as two sides of the same coin: analysis informs production; production informs analysis" (Wysocki et al. 2019: 19). Of particular importance here is the generative capacity of the differences among different communicative modes: gaps of signification open up between them, offering opportunities for re-conceptualization and re-articulation (Cope and Kalantzis 2009: 14).

HYBRID SUBJECT POSITIONS

Second, the *Iconoclastic Controversies* exhibitions demonstrated the complexity and hybridity of the subject positions that were involved. Cooperman's (2018: 22–23) writing about arts-based research nicely exemplifies this point: "We choose to risk that identity as part of undoing the systems of power which so neatly construct and produce who and what we are." Creating an assemblage of artistic and academic repertoires, with its photographs, its explanatory text panels, its deployment of the discursive-material knot to analyse the hegemony of antagonistic nationalism, its galleries and its visitors at least complicates the subject position of the academic. The authorship of the Iconoclastic Controversies photographs demonstrates how the subject position of the academic can be articulated with other subject positions, such as the subject position of the artist, affecting both subject positions through the articulatory process, without annulling the subject position of the academic. Even though both subject positions share elements (e.g. creativity and intuition, as Janesick (2001) argues), their explicit combination into what Sinner (2014) calls "artademics," for lack of a better term,[19] has a number of implications, which also became apparent through the authorship of the Iconoclastic Controversies photographs. Academic-artistic practices, as the Iconoclastic Controversies project made clear, demonstrate that both subject positions can be reconciled and that they are (thus) not mutually exclusive.

It is, in other words, possible to maintain an identification with an academic subject position, performing systematicity, a sense for precision and abstraction, an ethical positionality and transparency, and dialogical referentiality,[20] in combination with the deployment of artistic repertoires that do not lead to the instrumentalization of the artistic but instead respects its complex commitment to aesthetics, and the sense of abstraction, ethics and dialogical referentiality that also characterize the arts, albeit differently. Moreover, these practices demonstrate that this reconciliation is potentially beneficial, allowing for the enrichment of academic and artistic

communicative repertoires and for the development of knowledge in general. Third, these practices demonstrate that academia is not the exclusive site of knowledge production but that many different societal fields, including the arts, also engage in knowledge production and that the myth of a singular centre of knowledge production does not hold. It is, as Finley (2008: 73) writes, "an act of rebellion against the monolithic 'truth' that science is supposed to entail." Finally, the *Iconoclastic Controversies* exhibitions, as a form of knowledge communication driven by a hybrid academic-artistic subject position, allowed taking more charge of the communicative process, decreasing the dependency on knowledge brokers that is typical for the traditional knowledge dissemination approach. This renders the academic-artist more autonomous, avoiding what Fahnestock (1986) calls "scientific accommodations."

The previous paragraphs are not aimed to suggest that the reconciliation of these subject positions was easy. In particular, there is the issue of skills that are part of the performance of both subject positions as their absence might disrupt the hybrid subject position of the artademic. As Capous-Desyllas and Morgaine (2018: xii) write in their preface, "Some proponents of [arts-based research] stress that it is necessary for researchers to develop requisite skills and techniques in the chosen art form so as not to appear amateurish in their endeavors." Finley (2008), for instance, suggests training for those who are not sufficiently familiar with artistic practice. The same argument could be made for the academic component. Other strategies consist of the establishment of collaborative teams (Eisner 2008) or simply being less demanding, as, for instance, Leavy (2015: 30), suggests: "[Arts-based research] is not art for art's sake. It is a different thing that is artistic, but not only artistic." In the case of the Iconoclastic Controversies project, the first visual essay (Carpentier 2014), published in a cultural magazine, served as a test for the aesthetic quality of the photographs, later receiving further support by the interest of a respected cultural NGO, eventually leading to the second *Iconoclastic Controversies* in Limassol, in 2016.

DIVERSIFIED PUBLICS

Third, the *Iconoclastic Controversies* exhibitions also demonstrate the ability of these kinds of projects to reach diversified publics. A considerable part of the literature that deals with the five approaches expresses significant optimism about the ability of the non-written academic texts (or differently written texts) to reach different and/or larger publics. For instance, Leavy (2015: 292) writes that "the turn toward artistic forms of representation brings social research to broader and public audiences, mitigating some of the educational and social class biases that have traditionally dictated the beneficiaries of academic scholarship." Literat and colleagues (2018), writing about multimodal scholarship, use a similar argumentation, even though it is formulated more carefully. They write that "by communicating research conclusions in multiple modes and on multiple platforms, scholars can reach beyond traditional academic audiences" (Literat et al. 2018: 572). Accessibility of the content is, for Literat et al., key to achieving this increased reach, which in turn is said to offer citizens the opportunity to engage more and better with research findings.

An increased and more diversified public reach is not the only argument used in this context, however. As mentioned in the knowledge exchange approach discussion, participation in knowledge production – knowledge sharing – is also articulated as a possible outcome. In their article about multimodal scholarship, Literat and colleagues (2018: 568), for instance, point to the ability to "co-create knowledge with research participants." In some cases, the participatory argument is used in a broader sense as well, in which the possibilities of a recalibration of the power relations between the academic field and other societal fields are mentioned, opening up not only spaces for shared knowledge production but also opportunities for achieving more diverse interpretations (of knowledge communication), as Leavy (2015: 26) argues, when she writes that "research-produced artworks can democratize meaning-making and decentralize academic researchers as 'the experts.'"

The use of artistic repertoires opens up spaces for publics who are not employed (or studying in) academic institutions; however, art institutions are not necessarily accessible to all either. The *Iconoclastic Controversies* exhibitions did combine three very different spaces, one related to the Cypriot bi-communal peace movement, one arts space and one university space, but each space in itself created its own exclusions. Even if this should put a damper on the enthusiasm of some multimodal and arts-based scholarship proponents, we should not forget that the idea of a "general public," lumping together all non-academics, is an unhelpful myth and that we should think in terms of a diversity of publics (or target groups) with a diversity of characteristics that can only be imperfectly reached through a diversity of channels.

The *Iconoclastic Controversies* exhibitions did not live up to these high expectations when it comes to participatory knowledge production, as we can find in the knowledge exchange approa ch and in parts of the arts-based research approach. As photographer and exhibition curator, I remained firmly in control of the conception and construction process. It was still a highly structured theoretical text that explicitly shied away from being too open or too "readerly" (Barthes 1974: 4). Even if also "writerly" texts are open to interpretation, rendering the *Iconoclastic Controversies* exhibitions too readerly might have pushed them outside the realm of academic research communication. This is arguably one of the areas where the celebration of interpretative multiplicity and textual openness (Leavy 2015: 26) needs to be qualified. Still, to be able to witness visitors entering the exhibition spaces, looking at the photographs and reading the texts produced feelings of satisfaction that I hardly ever experienced as an author of written texts. Moreover, being able to guide visitors through the entire exhibition (as I was often present in the gallery spaces) and discuss their experiences was a unique, highly rewarding and pleasant experience that authors of written academic texts hardly ever encounter.

CONCLUSION

This is (obviously) not a call to abandon the written text, which has been proven vital in the century-old history of academic inquiry. The written text has particular affordances that work well with theory formation, argumentation and counter-argumentation, referentiality and more. It is, for instance, a conscious decision to combine the Iconoclastic Controversies exhibition photographs with written academic text, making an individual creative experimental experience visible and adding a layer of meaning to the ensemble of reflections by, and on, the photographs. Moreover, Jagodzinski and Wallin (2013: 21) have described the present conjuncture as characterized by post-alphabetization, warning for the consequences of reduced literacies. Arguably, there is a need for increased and accumulated literacies, not for less; from this perspective, there are good reasons to be careful for academics not to contribute to a logic of replacement. In other words, Murray's (2009: 8) argument for addition over substitution is more valid than ever.

At the same time, as this book argues, the alternative (artistic) modes of communication do have something to offer that is too promising to ignore at the levels of knowledge production, and its communication, hybrid subject positions, and diversification, interaction and participation of publics. But here, too, there are reasons for being careful and to avoid the overenthusiastic celebration of these alternative modes of academic communication. Given the complexity of reconfiguring the academic assemblage, doing the identity of work of hybrid subject positions, and acquiring and deploying the necessary extended skill sets, multimodal and art-based research scholarship should remain an invitation and not become a requirement. But, inversely, when academics do engage in these novel practices, there is a need for institutional appreciation and support, which are also still too often lacking (Leavy 2015: 266ff). Even if there is still a long way to go – in particular, in the field of Media and Communication Studies – carefully and critically moving forward, creating a critical mass of academics who are willing to engage in more experiments, will eventually also allow further enriching academia and its many fields.

NOTES

1. Various concepts are being used in these discussions, and no solution is perfect: Reid, Snead, Pettiway and Simoneaux (2016: 8) and Powell (2020) refer to the written text as the "alphabetic text"; Murray (2009) writes about the "hegemony of discursive text." Literat and colleagues (2018) use both "text-based" and "paper-based" academic formats. Here, the concept of the "written text" is considered to be the most appropriate, keeping in mind that the concept of the "text" is defined in a broad sense to "include every form of mediation in language, sound, smell and image" (Lewis 2008: 5).

2. Of course, written texts also frequently contain other communicative modes (see Elkins 2007) and also the oral mode is often used, for instance, for conference presentations.

3. These examples are structured following the five approaches, which are discussed later.

4. See, for instance, Sonia Livingstone's TEDxExeter talk at https://www.youtube.com/watch?v=SyjbDUP1o0g.

5. https://www.camrapenn.org.

6. https://tinyurl.com/hl4vrpq. The theme book of the 2017 International Communication Association conference (on

interventions) also has one chapter on the exhibition (Henderson, Hogan, Christian and Erni 2018).

7. https://oregon2018.iamcr.org/ecomedia.html.

8. Schiele et al. (2012: xxiii) retrace the deficit model to Snow's (1998) *The Two Cultures*, originally published in 1959, which was even in the 1960s extensively critiqued (see Leavis 2013).

9. http://www.unesco.org/new/en/natural-sciences/science-technology/sti-policy/global-focus/science-popularization/.

10. Multimodal academic practices are much older and widespread than the label itself, evidenced by the importance of the scientific illustration (see, e.g. Ford 1992); in the meanwhile, these practices have moved beyond the field of writing studies.

11. There are, of course, similar examples in the (hard) sciences. One example is the peer-reviewed *Journal of Visualized Experiments* (JoVE – https://www.jove.com/), whose articles "consist of high-quality video demonstrations and detailed text protocols which facilitate scientific reproducibility and productivity" (https://www.jove.com/about/).

12. In his conclusion of *Principles of Visual Anthropology*, Hockings (1995b: 515; emphasis in original), for instance, writes that "film can capture an external reality for future analysis in many contexts – analysis by many scholars and for many purposes – whereas a written ethnographic account can only capture KNOWLEDGE ABOUT that reality, whether it is the ethnographer's own knowledge or that of his native informants too." Mead's (1995) introductory text of this volume, even if she's critiquing anthropology for being a "discipline of words" and refers to the "criminal neglect of the use of film" (6) also tends towards an emphasis on data collection and less on academic communication, even if her own work with Bateson (Bateson and Mead 1942) can be easily interpreted differently.

13. http://www.videoethno.com/.

14. One concrete genre that Grady (1996: 18) suggests is the visual essay. A similar argument could be made about the essay film, which is discussed by Alter (2018: 5) as "filmed philosophy."

15. Arguably, arts-based research could be extended to practice-based research, but this is beyond the scope of this book. Also, different labels for arts-based research have been used. For instance, in Canada the label *research creation* is frequently used (see, e.g. Loveless 2015).

16. Arts-based research is not the only intellectual project that aims to integrate more artistic repertoires into academia. For instance, fictocriticism, a (mostly) feminist set of projects, aims to combine fictional writing, theory and critique (Gibbs 2003; Haas 2017). But arts-based research is particularly relevant here because of its shift away from the written text.

17. A part of this text was originally written for the analysis of another artwork, the *Mirror Palace of Democracy* (see Carpentier 2020), which was part of the Respublika! exhibition (see Carpentier 2019). It has been adjusted for the analysis of the *Iconoclastic Controversies* exhibitions.

18. Mitchell (1994: 48; emphasis in original) defines metapictures as "pictures that show themselves in order to *know* themselves." His chapter on metapictures is described in the following words: "[the chapter] looks at pictures 'as' theory, as second-order reflections on the practices of pictorial representation; it asks what pictures tell us when they theorize (or depict) themselves" (1994: 9).

19. There are alternatives, however. Finley (2008: 73), for instance, uses the term "artists as researchers/researchers as artists," which is a bit long to be used here.

20. Defined here as the explicit connection to a body of academic knowledge.

Chapter 3: On Antagonism and Nationalism – A Discursive-Material Re-Reading

As the Iconoclastic Controversies project focused on antagonistic nationalism, it is important to provide a theoretical grounding that allows us to gain an in-depth understanding of this concept. This is done here through the perspective of the discursive-material knot (Carpentier 2017), which allows highlighting the strong discursive dimension of nationalism, but also its material components (and how these are entangled). When analysing nationalism from this perspective of the discursive-material knot – relying heavily on Billig's (1995) work on nationalism – we can start by arguing that nationalism is a discourse that is particular, first because of the presence of two subject positions: the self and the other. This discourse's particularity (and the relation between self and other) is mediated through nationalism's connection with the signifier of the nation (the nodal point of the nationalist discourse, as de Cleen (2012) argued), where "[t]he term 'nation' carries two inter-related meanings. There is the 'nation' as the nation-state, and there is the 'nation' as the people living within the state. The linkage of the two meanings reflects the general ideology of nationalism" (Billig 1995: 24). This articulation of the nation-as-people and the nation-(as-)state is at the very heart of the nationalist project.

NATIONALISM AS A DISCOURSE

The specificity of the signifier nation does not annul that nationalism still uses an in-group and out-group logic, distinguishing between a self and one or more others. Billig (1995: 70) emphasized the centrality of the self in the following terms: "There is a case for saying that nationalism is, above all, an ideology of the first person plural," but he immediately added that nationalism "is also an ideology of the third person. There can be no 'us' without a 'them'" (1995: 78). But again, both self and other gain specific articulations in nationalist discourse. In the case of the self, the subject positions that are mobilized are the citizen, on the one hand (linking subjects to the nation-state), and the member of the national community, on the other (linking subjects to the people). The balance tends to be different, but both subject positions (or the interrelated concepts of state and community) are present. Weber's (1991: 176) definition of the nation is one illustration, when he wrote: "A nation is a community of sentiment which would adequately manifest itself in a state of its own; hence, a nation is a community which normally tends to produce a state of its own." We can find this combination also in Anderson's (2006: 6) book *Imagined Communities*, where he argued that the nation is both sovereign and a community. In the latter case, Anderson emphasized the notion of belonging that grounds community membership, as the nation is "always conceived as a deep, horizontal comradeship." He added that "it is this fraternity that makes it possible, over the past two centuries, for so many millions of people, not so much to kill, as willingly to die for such limited imaginings." When returning to Billig (1995: 73), we can see in the following example how the concept of nationality bridges the two subject positions:

> If "we" are to imagine "ourselves" as unique, "we" need a name to do so. [...] "we" must categorize "ourselves" with a distinctive label, so that "we" are "French," or "Belgian" or "Turkish" (or "Breton," or "Flemish" or "Kurdish"). The category not only categorizes "us" in our particularity – demarcating "us" as an "us" – but the category is to be categorized (or proclaimed) as a national label in its universality. There is, in short, a universal code for the naming of particulars.

Also, the other becomes specific in the nationalist discourse, with the subject position of the foreigner acting as a constitutive outside of the self. Here, Billig referred to Kristeva's (1991) book *Strangers to Ourselves*, arguing that the other-foreigner is the subject (position) that does not belong to the state that defines the self, as the other-foreigner does not have that state's particular nationality. Kristeva (1991: 96) indeed wrote that "[w]ith the establishment of nation-states we come to the only modern, acceptable, and clear definition of foreignness: the foreigner is the one who does not belong to the state in which we are, the one who does not have the same nationality." But Kristeva also aimed to move away from the legalist articulation of the other-foreigner subject position and offered a much richer discussion where the absence of belonging plays an important role. On the one hand, the other-foreigner is described in the following, rather depressing, terms: "Not belonging to any place, any time, any love. A lost origin, the impossibility to take root, a rummaging memory, the present in abeyance. The space of the foreigner is a moving train, a plane in flight, the very transition that precludes stopping" (Kristeva 1991: 7–8). But on the other hand, Kristeva (1991: 7) also wrote that "[t]he foreigner

feels strengthened by the distance that detaches him from the others [...]. In the eyes of the foreigner those who are not foreign have no life at all: barely do they exist, haughty or mediocre, but out of the running and thus almost already cadaverized." Later, she added: "Always elsewhere, the foreigner belongs nowhere" (Kristeva 1991: 10), again implying that this subject position is articulated outside the national community.

THE MATERIALITY OF NATIONALISM

Nationalist discourses are still part of assemblages that also have material components. Especially in the primordialist approaches of nationalism[1] (Özkirimli 2010: 49ff), the material becomes amply visible, even if their essentialisms (leading to the naturalization of nationalism) are theoretically problematic and irreconcilable with the discourse-material knot perspective used here. But the primordialist argumentation brings out the role of the material very clearly. In the more socio-biological versions of primordialism, kinship and common descent are seen as the material backbone of nationalism, as van den Berghe (2001: 274) argued: "In simplest terms, the sociobiological view of these groups is that they are fundamentally defined by common descent and maintained by endogamy. Ethnicity, thus, is simply kinship writ large." Ethnic groups and "races" are then seen as "super-families of (distant) relatives, real or putative, who tend to intermarry, and who are knit together by vertical ties of descent reinforced by horizontal ties of marriage" (van den Berghe 2001: 274). Writing from a more distant position, Connor (1978: 381) made a similar reference, but he added the important and often-used blood metaphor, referring to the material sharing of the "same blood" to the analysis: "It is the intuitive conviction which can give to nations a psychological dimension approximating that of the extended family, i.e., a feeling of common blood lineage."

Another material component is the homeland. As Özkirimli (2010: 51) wrote, nationalism sees "[t]he nation [as] the sole depository of sovereignty and the only source of political power and legitimacy. This comes with a host of temporal and spatial claims – to a unique history and destiny, and a historic 'homeland.'" Or, to use Billig's (1995: 8) words: "Having a national identity also involves being situated physically, legally, socially, as well as emotionally: typically, it means being situated within a homeland, which itself is situated within the world of nations." A third material component of nationalism is the material dimensions of a set of cultural practices, where language, religion and history are significant fields. For instance, Kristeva (1991: 178), in her discussion of Herder's work on the national genius (the *Volksgeist*), wrote: "one nevertheless finds in Herder the first and most explicit expression of such an anchoring of culture in the genius of the language." Geertz (1993: 259) mentioned, in his discussion of primordial attachments in decolonized states, "being born into a particular religious community, speaking a particular language, or even a dialect of a language, and following particular social practices." Özkirimli (2010: 51ff) also argued that history plays an important role in nationalist discourse, through the belief in the nation's continued existence (even if it is suppressed). Özkirimli (2010: 58) here referred to the perennialist version of primordialism, which is defined by Smith (1998: 159) in the following words:

> The perennialist readily accepts the modernity of nationalism as a political movement and ideology, but regards nations either as updated versions of immemorial ethnic communities, or as collective cultural identities that have existed, alongside ethnic communities, in all epochs of human history.

Özkirimli (2010: 52) provided us with an example of this perennialist logic, grounded in the idea that the nation has always been there, when he quoted the words of Adamantios Korais, who he described as "the foremost figure of the Neohellenic Enlightenment":

> In the middle of the last century, the Greeks constituted a miserable nation who suffered the most horrible oppression and experienced the nefarious effects of a long period of slavery. [...] Following these two developments [the opening of new channels for trade and the military defeat of the Ottomans] the Greeks [...] raise their heads in proportion as their oppressors' arrogance abates. [...] This is the veritable period of Greek awakening. [...] For the first time the nation surveys the hideous spectacle of its ignorance and trembles in measuring with the eye the distance separating it from its ancestors' glory. (Korais, cited in Özkirimli 2010: 52)

It is rather obvious that these cultural practices have a discursive component, but here it is particularly relevant to emphasize that cultural practices related to language, religion and history, but also to economy, also have material components, as they are performed in the present, even in the case of history, where the practices of memorialization are highly material. Finally, in discussing the material components of nationalism, we need to return to the nation-state, as also the nation-state apparatuses have strong material components, against the backdrop of particular economic and social (class) structures (Breton 1964; Findlay 1995), which are equally material. In his discussion of the nation-state, Billig referred to Giddens's (1985: 120, cited in Billig 1995: 20) definition of the nation-state as "a set of institutional forms of governance maintaining an administrative monopoly over a territory with demarcated boundaries, its rule being sanctioned by law and direct control of the means of internal and external violence," which nicely illustrates this material dimension.

NATIONALIST ASSEMBLAGES

As an ideological project, nationalism is easy to integrate into the perspective of the discursive-material knot, at least when focusing on the discursive component. Within academia, the idea that nationalism is a discourse (or a construction, or a narrative, or a rhetoric) is widely accepted. For instance, Özkirimli (2010: 206) wrote, after discussing the many different theories on nationalism: "I treat nationalism as a 'discourse', a particular way of seeing and interpreting the world, a frame of reference that helps us make sense of and structure the reality that surrounds us." He continued this part with an overview of references to this perspective, with Hall as one of his sources. Hall (1996: 613, cited in Özkirimli 2010: 207) is quoted here as saying that "a national culture is a discourse – a way of constructing meanings which influences and organises both our actions and our conception of ourselves." Moreover, nationalist discourses are recognized to have been, over time, strong forces of interpellation that have driven millions to their deaths. To use Žižek's (1993: 202) words: "Nationalism [...] presents a privileged domain of the eruption of enjoyment into the social field."

It was also Žižek (1993: 201) that offered a bridge from the discursive to the material component of nationalism, which is rare, as both components remain firmly segregated in most theories of nationalism. As mentioned before, primordialist theories do pay considerable attention to the material dimension of nationalism, but their irreconcilability with the discursive-culturalist approaches hinder the combination of discursive and material components in theories of nationalism. One example that illustrates these difficulties is this quotation from Connor (1978: 389), when he attributed an ex-post role to the material in the following way:

Any nation, of course, has tangible characteristics and, once recognized, can therefore be described in tangible terms. The German nation can be described in terms of its numbers, its religious composition, its language, its location, and a number of other concrete factors. But none of these elements is, of necessity, essential to the German nation. The essence of the nation, as earlier noted, is a matter of self-awareness or self-consciousness.

Žižek (1993: 201), with his psychoanalytical approach, opens the door for looking at the nationalist interactions of the discursive-material when he wrote that "[t]he element which holds together a given community cannot be reduced to the point of symbolic identification: the bond linking together its members always implies a shared relationship toward a Thing, toward Enjoyment incarnated." One of the other authors that thematizes the role of the material more, and brings together the rather dispersed reflections on materiality and nationalism – Kaygan (2012) – also commented on the scarcity of this kind of work:

> Ideological and discourse-analytical approaches to everyday nationalism have been mainly interested [in] the reproduction of the nation in the symbolic register – above all in political and media discourse, everyday talk and accompanying representations of the nation. Yet, nationalism in everyday life cannot be reduced to its representational aspects. (Kaygan 2012: 91)

The material does play a significant role, also in relation to nationalism, as Edensor (2002: vii) formulated it: "national identity is not only a matter of will and strategy, but is enmeshed in the embodied, material ways in which we live." Kaygan's (2012) overview touches upon the materiality of state apparatuses and the institutional basis of discourses of nationalism, in combination with the materiality of nationalist praxis and experience (see also Foucher 2011: 100), where he referred extensively to Edensor's (2002) discussion on the temporal and spatial organization of the nation. Kaygan (2012: 96ff) also initiated an analysis on the role of material objects in nationalist discourse, after critiquing Billig's (1995) *Banal Nationalism*[2] for not paying enough attention to the material: "Whilst he also refers to material objects such as actual flags, Billig's main interest is in discursive 'flagging', with examples from politicians' speeches, mass media and academic discourse" (Kaygan 2012: 87). In this part of the overview, Kaygan (2012) listed several types of material objects, including official state products (such as money and stamps), national cuisines and nationally branded and commodified products. Edensor (2002: 108) paid a lot of attention to fashion, arguing that the "most obvious material form in this regard, and that most closely associated with national identity, is clothing."

I would like to argue that these are examples of investment, where discourses provide meaning to material objects and these meanings enter (or are encoded) into the material. Coining is, for instance, the process where a coin die is used to strike an image on the metal, altering its form. Together with bank notes, with their images printed on paper, they become media that communicate elements of the "'national iconography', which encompasses state symbols, historical events and persona, the imagery of the dominant religion, etc." (Kaygan 2012: 98). Moreover, their (relatively) unrestricted use is limited to particular geographies, with more complicated systems set up to deal with money moving outside these boundaries (e.g. exchange rates, exchange offices, etc.). In the case of clothing, in particular, national or "traditional" clothing, Edensor (2002: 108) pointed to the national(ist) meanings attributed to them: "In ceremonies, folk dancing, tourist displays and official engagements, clothing becomes an important marker of national identity." But this also

implies that the textile is cut and combined in particular ways to produce the forms that are seen to emanate from the national identity.

At the same time, these materials also have agency, inviting particular meanings to be attributed to them. To give one example: Once a national dress has been produced, with its (more or less) characteristic form, it invites interpretation in particular ways. What Attfield (2000: 130) called their textility (not to be confused with textuality) affects the way clothes are produced, enabling particular forms to be created, and others not, particular types of material to be used, and others not. Textiles have an "ability to withstand and adapt to changing conditions, and still manage to retain vestiges of their original form" (Attfield 2000: 132). They also suffer from wear and tear, and – as Edensor (2002: 108) argued – they are inhabited, providing the bodies inside them with particular sensatory experiences, enabling these bodies to move in particular ways. Here, the material exercises its agency by offering, and sometimes imposing, particular "ways of moving and feeling, sitting and fiddling" (Edensor 2002: 108).

Also, the material and the discursive are embedded in the logic of contingency. Nationalist discourses change, as they are confronted with space and time. Even in primordialist approaches we can find references to contingency, as they refer to the "awakening" of nationalist sentiments or to the idea that "[p]articular nations may come and go" (Özkirimli 2010: 58). These discourses are also part of many different discursive struggles, with discourses defending and opposing the construction of national identities and other discourses struggling over the specific articulations of national identities. One of the many historical examples is provided by Kane's (2000: 246) analysis of the Irish national identity during the Land War (1879–82), where she retraced the "discursive struggle between the various, and often conflicting, groups which constituted the core of the movement – tenant farmers, nationalists, and the Irish Catholic church." This mostly discursive struggle "against landlords and British rule," paralleled by a discursive struggle within the movement, eventually allowed that "the Irish constructed new meanings, symbolic models, and shared understandings about themselves as a nation" (Kane 2000: 246). Simultaneously, existing nationalist projects can also be unsettled (or strengthened) by new projects (such as the European Union), as de Cillia, Reisigl and Wodak (1999: 150) remarked: "Apparently firmly established national and cultural identities have become contested political terrain and have been at the heart of new political struggles." These discursive struggles can also implicate the material, as is illustrated by the subcultural re-appropriation of style, which also implied a re-articulation of national identity. Edensor's (2002: 109) example deals with the re-articulation of Britishness: "Teddy boys recycled British Edwardian styles, and punks and Britpop bands have made ironic and celebratory use of older fashions."

Contingency can also originate from the material, where events can dislocate nationalist discourses or, in contrast, enable nationalist discourses to re/deconstruct older discourses. One example here is Norval's (1996: 51) analysis of the dislocatory force of a series of historical processes ("the Depression, the great drought and the war") that co-determined the construction of "an exclusivist Afrikaner nationalism." If nationalism is (seen to be) located in particular materials, then these materials are not that easily tamed. Bodies, but also blood and genes, travel in uncontrollable ways, always undermining the homogeneity of ethnic groups and their gene pools. Özkirimli (2010: 58) referred to Smith's (1995) critiques on the primordialist approaches, which can be used here as indicators of the agency of the material: "frequent intermarriage and the importation of scarce skilled labour [...], extensive trading links

with other areas and peoples, and the frequency of external conquests in history," which made it difficult for many ethnic groups to preserve "the cultural homogeneity and pure 'essence' posited by most primordialists" (1995: 33). Cultural practices related to language, religion and history, with their material dimensions, tend to be unstable, sometimes enhancing nationalism, but sometimes frustrating it. Objects invested with nationalist meanings can disappear or disintegrate, despite all conservation efforts, and new discoveries of objects considered significant can dislocate (or strengthen) nationalist discourses. Even territories produce their own contingencies, as geographies tend to change over time, not only by human intervention but also sometimes as part of natural processes such as the changes in the course of a border river.[3]

ANTAGONIST NATIONALISM

The other-foreigner in nationalist discourse, part of the nationalist discursive-material assemblages, can take on different positions, as not all other-foreigners are articulated alike. As Billig (1995: 80) argued, by referring to McDonald's work, "If the imagining of foreignness is an integral part of the theoretical consciousness of nationalism, then foreignness is not an undifferentiated sense of 'Otherness'" (McDonald 1993). "Obsessively fine distinctions can be made between different groups of foreigners." It is actually most helpful to cite Billig's (1995: 87) description of the diversity of otherness at length:

> In consequence, there are infinite discursive possibilities for talking about "us" and "them": and, indeed, "you." "We" are not confined to simple differentiating stereotypes, which downgrade the foreigner as the mysterious Other. Foreign nations are like "ours," but never completely alike. "We" can recognize "ourselves" in "them"; and, there again, "we" can fail to recognize "ourselves." "We"

can become allies, "they" becoming "you"; and "we" can become enemies. And "we" can debate amongst "ourselves" about the value of "our" allies. "We" can accuse "them" of threatening "our" particularity or of failing to act like proper, responsible nations like "we" do. And "we" can claim that "they," in threatening "us," threaten the idea of nationhood. In damning "them," "we" can claim to speak for "all of us."

The last sentences of this quotation show the presence of the other-foreigner as enemy, which produces a type of nationalism that we can label *antagonistic nationalism*.[4] This type of nationalism identifies the other-foreigner as a radically different and inferior actor, which is a threat for the self. This then legitimates the use of violent strategies in order to destroy (or at least neutralize the threat originating from) this other-foreigner. Simultaneously, in antagonistic nationalisms, the self becomes articulated through a solidified chain of equivalence that homogenizes the self, also by defining enemies-within, which then need to become purged for the nationalist chain of equivalence, for example, through the traitor signifier, which aligns the traitor with the other-foreigner-enemy.

To expand a bit on this notion of antagonism: In *Hegemony and Socialist Strategy*, Laclau and Mouffe (1985: 126) used it to theorize the "negation of a given order," where the antagonistic other becomes a constitutive outside that simultaneously produces the self and this outside. Antagonistic relations are (symbolically) violent in nature, as the self attempts to destabilize this other identity, although it ironically requires the very same other to construct its own identity. This construction of an outside, in Mouffe's (2005: 73) words, is very much part of the political: "there is no consensus without exclusion, no 'we' without a 'they' and no politics is possible without the drawing of a frontier," but in the case

of antagonism, the other becomes an enemy, to be excluded from the social order.

In this antagonistic process, the self becomes constituted through the creation of a chain of equivalence, which has a homogenizing impact on the self. Through the workings of this chain of equivalence, a series of discourses (and materials), linked to signifying and material practices, become articulated as representative of the self and as different from those of the constitutive other (see later). The different elements of the chain of equivalence do not naturally belong together, but they are assembled through the antagonism (which implies that the chain can be altered). Nevertheless, the particular assemblage of elements that support the identity of the self (in an antagonistic relation with an enemy) is often rather strong and supports the idea of a homogeneous self.

These antagonistic logics are not exclusively discursive but are grounded in assemblages that articulate the material and the discursive. In the case of violent conflict, violent practices are very present, in all their materiality. Killing the enemy remains a very material act. But signifying practices, legitimating these violent practices from within the antagonism between self and other, remain equally important. Here, we should keep in mind that "[t]he exclusionist discourse of violent conflict is not [...] confined to the battlefield," as Jabri (1996: 138) reminded us:

It is a discourse which politically legitimates and reproduces a categorisation based on those who are defined as legitimately within, against all external others, who are variously target of direct violence and/or institutionalised discrimination.

It is also important to stress that agency still plays a significant role in dealing with these discursive structures, and the interpellation of antagonism can be resisted, for instance through identifications with pacifist discourses (Jabri 1996: 145ff). Also, the discursive component intersects with the (very) materialist dimensions of violence, where particular actors (e.g. armies, police forces, irregular soldiers, weapons manufacturers, and traders, among others) align themselves with a vast and sophisticated range of proto-machines to unleash deadly force.

Finally, I also want to emphasize that these assemblages remain contingent. With a vague sense of irony, one could point out that the material destruction of the other is the ultimate moment of contingency, but the total destruction of the other is often more to be located at the level of the antagonistic fantasy. Actually, the unwillingness of the other to be completely destroyed generates more (or just as much) contingency, through the inability of living out the antagonistic fantasy of eliminating the other. To use Laclau and Mouffe's (1985: 125; emphasis in original) words: "Antagonism, far from being an objective relation, is a relation wherein the limits of every objectivity are *shown*." They continue:

> Antagonism, as a witness of the impossibility of a final suture, is the "experience" of the limit of the social. Strictly speaking, antagonisms are not *internal* but *external* to society; or rather, they constitute the limits of society, the latter's impossibility of fully constituting itself. (Laclau and Mouffe 1985: 125; emphasis in original)

Also, the idea of "a perfectly unified and homogenous agent" (Laclau and Mouffe 1985: 84), constructed through a perfectly stable and eternal chain of equivalence, is open to dislocation, as the complexity of these constructions often crumbles underneath their own (discursive) weight and have to deal with counter-discourses, in particular, in the case of long-lasting violent conflicts. Furthermore, at the material level, the antagonistic assemblages are vulnerable to contingency, ranging from military equipment

not living up to the expectations (of accuracy, for instance) to military personal refusing to engage in battle, arriving too late to the battlefield or dying of illness before they can do so.

AGONISTIC NATIONALIST DISCOURSE

As the long Billig (1995: 87) quotation in the previous part illustrates, the other-foreigner can also be articulated differently, for instance, as other-foreigner-adversary or as other-foreigner-ally. Here, the other-foreigner is dealt with through peaceful and non-violent actions, and both the self and the other-foreigner are accepted as part of the same symbolic space, even if they are still acknowledged as different. This conflictual togetherness is combined with a pluralization of the self, where the chain of equivalence of the self is combined with the logics of difference. This kind of nationalist discourse we can label an *agonistic nationalist discourse*, which builds on Mouffe's (2005, 2013a) work on agonism.

In Mouffe's perspective, the aim of democratic politics is "to transform an 'antagonism' into 'agonism'" (Mouffe 1999: 755), to "tame" or "sublimate" (Mouffe 2005: 20–21) antagonisms, without eliminating passion from the political realm or relegating it to the outskirts of the private. Later, in *Agonistics*, Mouffe (2013a: 109) argued that "antagonistic conflict can take different forms," in order to introduce the distinction between antagonism proper and agonism. While antagonism proper is grounded in the Schmittian friend/enemy relation, agonism is not (Mouffe, in Errejón and Mouffe 2016: 55). Agonism articulates the relationship between self and other as a "we/they relation where the conflicting parties, although acknowledging that there is no rational solution to their conflict, nevertheless recognize the legitimacy of their opponents" (Mouffe 2005: 20). Later, she also pointed to their sharing of ethico-political principles:

What exists between adversaries is, so to speak, a conflictual consensus – they agree about the ethico-political principles which organize their political association but disagree about the interpretation of these principles. (Mouffe 2013a: 109)

In other words, an agonistic conflict does not hide the differences in position and interest between the involved parties; they are still "in conflict" but share "a common symbolic space within which the conflict takes place" (Mouffe 2005: 20; see also Mouffe 2013a: 7). Still, antagonism proper[5] remains "an ever present possibility" (Mouffe 2013b), and societies can quite easily slip into antagonistic self–other relationships, where enemies need to be destroyed.

THE AGONIZATION POLITICS OF ICONOCLASTIC CONTROVERSIES

Iconoclastic Controversies is theoretically and normatively embedded in Mouffe's (2005, 2013a) analysis of antagonism and agonism, and the need to move away from antagonism proper. This shift towards agonism – what I would like to call agonization – is closely related to discussions about conflict transformation (Lederach 2003).

Both frameworks share the normative position that violent conflict is not desirable. The definition of conflict transformation used by Lederach (2003: 14), one of the conflict transformation concept proponents – which is seen to consist of "constructive change processes that reduce violence, increase justice in direct interaction and social structures" and that respond to "real-life problems in human relationships" – enhances this argument. Although Mouffe's work is grounded more in democratic theory, its focus on the transformation of antagonistic conflicts into agonistic conflicts is very similar. As argued before, in her approach, this transformation consists of the redefinition of the enemy into an adversary, who still shares the same symbolic space.

The second basic assumption these approaches share is that conflict is not restricted to violent conflict and that thus conflict does not necessarily disappear when a society (or situation) becomes agonistic. A conflict transformation approach actually emphasizes that "conflict is normal in human relations and conflict is a motor of change" (Lederach 2003: 5). Also Mouffe (2005: 4) puts considerable emphasis on "the ineradicability of the conflictual dimension in social life." Later, she would write:

The specificity of modern democracy is precisely its recognition and legitimation of conflict; in democratic societies, therefore, conflict cannot and should not be eradicated. Democratic politics requires that the others be seen not as enemies to be destroyed but as adversaries whose ideas should be fought, even fiercely, but whose right to defend those ideas will never be questioned. (Mouffe 2013b: 185)

Mouffe's (1996: 8) reflections about conflict are very much embedded in a democratic theory of diversity, where "the specificity of liberal democracy as a new political form of society consists of the legitimation of conflict and the refusal to eliminate it through the imposition of an authoritarian order." Conflict transformation, or the agonization of conflict, thus rejects the idea that an ultimate consensus (or resolution) can be achieved and argues instead that conflict transformation consists of the democratization of conflict. These approaches also imply that both conflict and conflict transformation are intensely political processes that cut through a variety of societal fields and are not limited to institutionalized politics. This is exemplified by Mouffe's (2005: 8) distinction between politics and the political, which supports this broadening of the democratic-political scope:

By "the political," I refer to the dimension of antagonism that is inherent in human relations, antagonism that can take many forms and emerge in different types of social relations. "Politics" on the other side, indicates the ensemble of practices, discourses and institutions which seek to establish a certain order and organize human coexistence in conditions that are always potentially conflictual because they are affected by the dimension of "the political."

As a consequence, also academic actors can engage and assist in these political processes of conflict transformation or agonization, as the Iconoclastic Controversies project does. The study of violent conflict has a long history, but academic activism (Evangelista 1999; Eschle and Maiguashca 2006) and academic diplomacy (Wallensteen 2009) in relation to violent conflict also have a substantial history. Moreover, action research, used also in conflict-affected societal contexts (McIntyre 2000; Life & Peace Institute 2014, 2016), incorporates a similar interventionist dimension.

Second, also the arts have been working with the objective of agonization (or conflict transformation). Obviously, the arts have a long history of communicating about and sometimes fiercely critiquing violent conflict (Hyvärinen and Muszynski 2006; Mesch 2013; Downey 2014; Segal 2016). We can use the work of Krzysztof Wodiczko to illustrate these dynamics, although many other examples exist. Wodiczko is most known for his large-scale projections on monuments, reflecting about memory and trauma but also critiquing the culture of war. For instance, the *Abolition of War* is an arts project that proposes to transform the *Arc de Triomphe* (in Paris, France), which celebrates the Napoleonic Wars, into the *World Institute for the Abolition of War* (Wodiczko 2012). Wodiczko's writings about the need for a

transformative avant-garde tackles the culture of war head-on, for instance when he writes:

> Building a war-free civilization demands dismantling the workings of the culture of war, disarming its symbolic arsenal, exposing war's human toll and fallout, and confronting our drive to enter war situations. An even more important task is to create and disseminate new and effective peacemaking and peace-securing projects. (Wodiczko 2014: 121)

Authors writing in the traditions of conflict transformation and agonization have taken on this challenge and have been addressing the capacity of the arts to contribute to agonization. Bergh and Sloboda (2010: 6) argue that this literature started developing in the 1990s and point to Liebmann's (1996) *Arts Approaches to Conflict Resolution* and the European Centre for Conflict Prevention's (1999) *People Building Peace*. The arguments behind this articulation of the arts and agonization are well captured by Lederach (2005: 73), when he writes, addressing the conflict transformation community: "We need to envision ourselves as artists. We need a return to aesthetics." He continues by emphasizing that academics still need to maintain discipline and respect the specifics of the artistic field, but also that "[a]esthetics helps those who attempt to move from cycles of violence to new relationships and those of us who wish to support such movement to see ourselves for whom we are: artists bringing to life and keeping alive something that has not existed" (Lederach 2005: 73–74). One example of this kind of analysis, in a Cypriot context, is Ungerleider's (1999) text from *People Building Peace* about the role of music and poetry in the Cyprus Problem. He argues for the capacity of the arts in the following terms: "Lyric music helps keep the vision of peace alive and deeply felt. It is a tool and impetus for communication, collaboration and celebration, cornerstones of a budding common culture, not Greek or Turkish, but Cypriot, non-divisive and hopeful – peace culture."[6]

The Iconoclastic Controversies project aimed to contribute to the process of agonization by deconstructing and de-naturalizing antagonistic nationalism but also by triggering societal debate, reflections and further initiatives, empowering the more agonism-oriented parts of society and offering opportunities for reflection to others, without overestimating the capacity of one project to achieve social change. Simultaneously, it is important to stress that academic interventions and action research remain political (in Mouffe's meaning allocated to the concept of the political). However valuable academic work is, regardless of its form and modes, its truth claims are not automatically accepted (Lyotard 1984). Academic interventions, more specifically, however truthful they may be, may be fiercely resisted, problematized and rejected. Or they may simply be ignored. Some of these rejections might be grounded in the refusal of the conflict transformative and agonistic assumptions or in the logics of antagonism itself (leading, for instance, to accusations of partiality). Other rejections might be related to critiques on academia in general (e.g. the ivory tower metaphor), on action research in particular or on the communicational tools and repertoires that are deployed (e.g. the use of photography).

Arguably, the responses to academic interventions, aimed at agonization, including its rejections, are important to study, as they allow to evaluate the interventions themselves, but also because they yield more information about the processes that are being studied and allow for the cyclical approach that is characteristic of action research (Dickens and Watkins 1999). We will return to this in Chapter 6, when the reception of the two Cypriot exhibitions is discussed.

NOTES

1. See Özkirimli (2010: 60ff) for a critique on these primordialist approaches.

2. To his defence: Billig (1995: 78) did pay attention to the material, for instance, when emphasizing that "countries are materially established in this world."

3. One example is the changing course of the river Semliki, which altered the Uganda–DR Congo border. See http://www.independent.co.uk/environment/changing-river-course-alters-uganda-dr-congo-border-1818532.html and http://www.theguardian.com/environment/2010/dec/07/climate-change-rerouting-semliki-river.

   Another changing river border is the Rio Grande between the United States and Mexico. See http://www.nytimes.com/1987/09/26/world/a-liquid-border-pays-no-heed-to-diplomacy.html.

4. Others have also used this concept; see, for instance, Kang (2012).

5. Their potential occurrence remains for Mouffe (2013a: 1) important, as this "impedes the full totalization of society and forecloses the possibility of a society beyond division and power," but this analysis is made without any hint of celebration for the existence of antagonistic self–other relationships.

6. Ironically, military songs, which may resound from both Greek Cypriot and Turkish Cypriot army barracks, would use exactly the opposite logic – deploying similar elements of lyrical music to promote a culture of war. It is impressive how sometimes the same melodies are sung by both armies – with different words, in a different language, addressing the respective enemy.

Chapter 4: The Discourses and Materialities of Cypriot Antagonistic Nationalism

Iconoclastic Controversies focusses on Cyprus, a small island in the Eastern Mediterranean, with a surface area of 9251 square kilometres and a population of about 1.15 million people.[1] Knowing that the country's political and historical complexity is the inverse of its size, it is important to discuss the characteristics of the different assemblages of antagonistic nationalism that can be found on Cyprus.

WRITING A CYPRIOT HISTORY AND ITS PROBLEMS

When Lawrence Durrell published his book *Bitter Lemons* in 1957, in which he wrote about his 3-year stay in Cyprus (from 1953 to 1956), he wrote that "the vagaries of fortune and the demons of ill luck dragged Cyprus into the stock market of world affairs" (Durrell 2012: 100). Without subscribing to Durrell's explanation of Cyprus's ill luck and to his rather exclusive focus on the international dimension of the conflict, this sentence still contains a hint of the dramatic and intense nature of what is often termed the "Cyprus Problem," to refer to the series of violent conflicts in the second half of the twentieth century and the resulting stalemate. Durrell's focus, and his omissions, also give a first idea of the difficulty of grasping the political complexity of the Cyprus Problem.

Any analysis of the Cyprus Problem, which is, given its long duration, necessarily historical, involves more than the traditional problems related to historical research. It would be naïve and arrogant, and in full contradiction with the discursive-material knot perspective used in this book, to assume that one particular historical analysis, academic or otherwise, can offer the final and ultimate interpretation of a specific set of practices and events from the past, even though this should not dissuade analysts from offering plausible attempts. Zooming in on the history of a particular region of the world also produces the risk of decontextualization, with practices and events in other parts of the world, sometimes interconnected with that region, disappearing into the background. For instance, global and long-term processes such as the Cold War; the process of decolonization; the conflicts in the Middle East, Africa and Asia; and the economic crises, all involved a wide variety of discursive-material assemblages, and assemblages of assemblages, that all impacted on the Cyprus Problem. The year that the Turkish Army invaded Cyprus, 1974, was one of the years of dislocation and destruction in Cyprus, but many other dislocatory, and sometimes destructive, events took place in that very same year. It was, for instance, also the year of the end of the OPEC (Organization of the Petroleum Exporting Countries) oil embargo, the Carnation Revolution in Portugal, the dethroning of the Ethiopian emperor Haile Selassie, a Provisional Irish Republican Army bombing campaign in the United Kingdom and the resignation of the US president Richard Nixon (following Watergate). The year before, the signing of the Paris Peace Accords implied the end of the US involvement in Vietnam and the 1973 Yom Kippur War raged in Israel and its neighbouring countries. Not all these processes and events can be addressed here, but, to use another formulation, the myopia that writing a particular history produces should at least be acknowledged.

In the case of the Cyprus Problem, there are a number of particular issues that are added to the more traditional problems of historical analysis. Even though it is hard to escape the impression that Cyprus never managed to attract much more than superfluous international consideration, the number of publications on the Cyprus Problem, also written by non-Cypriots, is simply impressive. Dealing with the abundance of literature on the Cyprus Problem is both a luxury and a problem, especially when one aims to generate an overview of the entire period related to the Cyprus Problem that is respectful of historical non-linearity and complexity, while many practical restrictions worked against one consulting primary sources.

Moreover, the Cypriot Problem itself impacts on the historical signifying practices, including some of the academic ones, because these signifying practices are often highly politicized. This implies that navigating through the literature on the Cyprus Problem feels a bit like meandering through an intellectual minefield, where one can only hope to make it through unscarred. From a discursive-material perspective, it is, of course, no surprise that the (re-)discursifications of practices and events – or, of discourses – from the past are part of discursive struggles, but this obviously does not make the analyst's life any easier, in particular when the differences between the historical signifying practices in the north and south of Cyprus are quite radical, as Richmond (1999: 42) also ascertained:

It is important to note that the two communities in Cyprus, and their motherlands, have completely different perceptions of the history of the island; "history" (i.e. the struggle for liberation) ended in 1974 for the Turkish Cypriots and began then for Greek Cypriots.

In particular, the nationalist interpretations of history tend to complicate the development of plausible academic-historical analyses. I (briefly) want to illustrate this problem by referring to two publications. The first example is Spryridakis's (1974: 164) book, *A Brief History of Cyprus*, in which he wrote: "The Turks[2] made no intellectual or cultural contribution worth mentioning." On the next page, he concluded his chapter, "The Role of the Archbishop of Cyprus as Ethnarch," as follows:

The Turkish rule of Cyprus ended in 1878. The scholar of the history of Cyprus [...] is forced to bypass 300 years of barrenness and desolation. The few oases flourishing in this vast desert of Turkish occupation are proofs of the undying and indomitable Hellenic faith in the human spirit. (Spryridakis 1974: 165)

In the history chapter of the *North Cyprus Almanack*, an official publication of the TRNC[3] (1987), we find a different evaluation of the Ottoman period:

The Turks were greeted as liberators by the local population, who were treated with consideration in return. They abolished serfdom, recognized the supremacy of the Orthodox community over all other Christian dominations, and restored the Orthodox Archbishopric. Above all, the Cypriots were integrated into that remarkable institution known as the Millet system [...] which for centuries provided members of religious minorities within the Ottoman Empire with more freedom than was enjoyed by such groups anywhere in Europe.

The presence of these kinds of nationalist sentiments is, of course, understandable in the context of the Cyprus Problem, but it still produces a challenge for those who want to write a fair and balanced academic historical narration. At the same time, a thorough and careful literature review, based on the identification of reliable Cypriot and non-Cypriot authors, and on a continuous engagement with the unavoidable contradictions between Greek Cypriot and Greek, and Turkish Cypriot and Turkish (academic) narrations, remains possible, resulting in the historical analysis that follows.

The argument here is also that nationalist discourses have been, and still are, a key driving force of the Cyprus Problem. For instance, Baruh and Popescu (2008: 80) wrote that "there is no question that Cyprus is a contentious issue prone to focusing nationalistic discourses in both countries." A slightly more careful version that still points to nationalism as a significant discourse can be found in Nevzat's (2005: 11) Introduction: "Nationalism, all agree, contributed to some extent at least to the conflict that wrought such havoc on the island during the twentieth century." These citations are indications of the importance of nationalism in Cyprus, but at the same time, the Cyprus Problem cannot be reduced to the workings of a particular discourse. The discourse-material knot perspective, deployed as an analytical strategy, offers a way to bypass this possible threat of reductionism, as it enables focusing on the nationalist assemblages, characterized by material presences (with their agencies), embedded in discursive struggles, and always affected by contingencies, at work at the level of both the discursive and the material. Even then, this part cannot (and definitely will not) claim to provide an all-encompassing analysis of the Cyprus Problem, given its complexity and intensity, and it complements the approaches oriented towards geopolitics (Ram 2015; Markides 2019; Tziarras 2019), political economy (Ioannou 2020) and psychoanalysis (Volkan 1979), to mention but a few. Modesty remains a very necessary attitude here.

THE TWO NATIONALISMS

When arguing that nationalism is a (or even "the") key driving force of the Cyprus Problem, further specification is needed, as two nationalisms, namely Greek Cypriot nationalism and Turkish Cypriot nationalism, come into play. In this approach, the Cyprus Problem is defined through – and can be analysed as – a confrontation between (antagonistic versions of) these two nationalisms, which were forms of Greek nationalism and Turkish nationalism, respectively. In turn, this statement needs two immediate historical qualifications. First of all, these nationalisms developed asynchronously, with the Greek Cypriot nationalism being consolidated much earlier, acquiring a hegemonic position on the island, forcing those who did not identify with this ideological project into a weakened (discursive) position. Later, a Turkish Cypriot nationalism developed, partially in response to the Greek Cypriot nationalist project but also partially fed by ideological changes in mainland Turkey. The second qualification, which might not come as a surprise, given the discursive-material perspective of this book, is that these nationalisms were constructed. Nevzat (2005: 11) explained that the construction of Greek Cypriot nationalism was not an immediate event, but a long process:

> It was not, however, a constant feature in this Mediterranean isle's history, nor did it emerge as an axis of tension in a sudden instant. Notwithstanding misconstrued appreciations of the nation as a virtually eternal entity, a fuller understanding of how and why rival Greek and Turkish national identities with conflicting political ideals evolved in Cyprus can only be acquired if the roots and evolutionary progression of these adversarial nationalisms are identified.

This ideological construction process took several decades and was part of a discursive struggle for hegemony with other identity projects (see below). A crucial element in the successful construction of Greek Cypriot nationalism was Greek independence, which provided the nodal point for Greek Cypriot nationalism: Greekness, or the subject position of the Greek. Anthias and Ayres's (1983: 62) quotation below shows that the material creation of the Greek state in 1832, after an uprising that started in 1821, and the following Greek state's expansion which lasted for more than a century,[4] provided the Greek Cypriot (leadership) with a nation-state with which they could identify and which they could call their "motherland":

> Since 1830, when Greece was freed from the Ottoman yoke, Greek-Cypriot leaders had wanted to become merged with the "motherland." Though not of itself chauvinist, the nationalist form that the desire for union [*enosis*] took was chauvinistic, romantic-idealist, thrived on the mythology of a glorious Hellenic past, and was aimed at the aggrandisement of the Hellenic world.

The exact starting point of this identity project may not be as clear as Anthias and Ayres (1983: 62) suggested. Brewer (2010: 139), for instance, placed the origins of *enosis* – the idea of the unification of Cyprus with Greece – later: "the demand for union with Greece, *enosis*, [...] began when the British took over the island in 1878." Still, the 1821 massacre of the Cypriot elite by the Ottomans in response to the Greek uprising, the protracted Greek independence process (Koliopoulos and Veremis 2010) and its expansionist ideology (the so-called Megali idea, which captured the idea of bringing all Greek-speaking people into the Greek nation), would strongly feed the desire for *enosis*. An equally important mobilizing set of events were the two Balkan Wars in 1912 and 1913 (Katsourides 2014: 35), in which about 1500 Cypriot volunteers joined (Kolev

and Koulouri 2009: 92; see also Papapolyviou 1997). Particularly important was that this Greek identity project was strongly supported by the Greek Orthodox Church of Cyprus, as Faustmann (2008: 48) wrote:

> The Orthodox community had gradually developed a Greek national identity based on ethic and cultural roots shared with the newly founded Greek state since the first half of the 19th century. Originally, this identity embraced by the small educated elite and the Church but it was soon passed on to the wider population. By the second half of the nineteenth century, Greek nationalism was clearly, "engulfing the lower strata."

The Greek Cypriot self was thus constructed in alignment with Greece and supported by claims about the material, in relation to a joint history, geography, language, religion and culture. Anthias and Ayres (1983: 64) also pointed to the constitutive outside that was created to support the Greek subject position: "it was an affirmation of 'Greekness', as opposed to 'Turkishness' or 'heathenism.'" This discursive construction of a new self (and its other) was not outside the material – it simply provided a new assemblage, which rearranged particular discourses (including subject positions) and materials, including some and excluding others. The new nationalist assemblage was discursively centred on Greekness and thus aligned with the geography of the island, with its territory demarcated by the sea and its geographical position in the Eastern Mediterranean (close enough to the Greek "motherland"), the material traces of the Aegean history (that are obviously present on the island), the many Greek-speaking bodies on the island, their religious practices structured by the Greek Orthodox Church of Cyprus and the strong presence of particular objects, in particular the Greek flag. Moreover, the institutional support for the Greek Cypriot nationalist project was extensive, and many organizational machines, with their material and signifying practices, mobilized to support the Greek Cypriot nationalist discourse: early Greek Cypriot newspapers "represented varying shades of Greek nationalism" (Katsiaounis 1996: 95) and "the orthodox Cypriots imported teachers and textbooks from Greece which promoted the idea of union of Cyprus with Greece" (Faustmann 2008: 48). Constantinou and Papadakis (2002: 83) referred to "the historical studies" produced by Greek Cypriots "proving their Greekness and continuity as a self-conscious actor who always resisted foreign domination," as part of the discursive struggle with the British colonizer about the Greek (Cypriot) subject position. As mentioned before, this institutional support included the Greek Orthodox Church of Cyprus, as one of *enosis*'s fiercest proponents.

At the same time, the nationalist assemblage became engaged in a discursive struggle with a series of contending discourses and had to deal with a number of potential dislocations, where the material threatened to disrupt the nationalist assemblage. This resulted in a series of successful exclusions and re-articulations countering these contingencies and preventing them from undermining the nationalist assemblage's discursive strength and hegemonic ambitions. One key exclusion was the possibility and/or desirability of non-nationalist Greek Cypriots. Crucial here is how "the different ways in which nationalism is naturalized," which is "central to understanding the ethnonationalist conflict that has divided the island," as Bryant (2004: 190) noted.

This naturalization of nationalism was part (and the outcome) of a discursive struggle against Cypriotism, which privileged a national identity that also spanned the island but privileged a different assemblage, which consisted of Greek Cypriots, Turkish Cypriots and other groups living in Cyprus, their combined organizational machines and cultural practices

(with an emphasis on their similarities; see Doob 1986: 391–92) and their histories of cohabitation. As Michael (2011: 40) remarked, Cypriotism was not a new phenomenon and some of the Cypriot organizational machines, mostly located within the Cypriot left, defended it. One witness is the slogan that the Cypriot communist party (KKK) used "from its inception": "A united anti-British front of Greek and Turks" (Anthias and Ayres 1983: 65). Katsourides (2014: 98) confirmed that the "[e]xamination of the [KKK's] official Party newspaper reveals many articles promoting the need for a united front with the goal of independence (or autonomy) for Cyprus."

When in October 1931 riots took place, partially driven by class conflict and partially by Greek nationalism, the British colonizer also started to promote Cypriotism as "an identity that would transcend cultural and linguistic affinities towards Greece and Turkey and pose no direct threat to British rule" (Morgan 2010: 133). The Cypriotist position turned out to be untenable and lost the discursive struggle for hegemony. Greek nationalism managed to claim the anti-colonialist position and integrate it into the nationalist chain of equivalence, as Anthias and Ayres (1983: 66) wrote:

> As Crouzet [1973] has shown, [...] both the right and left were drawn into the Enosis movement, for no group could denounce the form in which nationalism/anti-colonialism was articulated – since to be opposed to one was to oppose the other. It was the theoretical and necessary link established between these two analytically different positions that was responsible for this.

Other exclusions from the nationalist assemblage were the complexities that characterized the cultural practices from the Cypriot past and present, which potentially threatened to dislocate the nationalist assemblage and had to be re-articulated. The nationalist project divided the Cypriot history in periods with legitimate migrations (basically those who came from the Aegean) and illegitimate migrations (who were articulated as part of a process of occupation). In particular, the Ottoman period (but also earlier periods) became classified in the latter category, weakening the discursive positions of the populations that arrived in these "illegitimate periods." Also, the complexity of the island, caused by the presence of many different groups and beliefs, became simplified to enter the logic of the dichotomy.

Moreover, by privileging the national identity, other subject positions, in particular those related to class and gender,[5] had to be integrated into the nationalist chain of equivalence, but only in secondary positions, so that they could not threaten the main subject position of the Greek. This also implied that some of the earlier class-based revolts, which united Muslim and Orthodox peasants (Panayiotou 2012), had to be (re)moved to the margins of historical narration. Anthias and Ayres (1983: 61) described these – what they called – "solidarity bonds" as follows:

> There are other elements which appear to give some validity to the view that certain solidary bonds developed between Muslims and Christians, partly related to those families including both through the conversion process, but mainly structured by the common economic conditions of peasants. This is shown by a number of peasant revolts, under Christian or Muslim leaders, which included members from each faith.

The left-wing parties, in particular first KKK and later its (semi-)successor, AKEL, the Progressive Working People's Party, did not manage to prioritize a class identity (Anthias and Ayres 1983: 67) and eventually accepted the dominance of the national identity. Anthias and Ayres (1983: 69) wrote the following

about AKEL: "AKEL has always been extremely careful not to alienate popular nationalist feelings, justifying this theoretically by the need to maintain 'democratic' support." Still, these non-nationalist fractions of the Cypriot society continued to exist, producing counter-hegemonic signifying practices that could (potentially) disrupt the Greek Cypriot nationalist project.

Also, at a more everyday level, the dislocatory potential of the material had to be countered by the nationalist project. Here, too, exclusions had to be organized, for instance in relation to multi-linguistic practices. One should not forget that "a large number of Turkish Cypriots spoke Greek until 1964" (Soulioti 2006: 4). The specificity of the Greek Cypriot dialect matters as well, as it is "relatively distinct from SG [Standard Greek]" (Themistocleous 2015: 284) and has "incorporated many Turkish words and was spoken by Christians and many Muslims" (Anthias and Ayres 1983: 61). This material evidence of cohabitation and mutual influence, which rests uneasily with the Greek Cypriot nationalist discourse, was confirmed by Trudgill and Schreier (2006: 1886):

> Lexical borrowings from Turkish are numerous (Pavlou 1993), reflecting the fact that the two communities coexisted rather peacefully for four centuries and that, prior to the Turkish occupation of the northern area, mixing and interaction between Greek and Turkish Cypriots was by no means exceptional.

Papadakis (2005: 12) described the proximity of Cypriot Greek to Turkish from a more personal perspective:

> Speaking Turkish felt like a welcome liberation to my mouth. It often felt more comfortable than speaking Greek. In Cyprus, we mostly spoke the local Greek dialect. I now realized that it was full of

sounds similar to the sounds of Turkish, ones that the Greeks from Greece had real trouble with.

THE RISE OF TURKISH NATIONALISM ON CYPRUS

When Greek Cypriot nationalism prevailed, it also hegemonized its definition of the Turkish Cypriots as other. The Turkish Cypriot subject position became articulated to refer to those who frustrated the Greek Cypriot desire for *enosis* and homogeneity, which sometimes resulted in their conflation with Turkey as the "eternal enemy" (Bryant 2004: 224) of Greece and (Greek) Cyprus. In contrast, the Turkish Cypriots' identity politics were more complex, with Turkish nationalism being developed significantly later than the Greek Cypriot nationalism (Markides 2006: 27). In the earlier stages, at the end of the nineteenth century, Turkish Cypriots (or Muslim Cypriots, as they were labelled at the time) responded to the Hellenist nation-building process that threatened their position on the island, by (politically) mobilizing (Varnava 2009: 183). This response consisted of "inciting Cypriot Muslims against the Orthodox and Muslims they perceived ignoring it [the call for *enosis*]."

Nevzat (2005: 442) argued that "the rise of Turkish nationalism on the island had become appreciable by the time of the October Revolt of 1931." The idea of Cyprus joining Greece – "an arch-enemy of the Ottoman Empire – and, after 1923, Turkey" (Constantinou and Papadakis 2002: 83) – did not particularly appeal to the large majority of the Turkish Cypriots. The community "feared danger to its own existence," which was fed by examples of deportation, as, for instance, happened on the island of Crete (Kizilyürek 2006: 319). Moreover, the establishment of the Turkish state in 1923, on the ruins of the Ottoman Empire, provided the conditions for the development of Turkish Cypriot nationalism. Together with the state-building process, a particular Turkish nationalism was (further) developed, which paradoxically

"resulted in both a hostility towards and an imitation of Western ways [which] has accompanied the modernization process since the turn of the nineteenth century" (Kadıoğlu 1998: 185). Its Kemalist version combined an emphasis on Turkishness (in contrast to Ottomanness), laicism and republicanism, among others, as captured in the "six arrows" idea (see Parla and Davison 2004: 54ff for a discussion).

This Kemalist modernization project also had strong appeal in Cyprus (Akgün, Gürel, Hatay and Tiryaki 2005: 11) and supported the redefinition of Muslim Cypriots as Turks in the 1930s (Kizilyürek 2005: 26), "taking upon themselves an identity forged in the crucible of nationalism" (Bryant 2007: 116). For instance, in Cyprus, the Arabic alphabet (for writing Turkish) was replaced by the Latin alphabet in 1928, the same year that it was replaced in Turkey (Kizilyürek 2005: 25). Even if the modernization articulation was strong, the Turkish Cypriot nationalism "was a nationalism that incorporated them [the Turkish Cypriots] into the larger Turkish nation and minimised their relationship to their island home" (Bryant 2012: 188), using and developing the subject position of "the Turk." This is nicely illustrated by president Rauf Denktaş's[6] much later statement: "The only true Cypriots are the wild donkeys of the Karpas peninsula" (cited by Güven-Lisaniler and Rodríguez 2002: 183). Again, these nationalist discourses faced resistance. Here we can find a discursive struggle between Turkish Cypriot Kemalism, which had anti-colonial tendencies, and the traditionalist discourse, which was based on loyalty towards the British colonizer. Kizilyürek (2005: 25) described this struggle in the following terms:

This call on reform brought up a clash between the modernist and traditionalist elite groups, which, in fact, became a conflict about the power-distribution within the Turkish Cypriot community. On the one hand, there were the Kemalist modernists, who were aiming at a secular national education based on Turkish nationalism and on the other hand the traditionalist, who were loyal to traditional religious values and enjoyed the confidence of the colonial rule.

This discursive struggle, where the Kemalist discourse would eventually gain the upper hand, only slowly entered into the Turkish Cypriot community at large. After the Second World War and the Greek Civil War, Cyprus entered the international agenda, with both Greece and Turkey getting deeply involved in supporting "their" respective communities in Cyprus. Lacher and Kaymak (2005: 151) described how, in the 1950s, Turkish Cypriot nationalism consolidated its hegemonic status in the Turkish Cypriot community, which translated into broad support for the Turkish and Turkish Cypriot demand for *taksim* (or partition) of Cyprus:

> Among the Muslim population, by contrast, a similar turn towards an ethnonationalist identification as "Turks" (which they had customarily been called by Greek Cypriots) was mostly a response to the (failed) 1954 attempt by Greece to gain sovereignty over the island, and the subsequent launch of the Greek Cypriot anti-colonial struggle organized by EOKA. (Kizilyürek 2003: 222)

These two ideological projects, which eventually discursively (and later on materially) separated the Greek Cypriots and the Turkish Cypriots, were not disconnected from the Cypriot material structures. Even if Cyprus, with its mixed villages and towns,[7] was once characterized by "traditional coexistence" (Anthias and Ayres 1983: 60), where "if only occasionally, their relations had not been so thoroughly poisoned by the traditional enmity on the mainland, but had been semifriendly or even friendly" (Doob 1986: 392), the level of material integration was nevertheless limited. This facilitated the othering process, initially of Turkish Cypriots, as part of Greek Cypriot nationalism, and later in a more reciprocal form.

Historically, even though the Ottoman millet system created a (limited) power base for the Orthodox Cypriots, the Ottoman rule still strengthened "the Ottoman Muslims [who] were the colonial power and the Orthodox population was denied the freedom that its leaders, at least, desired" (Anthias and Ayres 1983: 60). Later, under British rule, an ethnic categorization was implemented, also in material policies, and the Cypriot society evolved differently at the socio-economic level: "Under British colonialism, Greek-Cypriots developed commercially, whereas Turkish-Cypriots remained mainly peasants or administrators" (72). Anthias and Ayres (1983: 63) also pointed to the different educational systems, in the following words:

> In education, Britain encouraged a rapid expansion of schools organised on religious lines (with separate schools for Muslims, Orthodox, Catholics, Armenians and Maronites), forcing the two main communities to become dependent for personnel and literature on mainland Greece and Turkey. This, in turn, exacerbated existing group differences and fostered national political elites concerned with protecting the political interests of their own communities.

At the more personal level, Greek Cypriot and Turkish Cypriot intermarriages remained rare, despite four centuries of coexistence (Polat 2002: 106). In short, "the two populations had different religious beliefs and practices, their own language, largely separate familial and social life and a low degree of intermarriage" (Anthias and Ayres 1983: 61).

THE ANTAGONIZATION OF NATIONALISM

Greek Cypriot nationalism and Turkish Cypriot Kemalism not only constructed each other as respective constitutive outsides but also defined the British colonizer as the other-foreigner. When the power of the Ottoman Empire receded, the island had come under the control of the United Kingdom, first as a protectorate (between 1878 and 1914), as part of an agreement between the United Kingdom and Turkey to protect the latter against Russian expansion (Mallinson 2005: 10). At the start of the First World War, the island was then annexed by the United Kingdom (on 5 November 1914) (Soulioti 2006: 4), a state of affairs that was recognized by Turkey in the Lausanne Treaty of 1923. In 1925 Cyprus became a British crown colony (Markides 2006: 32).

At first, as Katsourides (2014: 36) remarked, "Greek Cypriot nationalism was distinguished by its moderate approach towards the British. While demanding their freedom from the British Empire, Greek Cypriots were not anti-British." Even if the British were also frustrating the Greek Cypriot enjoyment of the Greek self by not ceding Cyprus to Greece, the Greek Cypriots chose, for a very long time (and with notable exceptions), to avoid violence, even though they continued their *enosis* campaign relentlessly. This situation was complicated by the articulation of the British as the best guarantee against *enosis* by one part of the Turkish Cypriot community, which resulted in the definition of the British colonizer as other-foreigner-ally, something that was gracefully accepted by the British. The British themselves were caught in an evenly complicated mixture of fascination for the Hellenic past of (Greek) Cyprus and their orientalist ideology of empire, which "imposed" a civilizing mission upon the British. Morgan (2010: 126) described the position of Ronald Storrs, the British governor between 1926 and 1932, as follows: "It would only be through a period of enlightened British government that Greek Cypriots could rediscover the values that underpinned their classical past – concepts of civic duty, public obligation, self-discipline and honour – from which they had been alienated for so many centuries."

This does not mean that all was peace and quiet on the island. The first inter-communal clashes between Greek Cypriots and Turkish Cypriots took place in May 1912. In a series of incidents, related to the Balkan Wars, several Cypriots were killed, and about 150 were injured (Varnava 2009: 189; see also Bryant 2004: 91–92; Mirbagheri 2010: xxviii). The October 1931 riots were triggered by nationalist sentiments and economic grievances (Faustmann 2008: 47–50; Richmond 1998: 70; Soulioti 2006: 17; Stefanidis 1999: 1). These so-called *Oktovriana* (October) riots again left several Cypriots dead, and the British Government House was burned down. The British regime responded by deporting some of those involved in the riots, imprisoning others, dismantling the Legislative Council (Cyprus's consultative body; see Akgün 2012), banning political parties, censoring the press, prohibiting the Greek flag being flown and (a few years later, in 1937) restricting the autonomy of the Cypriot Orthodox Church (Bryant 2004: 129; Calame and Charlesworth 2011: 126; Soulioti 2006: 17–18). But then, during the Second World War, more than 30,000 Cypriots volunteered to fight in the British Army (Asmussen 2006: 167, 170).

In the mid-1950s, a major shift occurred, and Greek Cypriot nationalism evolved from a mostly agonistic nationalism to an antagonistic nationalism, when EOKA (*Ethniki Organosis Kyprion Agoniston*, or the National Organization of Cypriot Fighters) launched its guerrilla war. EOKA was led by the right-wing Georgios Grivas, who had been an officer in the Greek Army, and politically supported by archbishop Makarios, who would later become the first president of the Republic of Cyprus. In 1955 the British thus became articulated as the other-foreigner-enemy that needed to be expelled from the island through the use of material force. This re-articulation affected all British inhabitants of Cyprus (civilians and military staff) but also Cypriots (and people with other nationalities) that were seen to "collaborate" with the British regime. This process of othering, grounded in EOKA's anti-colonialist project, legitimated not only the guerrilla warfare of EOKA against the British enemy but also the solidification of the Greek Cypriot chain of equivalence and the homogenization of the Greek Cypriot community in their fight against the British colonizer. The first and the last sentences of the oath of the EOKA youth organization illustrate, on the one hand, the construction of the British enemy and, on the other hand, the construction of the (potential) traitor as an enemy within, driven by the desire to purify the Greek Cypriot chain of equivalence:

> I swear in the name of the Holy Trinity that: I shall work with all my power for the liberation of Cyprus from the British yoke sacrificing for this even my life. [...] If I disobey my oath, I shall be worthy of every punishment as a traitor and may eternal contempt cover me. (EOKA Youth Organization oath, cited in Byford-Jones 1959: 57)

Quickly after the EOKA revolt was initiated, the other-enemy started to include Turkish Cypriots, triggered by the involvement of a considerable number of Turkish Cypriots in the British security forces, who were targeted by EOKA and whose deaths were then reported by "Turkish-Cypriot leaders and the press" as "Turks murdered by Greeks" (Asmussen 2011: 129). Moreover, the September 1955 riots in Istanbul targeting the Greek inhabitants of the city, and the formation of the Turkish Cypriot Turkish Resistance Organization (TMT) to combat EOKA, were very material impulses that supported the inclusion of the "Turks of Cyprus" in the articulation of the other-enemy. In his book *Guerrilla Warfare and EOKA's*

Struggle, Grivas described how in 1957 he "drew up plans for warding off Turkish [Cypriot] attacks in towns and villages" (Grivas-Dighenis 1964: 44):

> About the middle of July 1958, after plenty of preparation, I launched a counter-offensive against the Turk[ish Cypriot]s, having received information that their morale was at a low ebb and that their activities were on the decrease rather than the contrary because of the strong and persistent resistance put up on our side which they had not expected. (Grivas-Dighenis 1964: 45)

Furthermore, the nationalist desire for the homogenization of the self resulted in additional violence, with the left–right opposition playing a significant role in the EOKA period. More specifically, the right-wing and nationalist EOKA and TMT came to oppose the progressive members of Cypriot society. AKEL was viewed by EOKA as its opponent and also its members were, in some instances, effectively exposed to violence. TMT also killed left-wing opponents, with the execution in 1965 of two union members – the Turkish Cypriot Derviş Ali Kavazoğlu and the Greek Cypriot Kostas Misiaoulis – as emblematic examples. But as Nome (2013: 64) wrote, this strategy was used earlier: "During 1958, TMT was apparently responsible for a series of vandalism, shootings, killings and threats targeting Turkish-Cypriot leftists, which led hundreds of Turkish-Cypriot workers to withdraw from their ethnically mixed trade unions." TMT also used the logic of the enemy-within, as exemplified by the signifier traitor in their oath:

> I dedicate myself to resist against any attack from wherever it might come, which will threatens [*sic*] the lives, the freedoms, the properties and all that is sacred of the Turkish Cypriots. I will execute any duty given to me, even if it involves even my

death. I will protect until the very end whatever I would see, hear, know or would be entrusted to me. I will not reveal anything to anybody. I know that revealing anything amounts to treachery the punishment of which is death. I swear in the name of honour, dignity and everything sacred that I will follow all the above.[8]

The end result of these struggles was that the left-wing connection between Greek Cypriots and Turkish Cypriots was cut:

In the ensuing conflict between the two communities, the activities of EOKA and TMT finally split the tenuous horizontal links between Greek- and Turkish-Cypriots, as the two military organisations took up a distinctly anti-communist position so that Turkish-Cypriot workers were forced to leave PEO [the Pancyprian Federation of Labor] and AKEL. (Anthias and Ayres 1983: 69)

The 1955–59 independence war was characterized by intense violence, leading to considerable material destruction and loss of life. The material destruction of the other-enemy, whether these were British, Turkish Cypriots, Greek Cypriots or others,[9] continuously fed the processes of othering and the deep effects that supported these processes and, in turn, legitimated more intense forms of violence. As, for instance, Cobain (2012) has argued, the British also used excessive force, and this material violence again supported the construction of the enemy-other:

A young British army officer recorded seeing 150 soldiers indiscriminately "kicking Cypriots as they lay on the ground and beating them in the head, face, and body with rifle butts." The officer described how he "forcibly restrained several such groups of soldiers who had completely lost their heads. Many of them were screaming abuse and the whole area resembled a hysterical mob. [...] Several [Cypriots] appeared to be unconscious and bleeding profusely."

When EOKA announced in 1959 its (initial) acceptance of the Zürich and London Agreements, and an independent Cypriot state, the Republic of Cyprus, was established in August 1960, the levels of material violence decreased drastically and a brief period of pacification started. The foundation of the Cypriot state assemblage was a major re-articulation of the organizational machines that operated in Cyprus, with the withdrawal of the bulk of the British armed forces and the replacement of the British colonial state apparatus by that of the Republic of Cyprus. Even when the material framework of the Republic of Cyprus was (being) constructed, the identification with this new state was limited. One (very material) example was dislike of the new Cypriot flag, which was hardly used in the 1960s, as Papadakis (2005: 161; capital letters in original) explained: "Yellow was the main colour in the 1960 Republic of Cyprus flag, but this was despised as a symbol of defeat, the defeat of ENOSIS." Also, the idea of one Cypriot nation did not take root, something which is illustrated by Faustmann's (2006: 419) description of the independence celebrations: "The two communities celebrated separately, one celebrating the arrival of the Turkish [military] contingent, the other the return of the [EOKA] exiles. On the streets, mostly Greek and Turkish flags were used for decoration while hardly a Cypriot flag could be seen." For a short while, the other-enemy became an other-adversary, even if, soon after independence, the political conflict intensified again, fed by mutual distrust (Uslu 2003: 17). Reddaway (1986: 8) pointed out that the constitutional structure was unworkable, because "it depended on a degree of goodwill from the leaders of both communities," which was lacking. Moreover, "it was deliberately wrecked either by the Greek

Cypriots in the continuing pursuit of Enosis or by the Turkish Cypriots in the continuing pursuit of partition, or by both" (Reddaway 1986: 8). Here, Greek Cypriot nationalism impacted on the prevailing democratic discourse. This articulation of nationalist and democratic discourses produced a particular, majoritarianist perspective on democracy. Uslu (2003: 18, emphasis added) wrote:

> It should be noted that the Greek majority had the upper hand in choosing its own way and the Turkish Cypriots could not do anything more than trying to protect their constitutional rights. [...] The present condition suited the interests of the Turkish community but irritated the Greeks [Greek Cypriots] since they were extremely unhappy on not governing the island as they wished *in spite of their majority position.*

The majoritarianist democratic articulation of democracy that Greek Cypriots were using led to a "theorisation of Turkish-Cypriots *not* as a political representational group but as a 'minority'" (Anthias and Ayres 1983: 69; emphasis in original). This articulation of the other conflicted with the Turkish Cypriot desire for a degree of self-control (e.g. in the municipalities) but also fed the Greek Cypriot frustration with the Cypriot constitution, which was based on a consociational democratic model. This type of democratic model "shares governmental decision making between political representatives of the disputant groups" (Yakinthou 2009: 25), in order to prevent antagonistic conflict. The trigger for the collapse of the 1960 constitution was, not accidentally, president Makarios's proposed constitutional reform, which would steer the Cypriot democratic model into the direction of a majoritarianist democratic model, removing some of the institutional safeguards that had been implemented to protect the Turkish Cypriot community.

POST-INDEPENDENCE ANTAGONISTIC NATIONALISM

In December 1963, after only a brief pause, Cyprus re-entered the domain of antagonistic nationalism, with the intense collective violence of 1963/1964 and 1967, and with yet another major restructuring of the Cypriot state assemblage, caused by Turkish Cypriot material withdrawal from the Cypriot state apparatus. The Turkish Cypriot security concerns led most Turkish Cypriots to withdraw into fortified enclaves scattered over the island. In an attempt to contain the conflict, a United Nations peacekeeping force, UNFICYP, was also established in March 1964.[10] Morag (2004: 601) argued that the "enclave period" implied a de facto partition of the island. At the same time, this material rearrangement (and concentration) of Cypriot bodies on the island posed a continued frustration of the Greek Cypriot desire for a Greek Cyprus, as the Turkish Cypriot presence was still conflicting with the nationalist interpretation of the nation-state. Moreover, the forced relocation of Turkish Cypriot refugees deeply frustrated the possibility of Cypriot togetherness. According to Morag (2004: 601), in this era, the Turkish Cypriot community came to control "about four percent of the territory of the island," with 39 enclaves dispersed all over Cyprus.[11] Many of the mixed villages were abandoned by one of the communities.[12] This material segregation facilitated the construction of the other-enemy, as Morag (2004: 601) wrote:

> The enclave period significantly contributed to the further deterioration of relations between the two national communities. Most Turkish Cypriots had no contact with Greek Cypriots and vice versa making it easier for each side to demonize the other. The congestion and tension within the Turkish Cypriot enclaves led to an externalization of tensions within the community and an exaggeration of national unity, with the authorities

constantly reinforcing the belief that the Greek Cypriots were a serious threat.

But after 1967 the violence between Greek Cypriots and Turkish Cypriots paused, assisted by the official renouncement of *enosis* by Makarios in 1968 and the start of bi-communal talks. This did not imply the cessation of the violence on Cyprus, though. The establishment of the military junta in Greece in April 1967 had further complicated *enosis* (as not all Cypriots wanted to join a dictatorship), and it strengthened the tensions within the Greek Cypriot community. The assassination attempt on Makarios in March 1970, unrelated to Turkish Cypriots or Turkey, made these intra-communal tensions very visible. When former EOKA leader Grivas became more active again (founding EOKA-B and returning to Cyprus in September 1971), it further fed the conflict, with Makarios and Grivas fiercely opposing each other: The "bloody clash between Grivas's and Makarios's supporters dragged on until 1974" (Faustmann and Ker-Lindsay 2008: 68). As a consequence, the subject position of the unified and homogenized Greek Cypriot self was shattered through the dislocation caused by the intra-communal violence within the Greek Cypriot community. Instead, two Greek Cypriot fractions, both nationalist, fought over the control over the Republic of Cyprus (while part of the Greek left still tried to resist Greek Cypriot nationalism). Henn (2004: 172) described how Grivas first demanded Makarios's resignation for waging peace talks without *enosis* as objective. When this failed, EOKA-B resorted to violence, which reached a peak in 1973:

> Attacks were made on police stations (some were destroyed and the weapons in them stolen), pro-government newspaper offices were bombed, cars were set alight and other acts of intimidation against government supporters and policemen.

THE 1974 COUP D'ÉTAT

The intra-communal violence within the Greek Cypriot community reached its peak with the failed 15 July 1974 coup d'état against Makarios by the Cypriot National Guard and the Greek junta, which had the support of EOKA-B. Again, the internal division within the Greek Cypriot community became apparent and dislocated the nationalist discursive claim on homogeneity and unity. This attempt to yet again alter the Cypriot state assemblage failed, but soon after, the coup did result in the modification of two state assemblages – the Greek and the Cypriot, in a dramatic example of the logic of contingency. The coup immediately triggered the Turkish invasion in Cyprus – on 20 July 1974 – which resulted in Turkey occupying a month later the entire northern part of Cyprus (Faustmann and Ker-Lindsay 2008: 68), including the north of Nicosia. This material reconfiguration of the island's geography and demography caused severe material destruction and harm, deeply dislocated hegemonic discourses related to safety and ownership and, also, structurally altered the Republic of Cyprus state apparatus, as the latter lost control over more than one-third of its territory. The Greek state assemblage was also transformed, as the Greek junta collapsed, three days after the Turkish military invasion, immediately followed by the collapse of the coupist regime in Cyprus (both on the same day, 24 July 1974). While the Turkish "motherland" was seen to come to the rescue of the Turkish Cypriots, the Greek "motherland" was unable to successfully assist the Greek Cypriots. One attempt, to send a small group of reinforcements from Crete to Nicosia airport ("Operation Niki"), ended in disaster when Greek Cypriot air defence shot down one of the Greek troop-carrying planes.[13]

With the Turkish military invasion, the Turkish Cypriot and Turkish partition signifier, part of the nationalist discourse, became a material reality. An estimated 10,000 people were killed, with a substantial number of them not having their bodies recovered until decades later. The Buffer Zone, protected by the United Nations, replaced the 1974 front line and divided the island into two geographical entities, separated by a highly fortified and militarized frontier. In some cases, with the Varosha suburb of Famagusta as a well-known example, living spaces were transformed into ghost towns (and villages) because the material access to them was blocked. Large portions of the two populations became refugees; lost their homes and belongings (and family members); and fled to "their" respective parts of Cyprus. The numbers vary between 160,000 and 200,000 Greek Cypriots that were displaced and between 40,000 and 50,000 Turkish Cypriots that were displaced.

Behind each side of the Buffer Zone, the two communities would (further) develop their own state apparatuses, one as part of the internationally recognized Republic of Cyprus and one as a de facto state, that would in 1983 become the Turkish Republic of Northern Cyprus (TRNC), only recognized by Turkey. These new assemblages would become responsible for the government of "their" territories and their nations, with, in the case of the TRNC, considerable material support being provided by Turkey. This relationship of material dependency affected the power balance between the TRNC and Turkey, exemplified by the Turkish habit of referring to the TRNC as the "babyland" (*yavruvatan*) and to Turkey as the "motherland" (*anavatan*) (Canan-Sokullu 2013: 113).

One additional particularity is the widespread ritualistic signifying practices that Greek Cypriots use to refer to the institutions of the TRNC. In order to avoid any possibility of suggesting that the Turkish Cypriot state structures are recognized, either quotation marks or the pseudo-prefix is used. This form of what Anastasiou (2007: 127) called "exclusionary language" is a modest type of symbolic violence and part of the semantic war that continues to be waged today.

In discussing some examples, Hannay (2005: 232) argued that the Turkish Cypriot community also tends to be selective when it comes to the choice of particular signifiers:

The TRNC was the "pseudo state," its land "the occupied territories," its people "the Turkish Cypriot community," its politicians "so-called ministers" and so on. In the north there were some equally egregious examples, the Turkish military intervention of 1974 being invariably referred to as "the peace operation" and Greek Cypriot harassment referred to as "genocide." Turkish Cypriots were slightly less devoted to the textual exegesis of their visitors' statements than were the Greek Cypriots. [...] All this was translated by the politicians on both sides into highly vitriolic political discourse about the others.

As a consequence of the military invasion of 1974, the Greek Cypriot articulation of the Turkish Cypriot subject position changed, as they became (co-)responsible[14] for the suffering of the Greek Cypriots, through the material destruction of Greek Cypriot lives and properties, through the "hiding" of the missing Greek Cypriots and through the appropriation of Greek Cypriot houses and businesses in the north (and, in particular, in Varosha). They remain articulated as a threat because of the "Turkish expansionism" (Bryant 2004: 226). This articulation was sometimes combined with, and strengthened by, the articulation of Turkish Cypriot (economic) underdevelopment and primitiveness, linking up to orientalist discourses. From a Turkish Cypriot perspective, the Greek Cypriot other-enemy continued to be a threat to their security and their societal position. Bryant (2004: 224) wrote:

Turkish Cypriot officialdom consistently describes their neighbours as "fanatic" nationalists who still aim at uniting the island with Greece. When they do not so aim, they at least aim at destroying the hard-won freedoms of their Turkish Cypriot neighbours. In these portraits, Greek Cypriots ignore the "realities" of the situation – the long-standing division of the island and the presence of the Turkish military – in their pursuit of an ethic ideal.

Bryant (2004: 226) continued a few pages further: "many Turkish Cypriots interpret everything done by their Greek [Cypriot] neighbors as a move toward enosis, despite the fact that enosis died after 1974." In both cases, two subject positions merge: The self becomes the victim, through the violent practices of the other, but also "of international conspiracies [...], victims of British colonial policy [...], victims of the 'mother countries,' [...] or victims of their own leaders" (Bryant 2004: 187). This articulation of self and victim as part of the same chain of equivalence by both Greek Cypriots and Turkish Cypriots (with variations in some of the actual articulations but not in the main structure) blocks the possibility for empathy with the other's suffering (something that Papadakis (2006) called "ethnic autism"). It also inhibits that responsibility is taken for the violent practices perpetrated by the members of the self. Obviously, as Bryant (2004: 187; emphasis in original) remarked: "Cypriots have certainly been victims, they have not *only* been victims," but this perpetratorship is erased. Ironically, the Greek Cypriot slogan "I don't forget," which became educational policy (Zembylas, Charalambous and Charalambous 2016: 61), focused on a very selective remembering driven by Greek Cypriot victimhood, which obscures Turkish Cypriot suffering. This articulation is supported by a series of affects, as Zembylas (2015: 190) described in relationship to the socialization of Greek Cypriot children:

The "us-versus-them" frame of reference is linked to a number of emotions: "pride" for being Greek, feelings of obligations to struggle for the liberation of Cyprus; "empathy" for refugees and the relatives of missing persons; and "resentment" and "bitterness" for being victims of injustice.

The logic of victimization, present in both the Greek Cypriot and Turkish Cypriot discursive positions, is also translated into the demands formulated by the two communities, which were summarized by Bryant (2004: 219) as demands for justice and respect: "Greek Cypriots have demanded justice through those [popular] politics, while Turkish Cypriots have called for respect." The Turkish Cypriot demand for respect is articulated by, and grounded in, the "contingencies of daily life and the humiliations that Turkish Cypriots recall with vividness and feeling today" (Bryant 2004: 229). Partially, some argue, this demand for respect can be traced back to "their self-concept of lordliness and mastery" (Volkan 1979: 38), where – during the Ottoman rule – the Turkish Cypriot community had a more privileged position. But, as Bryant (2004: 231; emphasis in original) argued, it is also articulated with the notion of toleration that also originated from the Ottoman Empire, where "religious and juridical – as well as a certain amount of political – freedom was supposed to be granted to members of different *millets*, or religious communities, within the empire." From a Turkish Cypriot perspective, this discourse of respect was violated through the Greek Cypriot propagation of *enosis*, but even more through the material violence of Greek Cypriots, in particular the violence that was inflicted on Turkish Cypriots in 1963/1964 and 1967.

In the Greek Cypriot community, before 1974, the discourse of justice was articulated as a right to control the island as it had been "Greek for 3000 years." This right was "absolute, framed in terms of universal justice" (Bryant 2004: 237). The Ottoman rule became defined as an occupation, and its end as a liberation, in relation both to Greece and to Cyprus. *Enosis* was legitimated as a natural and just course for the future, also through the Greek struggle for independence and its long process of nation building, with, for instance, the island of Crete joining the Greek state only in 1913 (even though Cretan *enosis* had already been proclaimed in 1908). After 1974 the discourse of justice became re-articulated, referring to the need to end the injustice of the occupation of the north by the Turkish Army, and the return of the Greek Cypriot properties – confiscated in the north – to their Greek Cypriot owners. Also, the missing Greek Cypriots play an important discursive role here, as Turkey and the TRNC are accused of withholding information about missing Greek Cypriot soldiers and civilians who "might still be alive."

Between 1963 and 1974 around 2000 Cypriots disappeared, some three quarters of whom were Greek Cypriots. But whereas on the Turkish Cypriot side the death of the missing is accepted and the missing are viewed as martyrs, the Greek Cypriot missing – as Sant Cassia (2005) contended – were kept alive for decades by (artificially) feeding the hope of their return. An illustration of this process is the so-called Five of Tziaos: five Greek Cypriot soldiers who were captured by the Turkish Army, handed over to and shot by Turkish Cypriot irregular fighters. Photographs made by Turkish war reporter Ergin Konuksever fell into the hands of the Greek Cypriot Army when he was taken prisoner (together with another photographer, Adem Yavuz). However, the bulk of the photographs, including those of the executed soldiers, disappeared and the remaining photographs of the soldiers – on which they were still alive – became one of the ultimate symbols of the missing. Later on, testimonies about the death of the five by the photographer, the Turkish Army commander, inhabitants of Tziaos and Greek Cypriot soldiers were ignored. It was only in 2009, when their remains had been found, identified and returned to

the families, that their deaths were officially recognized (see Galatariotou 2012: 257ff).

AFTER 1974 – THE DIVIDED ISLAND

The Buffer Zone materially separated the belligerent parties, with the discursive constructions of the other-enemy also remaining firmly in place for a considerable amount of time. The cultural trauma[15] inflicted upon both communities after decades of discursive and material violence – even when both communities locate pain and blame in different eras – created a fertile soil for the discursive continuation of antagonistic nationalism. This antagonistic nationalist discourse articulated the Turk/Turkish Cypriot and the Greek/Greek Cypriot still as radically different, out for the destruction of the self, where Turkish Cypriots find evidence in the 1963/1964 and 1967 events and where Greek Cypriots see 1974 as evidence. These Cypriot nationalist discourses are strongly supported by the signifying practices of key institutions, with their capacity to coordinate, synchronize and harmonize different voices, even though, slowly but surely, the homogenization of the self becomes dislocated by material practices and contested by signifying practices, both providing evidence of internal plurality. Nevertheless, the homogenization of the self remained strongly protected by institutional actors, branding those who disagreed as traitors or as serving the enemy (something that continued well into the 2000s). The Cypriot mainstream media play an important role in this process, as illustrated by Christophorou, Şahin and Pavlou (2010: 7):

With the passage of time, intra- and inter-community polarisation appears to have deepened, with a blame-game directed by some not only against the "other" side but also against those with different views as well. Any view diverging from the official line was sometimes seen as damaging and undermining the community's cause to the benefit of the "enemies"; also, responsibility for unfavourable developments in one's own community was attributed to those with views different from the official view.

The material separation of the Buffer Zone has not been totally impregnable, as was also the case before the first crossing was opened in 2003. First of all, there are several villages within the Buffer Zone, with the mixed village of Pyla as the ultimate symbol of continued cohabitation. (Bi-)communal life in Pyla has not been easy, but at the same time, the local villagers have managed to keep the village mixed (and the door into the Buffer Zone open), despite severe outside pressures. Papadakis (1997: 366) described two incidents that show how localistic solidarities overruled antagonistic nationalism. The first incident took place in the early 1960s when (outside) Turkish Cypriot irregulars came to attack local Greek Cypriots, who were then protected by the local Turkish Cypriots. The second incident happened in 1974, immediately after the coup. Here, (outside) Greek Cypriot irregulars wanted to attack local Turkish Cypriots but were stopped by local Greek Cypriots. The latter, also supporters of the coup, were engaged in rounding up the local Greek Cypriot communists, who were then questioned and released again. These events show the importance of localistic identifications[16] and how localism can counter (antagonistic) nationalism. Localism is grounded in the intimate connection between material practices, places (Pyla in this example) and a discursive structure that organizes belonging in relation to a community, even though, sometimes, localism becomes articulated as backward, primitive and marginal (Herzfeld 2003: 281; Nadel-Klein 1991: 503). In our case, Pyla is a place of agonistic localism in the middle of the Buffer Zone, the material outcome of antagonistic nationalism.

The Buffer Zone also turned out to be less impregnable in more dramatic ways, with the militarized landscape having its own agency. Incursions into the Buffer Zones did happen and were sometimes met with lethal violence. Some casualties were caused by landmines, which have their own deadly agency (see Human Rights Watch 1999: 706). In other cases, people that entered the Buffer Zone were killed by (para-)military personal, as the deaths of Petros Kakoulis, Tassos Isaak and Solomos Solomou sadly illustrate. The Isaak and Solomou killings in particular demonstrate the fierce struggle for the material space of the Buffer Zone and how its entry is both possible and heavily policed (with deadly violence). At the same time, the Buffer Zone is a space overloaded with meaning, part of the discursive frameworks that give meaning to the self and the other as enemy and that articulate this space as a space to be (re-)conquered and defended (see Papallas 2016). It is highly significant, and deeply tragic, that Solomou died trying to remove the flag of an enemy and that his killers shot him in order to protect the flag they identified with, a situation that is reminiscent of a century-old, but virtually disappeared, tradition of protecting the flag on the battlefield.[17]

Also other – less lethal – material and signifying practices were developed to overcome the divide. The negotiations between the representatives of the two states (not recognizing each other) consisted of material meetings (even though these representatives did not always share the same room). They started soon after 1974, as part of the UN Good Offices Missions, and resulted, for instance, in two High-Level Agreements in the 1970s, although they were severely criticized in Cyprus (see, e.g. Richmond 1999: 52) from the respective dominant antagonistic nationalist positions. These endlessly ongoing negotiations were, at times, purely ritualistic, aimed at avoiding the fact that the self and the international community blamed one community for an unwillingness to engage in a dialogue with the other-enemy. This rendered the negotiations strategic and more of a confirmation of antagonistic nationalism than a means of overcoming it, still triggering cycles of hope and anxiety. As Jarraud, Louise and Filippou (2013: 45) wrote, "attempts to find accommodation between the Greek Cypriot and Turkish Cypriot leadership have frustrated the peacemaking efforts of successive professional mediators and the division of Cyprus has become synonymous with intractability." At the more local level, collaboration remained possible, exemplified by the shared sewage treatment system in Nicosia, completed during "a period of high political tensions between the two communities" (Calame and Charlesworth 2011: 182). Here, political pragmatism, driven by the material scarcity of resources, overruled antagonistic nationalism: "two sewage treatment networks were simply not affordable, and a cooperative scheme was necessary despite unfavorable political and diplomatic circumstances" (2011: 182), although one of the Turkish Cypriot civil engineers that Calame and Charlesworth quoted also added elements of agonism and humanism (even when still using the signifier "Turk"):

> The Turkish people are using the treated water from the south in their farms to grow crops and make money to survive. The south side residents also benefit because their wastewater gets treated, which is important for health. Symbiosis. You don't have to talk about nationality. You just have to say, "I'm a human being and I love my country. I love my environment." (Öznel, cited in Calame and Charlesworth 2011: 182)

The more formal, state-related initiatives to overcome the divide were complemented by civil society initiatives, which would eventually propagate an agonistic discourse of peace and reconciliation. Early peace activists, and the later-established bi-community peace movement, managed to overcome the material separation of the Buffer Zone, initially by meeting abroad or in Pyla. Jarraud, Louise and Filippou (2013: 48) quoted an anonymous peace activist describing the material difficulties of organizing these meetings: "In the early days you needed to be brave to get involved as anyone from the other community was considered the enemy. There was no easy way of meeting and the authorities had to grant us permission to enter the UN buffer zone." Through later initiatives, from the mid-1990s onwards, "thousands of Cypriots from across the island took part in bi-communal activities" (Jarraud, Louise and Filippou 2013: 49; see also Broome 2005: 12), again overcoming the material divide but also weakening the hegemony of antagonistic nationalism. As Anastasiou (2008a: 15) wrote,

> By the year 2000, a bicommunal citizen peace movement [...] reached maturity as it developed a recognizable voice. Having joined efforts: [Greek Cypriot] and [Turkish Cypriot] citizens gradually introduced into the hitherto nationalist cultures of Cypriot ethnocentric politics, an alternative culture of peace and reconciliation as the indispensable foundation of civil society and multiethnic democracy.

THE RISE OF CYPRIOTISM

It is also important to stress that discursive hegemony is never total. On Cyprus, an identity discourse contending with Greek and Turkish Cypriot nationalism, Cypriotism, never completely disappeared. Doob (1986: 390) observed the continued presence of the Cypriotist ideology, or what he called "Cypriot patriotism":

> Symptoms of Cypriot patriotism that transcended Turkish and Greek Cypriot patriotism and nationalism remained, even as persons on both sides

could and would not forget their heritage as well as the economic and military assistance and encouragement received from the mother countries. They realized that they shared the same small island, in spite of the salient reality of their inability ever to cross the Green Line and of the existence of several new airports that were less efficient and more dangerous than the single one formerly serving the entire country. Without necessarily being unfriendly, Cypriots were curious concerning events and people on the other side.

Moreover, despite AKEL's sometimes ambiguous stance, this organizational machine can be seen as one of the long-term protectors of Cypriotism (Mavratsas 1997; Papadakis 1998) and one of the key actors in the post-1974 discursive struggle between Greek Cypriot nationalism and Cypriotism.[18] Mavratsas (1997: 720) argued that in the first years after 1974, Greek Cypriot nationalism was weakened, "precisely because nationalism was seen as at least partly responsible for the events of 1974," which, for instance, led to the Greek Cypriot negotiators' acceptance of a federal solution (in the High-Level Agreements of the late 1970s). Mavratsas (1997: 720) added that "Communist AKEL [...] went beyond the discourse of the peaceful coexistence of the two communities and even talked about the 'brotherly' bonds between the Greek and the Turkish Cypriots."

But writing at the end of the 1990s, Mavratsas (1997: 726) also argued that "[s]ince the mid 1980s, Greek-Cypriot nationalist forces have returned to the forefront and to a considerable degree have again started to represent the political mainsteam [*sic*] of the Greek-Cypriot community." In the case of the Turkish Cypriot community, Loizides (2007: 180) wrote that "Turkish Cypriots felt closely attached to Turkey immediately after 1974, in the following years, Cypriotism was on the rise, taking a politicized form." Cypriotism here implied an "emphasis

on the differences between mainland Turks and Turkish Cypriots, paying particular attention to the cultural and linguistic similarities with Greek Cypriots" (Güven-Lisaniler and Rodríguez 2002: 183). One specific element that strengthened Cypriotism in the north were tensions about the so-called Turkish "settlers" in Cyprus. Navaro-Yashin (2012: 59) described this power struggle as follows:

> Turkish-Cypriots employed their status, lifestyles, income levels, and claims to autochthony in their differentiation tactics vis-à-vis the settlers. In turn, some settlers (those who could) attempted to overcome their sociocultural marginalization in Cyprus by declaring their alliance with Turkey as its citizens, assuming a Turkish nationalist discourse, or voting for the right-wing parties of the trnc regime.

This power struggle generated difference, which was then – as Navaro-Yashin (2012: 55) wrote – played out by "using terms that signify cultural difference and social class." In some cases, "settlers" (who had sometimes "settled" for a long time and, for instance, included Kurdish people) even became "conflated or confused" with the Turkish soldiers (Navaro-Yashin 2012: 55), using an other-foreigner articulation. As a consequence, the Turkish Cypriot nationalist homogeneity became dislocated, and a Cypriot identity – distinct from the Turkish one – was strengthened. We can find this discursive-political struggle, despite Denktaş long-lasting strong position in the TRNC, also at a more institutional level, where political and journalistic voices represented the Cypriotist ideology in the north of Cyprus. One example mentioned by Loizides (2007: 180) is the Communal Liberation Party (*Toplumcu Kurtuluş Partisi* – TKP) of Alpay Durduran, an opposition party established in 1976, which supported the establishment of a federal state (Kizilyürek 2012).[19] In sum, and as Loizides (2007: 177) argued, at first the majority of the "Turkish Cypriots saw the motherland troops as liberators," but then

> these feelings waned in the following years, because of the resulting international isolation, Turkey's interference in Turkish Cypriot community affairs, economic stagnation, and the colonization of Cyprus by Turkish settlers (Lacher and Kaymak 2005). Ultimately, the new conditions led many Turkish Cypriots to reconsider their unconditional loyalty to the policies of the national center.

THE ANNAN PLAN AND THE CONTINUED HEGEMONY OF NATIONALISM

Even if the dominant nationalisms were contested, these discourses managed to protect their hegemonic position for several decades. In 2001, Fisher (2001: 321–22) described the situation in Cyprus as follows:

> Antagonism is expressed, but is not used as a springboard for reflexive reframing, invention or action planning. The parties are caught in self-defeating processes of antagonism, including blaming the other side, attributing negative qualities to them, and polarizing one's own side against them.

The Buffer Zone, with its guards and fortifications that cut through the island, remained the materialization of the antagonistic nationalist discourse, created out of the desire to separate Turkish Cypriots and Greek Cypriots. The guards, and their rules of engagement, still contain the threat of material violence, grounded in this nationalist logic. Second, and relatedly, the material inability of the refugees to return and reclaim their properties is another materialization of the antagonistic form of nationalism that continues to structure the island's geography, demography and economy, until today. And finally,

the existence of two clusters of state apparatuses, labelled as the "Republic of Cyprus" and the "Turkish Republic of Northern Cyprus," is also a materialization of the antagonistic nationalist discourse.

None of these three materializations have disappeared, but in 2003 the Buffer Zone's (almost) impregnable status changed significantly. Days after the Republic of Cyprus signed the EU Ascension Treaty, and under the pressure of the Turkish Cypriot's "This country is ours" platform, the TRNC regime announced the easing of the Green Line crossing restrictions. The opening of the first crossings in April 2003 allowed Cypriots to enter and pass through the Buffer Zone without being exposed to material violence. As Dikomitis (2012: 117) wrote, "The first border crossing was historic, life changing and also confusing for many Cypriots." Although some Cypriots were (and some still are) hesitant about crossing (see Dikomitis 2012: 118ff) into the "other" side, and the encounters did not always produce the desired outcomes (Scott 2013: 127), the material permeability of the Buffer Zone has allowed for increased levels of contact between Greek Cypriots and Turkish Cypriots, also at an organizational (civil society) level.[20] Even more unexpected meeting places, such as casinos,[21] "operate as a particular kind of bicommunal space, very different from those spaces promoted by international agencies" functioning "as places for the rediscovery and exercise of cultural intimacy" (Scott 2013: 127). Most importantly, the other-enemy was no longer hidden behind the Buffer Zone and was seen to share the same material space, which, in most cases,[22] allowed for the re-articulation of the subject position of the other, in a variety of ways, ranging from other-foreigner over other-ally to part of the self.

Also, material collaboration at the grassroots level was facilitated, as is exemplified by work of the relatives of the missing. Efthymiou[23] (2014) described how the relatives of the missing persons from both sides of the divide started crossing the dividing line in search of information for the fate of their relatives. The work of journalists working on the issue and spaces created by bi-communal activities provided the opportunities for relatives of the missing from both sides to meet and exchange experiences and information. Very soon these people identified with the pain of each other and remarkable friendships formed. [...] The victims of the massacres and atrocious crimes from both sides were coming together to challenge society to stop using their pain to enhance nationalism but face the realities of the violent past and work so that no families in the future will again have to go through the same trauma.

This led in 2006 to the establishment of the "Bi-Communal Initiative of Relatives of Missing Persons, Victims of Massacres and Other Events 1963–1974" (later renamed "Together We Can"). Kovras (2012: 97) wrote about this initiative: "The 'open checkpoints' policy created an unprecedented opportunity for relatives of missing persons to build an effective organization structure, meet and exchange ideas regularly and organize collaborative events." The (early) activism of the relatives coincided with, and possibly contributed to, the reactivation of the Committee on Missing Persons in Cyprus (CMP) in 2004 (Kovras 2012: 89), after being dormant for almost 25 years. CMP has played (and still plays) a crucial role in the identification of the bodies of (a considerable part of) the missing, supporting closure for the families, even though it cannot raise "issues of legal, moral or political accountability" (2012: 100).

In the same period, one more crucial event took place, which merits our attention, as it demonstrates the role of nationalism in Cyprus in this period. A plan for unification of the island, the so-called Annan Plan – actually, its fifth version – was submitted to

an island-wide referendum on 24 April 2004, in yet another failed attempt to change the Cypriot state assemblage(s). The Annan V Plan was rejected by referendum in the Greek Cypriot community (with more than 75 per cent voting against it) and accepted in the Turkish Cypriot community (with almost 65 per cent voting in favour) (Michael 2011: 180). The Annan Plan period was a crucial moment in the contemporary history of Cyprus, because it showed the strength of the nationalist discourse in the twenty-first century, at least in the Greek Cypriot community, and its capacity to still mobilize large parts of the population. In the north, the Annan Plan demonstrated the relative weakness of nationalism and the contingency of its hegemony – in practice, it meant the political *fin de carrière* for president Denktaş and the coming of a new generation of more moderate political leaders. Still, the Annan Plan mobilizations also showed that there was no total consensus in either of the two communities, uncovering the lack of homogeneity. Moreover, the referendum, and the absence of inter-communal violence, illustrated how the antagonistic forms of nationalism remained at the discursive level.

Anastasiou's (2008b) analysis of the "no" campaign for the Annan Plan referendum shows the role of institutionalized politics, mainstream media and the Greek Orthodox Church of Cyprus in enhancing the Greek Cypriot nationalist discourse and consolidating its hegemony. In the case of the Orthodox Church, Anastasiou (2008b: 155) argued that this organization has been "[h]istorically influenced by the rise of Hellenic nationalism during the nineteenth century," which led to the "uncritical assimilation of impassioned ethnocentrism." He illustrated this by citing the words of Bishop Pavlos of Kyrenia, who declared before the 2004 referendum took place that "those who say 'yes' will be party to this injustice, will lose their homeland and the kingdom of heaven!" (2004: 157). Also, many of the Greek Cypriot political parties identified with a nationalist discourse, including President Tassos Papadopoulos's DIKO party, the socialist party EDEK, the communist party AKEL[24] and the Green Party. Anastasiou (2008b: 142) illustrated the workings of the nationalist discourse within the realm of institutionalized politics by analysing the Republic of Cyprus president Papadopoulos's crucial speech on 7 April 2004, which "was tearful and impassioned." In this speech, the Greek Cypriot president (involved in the Annan Plan negotiations) called upon the Greek Cypriots to reject the Annan Plan. Anastasiou (2008b: 144) argued that Papadopoulos used two sets of signifying practices:

> First, he tapped into the dormant nationalist memory and sentiments of the [Greek Cypriot] community, stirring, reactivating, and amplifying nationalism to the point of saturating the public debate and drowning out the pro-solution voices. Second, he reawakened the [Greek Cypriot's] sense of victimization and reintegrated it into the nationalist framework, thus re-associating the [Greek Cypriot's] sense of injustice with the typical reactionary culture of adversarial nationalism.

Also, the Turkish Cypriot sphere of institutionalized politics supported a nationalist discourse during the Annan Plan period. This support for a nationalist discourse was personified by Denktaş, at that time still president of the TRNC, even if his position was severely weakened after the 2002 protests and the 2003 parliamentary elections. Anastasiou (2008b: 122) referred here, for instance, to Denktaş's statement "that the Annan Plan was nothing but a trap for the TCs [Turkish Cypriots]." Anastasiou (2008b: 162) continued to argue that both Papadopoulos and Denktaş "chose to opt for ethno-centric agendas and approaches that perpetuated the captivity of their people to the divisive and belligerent remnant of their nationalist past." But, in contrast to the sphere of institutionalized politics, popular support for the Turkish Cypriot nationalism "had already been on the wane in the 1990s, even with a simultaneous hardening of the official position" (Tesser 2013: 123).

In the Annan Plan period, the signifying practices that entextualized nationalist discourses tended more towards antagonism, even though the calls for destruction remained at a discursive level. Anastasiou's (2008b: 162) summary of the negotiations leading up to the Annan V Plan offers an indication of this kind of antagonism, where Papadopoulos (and the institutional actors backing him) aimed at the dismantlement of the TRNC and Denktaş (again, with institutional support) opted for the dismantlement of the Republic of Cyprus:

> The reality was that at the forefront of events were two adversarial nationalists with maximalist approaches to negotiations; the TC [Turkish Cypriot] leader was still attempting to "negotiate" a secessionist solution and the GC [Greek Cypriot] leader was still pursuing a "settlement" that resembled the unitary state of the pre-1974 era.

In addition, the antagonism was also translated in a series of violent attacks, and it is important here to quote Anastasiou's (2008b: 160–61; emphasis in original) description of these events at length, as this description demonstrates that these violent acts were intra-communal and – as Anastasiou (2008b: 162) also emphasized – not inter-communal. In this stage of the conflict, the antagonistically defined other-enemy was purely situated within the self, both in the Greek Cypriot and in the Turkish Cypriot community, again leading to material destruction:

> The head of the DISY party, the first to declare formally its support of the UN proposal, had a hand grenade thrown into his house. Alecos

Constantinides, the chief editor of the center-right newspaper *Aletheia*, received anonymous calls "threatening his life and expressing anger at the line the newspaper was following during the referenda." [...] These events in the [Greek Cypriot] community paralleled phenomena in the [Turkish Cypriot] community during the run-up to the referenda. The most notable were the heavy beatings of pro-peace youths by the Grey Wolves, an extremist nationalist group rooted in Turkey's far-right nationalist past. Furthermore, [Turkish Cypriot] militants bombed the house of Mehmet Ali Talat, Republican Party leader and pro-peace "prime minister" supporting the Annan Plan. Reactionary forces also bombed the offices of *Kibris*, a newspaper known for promoting peace with the [Greek Cypriots], supporting a negotiated settlement to reunify the Island, and criticizing the intransigent nationalism of the Denktash regime.

POST-ANTAGONIST NATIONALISM IN CYPRUS?

With the title of her conclusion of her book *Imagining the Modern*, Bryant (2004: 249) raised the question of whether 2003 marked the start of Cyprus's evolution towards a "postnational" condition. She legitimated this question (and its possible positive answer) as follows: "Since the beginning of 2003, Cyprus has experienced tremendous change, much of it following upon the opening of the buffer zone and the opportunities for interchange that followed." The failure of the Annan Plan to reunite the island also triggered "a revolution that has marginalized their [the Turkish Cypriot's] long-time leaders" (2004: 249), who in the past have provided significant support for the nationalist discourse, including its antagonistic version. Further support for this position can be found in the quasi-absence of material violence in the past two decades.

Even though it might be better, at least within the context of this book, to refer to a post-antagonistic

nationalism (and not to a "postnational Cyprus," as Bryant did), there are still more arguments that can be mobilized to support Bryant's thesis. Contemporary signifying practices about the history of the Cyprus Problem, and about its possible solutions, continue to contain references to the enemy-other, but this enemy-other, in most cases, is situated in the past, even if the anxiety that the past might repeat itself has not disappeared (Cyprus 2015 Initiative 2011: 45). Still, the (possible) antagonistic nature of the contemporary other is articulated through the events from the past and not so much through the more recent behaviour of that other. One anonymous Turkish Cypriot stakeholder panel participant, cited in the Cyprus 2015 Initiative (2011: 92) report, formulated this concern as follows: "We have to accept our mistakes and understand each other's concerns. It's true that Greek Cypriots attempted to cleanse the island from Turkish Cypriots. They have to accept this and respect our security concerns." Another source of anxiety are so-called "extremists," as they are labelled in the Cyprus 2015 Initiative (2011: 98) report. This brings in another discursive logic, where the separation of normalcy and extremism shows the exceptionalism of antagonistic nationalism. This concern is formulated by another anonymous Turkish Cypriot stakeholder panel participant in the Cyprus 2015 Initiative (2011: 98) report:

"There are parties on each side whose interest lies with conflict and clashes in Cyprus" argued a Turkish Cypriot stakeholder. "These people will try to make the new state of affairs collapse. We have to keep this in mind and do not let them escalate a minor event into a communal strife."

In addition, there is also a tendency, in particular in the Cypriotist discourse, to shift the responsibility (and with it, the subject position of the other-enemy) outside Cyprus. For instance, in Zembylas,

Charalambous and Charalambous's (2016: 9) list of characteristics of Cypriotism, "proclaims Turkey as the aggressor" is mentioned. This implies a disarticulation of the Turkish Cypriot community from the other-enemy chain of equivalence, allowing it to become (at least) an other-adversary (or even a part of the self). There is a long history of disconnecting Turkish Cypriots from the Turkish enemy, where they sometimes – as Bryant (2004: 224) contended – become seen as victims of the Turkish state, which, in turn, strengthens the evilness and otherness of the Turkish enemy. One example is the missing, where "the Greek Cypriots [...] have long maintained [...] that the main culprits are not the Turkish Cypriots but the Turkish army occupying half the island" (Sant Cassia 2005: 23). Even if this articulation does not do justice to the complexity of the history of Cypriot antagonism, and is sometimes used to fragment and inferiorize the Turkish Cypriot other-enemy, it still has the potential to support a more agonistic discourse. Similarly, the conspiracy theories that blame the United States (and, to a lesser extent, the United Kingdom) for the antagonisms on the island are, intentionally or not, part of a politics of blame, which removes responsibility (at least partially) from the Cypriot people and its organizational machines. One version of this conspiracy theory[25] is that "both British passivity and a United States-led alliance actively colluding with Turkey in the invasion" paved "the way for the de facto partition" (Trimikliniotis 2012: 31). Even if their historical accuracy is highly debatable, these articulations of an enemy-other outside Cyprus (potentially) reconfigures the Cypriot other as non-enemy.

Also, the self has become more heterogeneous, both at the level of identifications with national identity discourses and at the level of political practice. Identifications with the different national(ist) discourses occur, and the merging of these identifications has become more intense, resulting in multiple subject positions. Vural and Rustemli's (2006) article on what they call "identify fluctuations" within the Turkish Cypriot community discusses the combination of Turkishness and Cypriotness, combined with Europeanness and being Muslim. They wrote:

> As expected, ethno-national identity is the most frequent among the late adult and elderly generations, of whom most had experienced intercommunal conflicts and were trained as "mujaheddins." The adults who had little direct experience of the inter-communal struggles exhibited a preference for "Cypriotness" over "Turkishness." The youngest generation showed a split between "Turkishness" and "Cypriotness." (Vural and Rustemli 2006: 343)

Muslim and European identities are much less present than Turkishness and Cypriotness, but the point that needs to be made here is that Turkishness is no longer the dominant identification, or, in other words, the Turkish Cypriot nationalist subject position has lost its hegemonic position. Turkish Cypriot nationalism is now, much more than in past decades, part of an intra-communal discursive struggle. This, in turn, implies that *within* the two communities, diversity and pluralism has increased. In particular, the role of religious identities has become more complicated. In the Greek Cypriot case, the Orthodox Christian faith was a significant component of the Greek Cypriot nationalist chain of equivalence, with Greekness as its nodal point. Even though, as Roudometof (2009: 64; my translation) showed, an "overwhelming majority" of the Greek Cypriots still believe in God, at the same time, the process of secularization has taken root in Cyprus: "following the modernization of the Republic of Cyprus, the evolution of religiosity took the typical form of an intensification of the cleavage between a more conservative and religious wing, and a more secular wing" (Roudometof, 2009: 64; my translation). Again, this is an argument that supports the pluralization of the Cypriot society. In north Cyprus, because of the historical dominance of the Kemalist secular tradition, religion did not play a very significant role in the Turkish Cypriot nationalist chain of equivalence. Until today, the role of religion in north Cyprus has been fairly limited. In an article, based on data from 2006, Yeşilada (2009: 58) concluded that "the Turkish Cypriots are some of the most secular Muslims in the world." Nevertheless, more recently, we can also find traces of an ongoing discursive struggle between different groups in the TRNC over the role of Islam in Turkish Cypriot society, with more traditional fractions and more secular fractions. Dayıoğlu and Hatay (2015: 159), for instance, referred to what they called the "public debates" over religious education for children and the question of whether Qur'an summer courses could be organized by mosques (or only schools). Again, these struggles demonstrate the diversity of Turkish Cypriot society.[26]

A similar diversity of (overlapping) identifications can be found in the twenty-first-century political party landscape in Cyprus. Long-established political parties in the south, such as DIKO and EDEK, still identify with a nationalist discourse, but also the Green Party (KOSP), the fairly new Citizens' Alliance (SYPOL, established in 2013) and the still new Solidarity Movement (established in 2016, incorporating the European Party – EVROKO) take a strong nationalist position, and so does the extreme right-wing party ELAM. This explains Charalambous and Ioannou's (2015: 271) short summary: "nationalism has neither been defeated nor limited to the margins." But other political parties, such as AKEL and DISY (with the latter providing the current president of the Republic of Cyprus, Nicos Anastasiades, re-elected in 2018), are much less inclined to strongly defend nationalist positions, which produces more diversity – or more fragmentation, as Triga et al. (2019) label it – within the sphere of institutionalized politics in the south. In the TRNC, we find a similar

ideological diversity, with Democratic Party (DP), National Unity Party (UBP) and Rebirth Party (YDP) on the nationalist side of the political spectrum. DP is led by the son of former president Rauf Denktaş, Serdar, and UBP has the current president, Ersin Tatar, among its ranks. On the other side of the political spectrum (see Baruh Popescu 2008: 83), we find the social-democrats of the Republican Turkish Party (CTP) and the Communal Democracy Party (TDP), with the latter party having provided the previous president of the TRNC, Mustafa Akıncı. There is also the more centrist anti-corruption People's Party (HP), established in 2016. Again, important here is that, in both communities, this diversity has enabled different coalitions, for instance bringing different government departments into the hands of different ministers.

Not only were Cypriot policies affected by the internal heterogenization, but also links with the two "motherlands," which were, in the past, an intimate part of the hegemonic Greek Cypriot and Turkish Cypriot nationalist equivalential chains, became more complicated. After the fall of the junta, Greece became less involved in Cyprus (even if the connections were never severed). Greece's relationship with Turkey remained problematic until both countries were hit by successive earthquakes in 1999 and the caring responses intensified the already existent détente (Ker-Lindsay 2007). But in the "post-kemalist" (Michael 2011: 198) era of Turkey, tensions between Turkey, Greece and the entire European Union have increased again, for a variety of reasons, including the continuation of the Aegean dispute, the long and difficult Turkish ascension process into the European Union, the increasingly authoritarian rule in Turkey, the Syrian Civil War (with its many refugees) and the economic conflicts over the Aphrodite gas field exploitation (see Michael and Vural 2018; Heraclides and Alioğlu Çakmak 2019). In Cyprus, Turkey has kept a firm grip on the TRNC, both materially and discursively, although there have always been tensions. Isachenko (2012: 75–76), for instance, described the conflict that erupted when, in July 2000, Mustafa Akıncı (then-leader of TKP and deputy prime minister) raised the question whether it was still appropriate for a Turkish general to control the Turkish Cypriot police and fire brigades, which resulted in accusations of treason by the Turkish military.[27] These events fed into the "This country is ours" platform. The very same Mustafa Akıncı said during his victory speech after the 2015 presidential elections that the relationship between Turkey and the TRNC would no longer be that of "motherland" and "babyland," but would be based on an equal "relationship between brothers." When Akıncı repeated the same message on CNN Turk, Erdoğan responded as follows:

> "Mr. President's ears should hear what comes out of his mouth. Working together even as brothers has its prerequisites. This country has paid a price for Northern Cyprus. We've sacrificed martyrs and we are continuing to pay a price. We spend about $1 billion for them annually," Erdogan said. "Who is waging the battle for Northern Cyprus in the international arena? Can Mr. Akinci wage this battle on his own? [Turkey] will continue to see [the TRNC] just like a mother sees her baby."[28]

The ascension of Cyprus into the European Union[29] added another significant state assemblage to the equation, further disrupting the structural "Republic of Cyprus and Greece" versus "TRNC and Turkey" dichotomy. Cyprus's connection with the European Union produced outcomes that can be considered more positive, as Cyprus moved symbolically closer to the other countries in the European Union, increasing its visibility, although Cyprus remained in a peripheral position. Still, the material consequences were considerable: As the entire island joined the European Union, (with the EU legislation suspended in the north), all Cypriots, also those living in the TRNC, became EU citizens, which offers possibilities for adding the identification with the European identity to the portfolio of possible identifications. EU citizenship also has material consequences, as it facilitates material movement through the possession of an EU passport. Moreover, some of the European Union's material resources became available to Cyprus, again including the north.[30] For example, from 2007 onwards, the European Union has supported the Committee on Missing Persons in Cyprus (CMP).[31] And third, as Kyriakides (2014: 165) argued, "the Court of Justice of the EU and the domestic courts of EU member states have been added to the architecture of the 'Cyprus Question,'" which produces more authoritative signifying practices that impact on, for instance, the ownership rights in relation to the Greek Cypriot properties in the north.[32]

The evaluation of the role of the European Union might be less positive when in 2012–13 the economic crisis hit the south of Cyprus and the Republic of Cyprus was forced to negotiate a bailout agreement with the so-called troika (the European Union, the European Central Bank and the International Monetary Fund). This agreement consisted of "a €10 billion bailout and a – later finalized – 47.5 per cent 'haircut' of all deposits above €100,000 in Cypriot banks (bail-in), combined with the shutdown of the second largest bank on the island, Popular Bank of Cyprus ('Laiki Bank'), whose depositors lost all their 'unsecured' savings (above €100,000)" (Doudaki, Boubouka and Tzalavras 2019: 354). This crisis dislocated not only the centrality of the Cyprus Problem but also the articulation of the Greek Cypriot subject position as economically superior (in relation to the north). Although very depths of the economic crises in the Republic of Cyprus have been left behind (even if precarity remains; see Ioannou 2017), and the dislocation of the centrality of the Cyprus Problem has been reduced again (see, e.g. Triga et al. 2019), the 2012–13 economic crisis altered the Cypriot horizon, even when this alteration was only (semi-)temporary.

Despite these changes in the Cypriot discursive and material spaces, and the changing international contexts, the material configuration of Cyprus has not changed drastically over time. The island remains divided by a militarized Buffer Zone, with all its material consequences, including the displaced Cypriots' inability to do more than visit their properties and the TRNC's political and economic isolation (Talmon 2001).[33] Also, the division of the Cypriot communicational spaces, with Cypriot mainstream media in most cases using either Turkish or Greek, does not facilitate inter-communal dialogue (Tringides 2013: 42). Although there have been some material attempts to bridge the divide, for instance at the times of the Florakis Naval Base and Karpasia

oil disasters, many other issues (in particular those related to the Aphrodite gas field exploitation) have created a substantial number of new tensions. Also, the discursive environment has proved to be more rigid than the above-discussed changes might indicate, as the discursive divide between north and south, still grounded in what one could call post-antagonistic nationalist frameworks, continues to exist and the voices to consolidate the partition have been growing stronger (this time also in the south; see Ioannou 2020). The many negotiations between Turkish Cypriot and Greek Cypriot political representatives (and international actors) – with the last major round having taken place in the Swiss resort of Crans-Montana in the summer of 2017 – have produced many signifying practices but no material peace agreement.

NOTES

1. In 2014 the population in the south was 847,000 (Press and Information Office for the Statistical Service 2015); in the north, a 2013 estimate suggests a number close to 295,000 (Encyclopaedia Britannica 2014: 143).

2. Some authors use "Turkish" for the Ottoman period. In this book, "Ottoman" is preferred.

3. TRNC refers here to the Turkish Republic of Northern Cyprus, the de facto state in north Cyprus. In the south of Cyprus, it is customary to add citation marks to TRNC, or to refer to it as a "pseudo-state." The reader will have to forgive me for not indulging in this signifying practice, although this practice will be briefly analysed further on in this chapter.

4. The Dodecanese (including Rhodes) were ceded by Italy and joined the Greek state in 1947.

5. See Hadjipavlou (2010) for one example of an analysis of gender and the Cyprus Problem.

6. Rauf Denktaş was the first president of the Turkish Republic of Northern Cyprus. He was in office from the declaration of the de facto state in 1983 until 2005.

7. For instance, in the case of Limassol, the Ottoman census of 1831 counted 303 male Muslim Cypriots and 345 male Orthodox Cypriots. Later, the percentage of Turkish Cypriots decreased to about 20 per cent to 25 per cent, but until 1974 there was a considerably sized Turkish Cypriot community

in Limassol. See http://www.prio-cyprus-displacement.net/default.asp?id=406.

8. See https://tr.wikisource.org/wiki/T%C3%BCrk_Mukavemet_Te%C5%9Fkilat%C4%B1_Yemini (in Turkish). A rare translation in English has been included in the transcript of a CyBC television program, entitled "*TMT: With Blood and Fire.*" This translation was used here.

9. One instance is the killing of Bonici Mompalda, a Maltese shop manager, who was also a special constable.

10. This was based on the United Nations Security Council Resolution 186 which was passed on 4 March 1964.

11. Lytras and Psaltis (2011: 15) mentioned 42 Turkish Cypriot enclaves.

12. Lytras and Psaltis (2011: 17) referred to data collected by Patrick (1976) that indicated that in 1891 the number of mixed villages was 346. In 1960 the number had declined to 114, and in 1970 there were 48 mixed villages left. Lytras and Psaltis (2011: 17) remarked that not only "inter-communal frictions" but also urbanization processes are responsible for this decrease. The number in the mid-1960s is likely to have been even lower, as "by 1971 [and according to Patrick's (1976) data], 2000 Turkish Cypriot refugees had returned to 19 mixed villages and to 5 Turkish Cypriot villages while 57 formerly mixed villages had become inhabited solely by Greek Cypriots"

(Lytras and Psaltis 2011: 18). Still, "relations between the ethnic quarters of most mixed villages were characterised by 'outright hostility'" (Patrick 1976: 8, cited in Lytras and Psaltis 2011: 17).

13. Also on the Turkish side, friendly fire – a dramatic example of human error, military tactics and material agency – took its toll, as Turkish war planes sank the Turkish destroyer D-354 Kocatepe (http://www.worldnavalships.com/turkish_navy.htm) and damaged the D-353 Adatepe and the D-355 Tinaztepe.

14. Bryant (2004: 224) argued that sometimes Turkish Cypriots "are portrayed as unwilling captives of Denktas [then the leader of the Turkish Cypriots] and the Turkish military."

15. A cultural trauma is more than an aggregate of individual traumata (see Kansteiner 2004: 209). It is a cultural phenomenon that "appears in the aftermath of a particular type of social change" (Sztompka 2000: 452).

16. Nadel-Klein (1991: 502) provided the following working definition of localism: "the representation of group identity as defined primarily by a sense of commitment to a particular place and to a set of cultural practices that are self-consciously articulated and to some degree separated and directed away from the surrounding social world."

17. Gentles (2007: 94) described the military importance of the flag ("the colours"), referring to a quote from Captain Thomas Venn from 1672: "To lose one's 'colour' was regarded as a disgrace worse than death. 'Indeed, a greater act of cowardice cannot be found', declared Captain Thomas Venn, 'than the colours to be lost.'"

18. We should here bear Mavratsas's (1997: 723–24) words in mind: "Cypriotist elements and orientations can be found in almost all political parties, and it should be clear that the reduction of the contest between nationalism and Cypriotism into a left-right opposition cannot be fully sustained and can only oversimplify the picture."

19. The Communal Liberation Party merged with the Peace and Democracy Movement into the Communal Democracy Party (*Toplumcu Demokrasi Partisi* – TDP), and the latter had Mustafa Akıncı elected as president of the TRNC in April 2015. Akıncı's mandate ended in 2020.

20. Witness the current set of civil society activities within the Ledra Palace crossing.

21. At that time, casinos were illegal in the Republic of Cyprus, but many casinos operated in the north. On 10 March 2016, the Republic of Cyprus parliament voted for a law allowing one integrated casino resort to be established. A regulator became operational in 2018, the National Gaming and Casino Supervision Commission of Cyprus (http://cgc.org.cy/). According to the regular's website: "The first ICR in Cyprus is currently under construction and is scheduled to open in the first quarter of 2021" (http://cgc.org.cy/en/integrated-casino-resort).

22. There are still cases of violence against the other. For instance, on 17 May 2016, a *Cyprus Mail* news report referred to three Turkish Cypriots being attacked in their car in the southern part of Nicosia on 15 May 2016, by a group of Greek Cypriots, believed to be APOEL (soccer) fans. The damage to the car, which had a TRNC license plate, was estimated at €500. See http://cyprus-mail.com/2016/05/17/police-investigate-claim-football-fans-attacked-turkish-cypriots/.

23. Christos Efthymiou is, together with Sevgül Uludağ, coordinator of Together We Can.

24. Anastasiou (2008b: 163ff) spent a lot of time analysing the position of AKEL. AKEL's "long-standing, interethnic rapprochement policy and ongoing contact and dialogue with the TCs [Turkish Cypriots]" (Anastasiou 2008b: 163) made its decision to support the "no" camp surprising, even though Anastasiou (2008b: 163) also argued that a strong push by a nationalist AKEL faction caused the party leadership to revise its original support to the Annan Plan and eventually reject it. The internal AKEL struggle illustrates how organizational machines harmonize signifying practices.

25. For a more plausible analysis of the role of the United States in 1974, see Constandinos (2012). Stearns's (1992: 11) summary about the earlier stages of the conflict points to a similar argument, describing the US initiatives as "firefighting operations designed primarily to prevent general hostilities between Greece and Turkey or secure other short-term objectives."

26. These changes raise concerns in the south of Cyprus, as this online article shows: http://www.newsincyprus.com/news/16061/religious-pressure-in-north.

27. The Turkish brigadier-general Ali Nihat Özeyranlı also requested the dismissal of some of the directors of the public service broadcaster BRT and the public news agency TAK and had an editor of the Turkish Cypriot daily *Avrupa*, Şener Levent, and three other journalists, arrested. See http://www.economist.com/node/6632.

28. http://www.al-monitor.com/pulse/originals/2015/04/turkey-greece-cypriot-baby-grow-up.html.

29. Sometimes the rather awkward term the "Europeanization of Cyprus" is used to describe this process.

30. For instance, on 27 February 2006, the European Council approved the establishment of a 5-year aid program for the Turkish Cypriot community, consisting of €259 million euros. Between 2006 and 2020, €591 million have been allocated, and in August 2020, the European Commission approved a second Annual Action Programme for a total amount of €31.6 million, in addition to the €5 million that had been approved earlier in

2020. See https://ec.europa.eu/commission/presscorner/detail/en/IP_20_1490 and http://ec.europa.eu/cyprus/turkish_cypriots/index_en.htm.

31. A 2012 European Commission report mentions 6.5 million euros (European Commission 2012: 26). For 2020, the CMP website mentions €2.6 millions EU contribution and a total of €28.1 millions EU contribution. See http://www.cmp-cyprus.org/content/donors.

32. Kyriakides (2014: 165) referred here to the Court of Justice's re-affirmation of property rights in the Apostolides cases.

33. Isachenko (2012: 157) added here that "de jure isolated, informal states are nevertheless embedded in the network of international politics" and "they find ways to escape isolation."

Chapter 5: The Iconoclastic Controversies Photographs

The violent confrontations in the second half of the twentieth century have left their mark on the Cypriot landscape, not only because of the Buffer Zone that cuts across the entire island. Memorials and commemoration sites are also very visible parts of the nationalist assemblage, spread all over the island. On the basis of a mapping project in the south of Cyprus, Karaiskou (2014: 20) refers to "nearly six hundred memorials spread over an approximate 5,750 square kilometers of the island's southern portion (an average of one monument per ten square kilometers)." In many cases, these memorials and commemoration sites are part of the (post-)antagonistic nationalist assemblage, with materialities that invite for a reading that supports the heroism and sacrifice of Cypriots and that celebrate the military victories of EOKA in the south (in the independence war) and of Turkey in the north (in 1974). In the south, they commemorate the defeat and losses of the Greek Cypriot communities (in 1974).

INDEPENDENCE: MATERIALIZATIONS OF A HEGEMONIC DISCOURSE

When we focus on the southern part of Cyprus, the independence war memorials form materializations of the hegemonic antagonistic nationalist discourse, based on nodal points such as freedom and liberation, justice, unity and heroism. The emphasis on self-sacrifice and suffering, which support this notion of heroism, forms a significant nodal point of this hegemony, as each contestation or nuance would inevitably undermine the very meaningfulness of self-sacrifice.

Many statues and commemoration sites in relation to the independence war celebrate the fighters of EOKA, the (Greek Cypriot) National Organization of Cypriot Fighters and their leader Georgios Grivas. These statues and commemoration sites not only accentuate the fighters' heroism and willingness to sacrifice themselves but equally – albeit implicitly – construct the evilness of the enemy. Abstraction is seldom used; the statues are frequently mimetic and individualized in nature, although symbolism is rarely shied away from.

One example is the *Memorial for EOKA 1955–1959 Heroes* in Avgorou, with an entrance that resembles an Ancient Greek temple, conveying EOKA's Greek nationalism and their desire for *enosis*. The large-scale complex in the Cypriot countryside has a long avenue leading up to a dome-shaped building, flanked by a church. Inside the main building, the sculpted heads of the killed EOKA fighters are displayed and in the centre is a separate small memorial for Tassos Isaac and Solomos Solomou, two Greek Cypriots killed in 1996.

Another example is the *1955–59 Heroes' Grove*, a memorial complex in the Troodos Mountains, again displaying references to Ancient Greek architecture at the entrance, in combination with bronze representations of the heads of Makarios, the first president of the Republic of Cyprus, and Grivas, the leader of EOKA. These are followed by the names of the EOKA dead, which have been carved into marble. The website of the community council of Pelendri, which describes the *1955–59 Heroes' Grove* in great detail, legitimates the presence of these names as follows: "They are there to remind us all those that were killed at the duration of the EOKA fight from the fires of the English army, by the Turks or by others."[1] Past the marble list of names, the visitor comes across the *Room of the Fighters* with the monumental painting the *Anthem of Freedom* by Andreas Makariou, in its basement, which once again celebrates the EOKA struggle (and its leaders). Further on, the visitor encounters 108 steps with the names of the 108 dead EOKA fighters carved in marble. At the top of the stairs stands a chapel which symbolizes the alliance of the struggle for independence and the Greek Orthodox Church. There is also the *Monument of Freedom* by Greek sculptor Evangelos Moustakas,[2] consisting of a wall with relief carvings about the struggle for independence combined with a high column on the right. One of the most striking scenes of the relief is the execution by hanging of nine EOKA fighters.

Another example of the celebration of EOKA's heroes, feeding the Greek(-Cypriot) nationalism, is the series of memorials in and near the Machairas Monastery, where the death (and life) of Grigoris Afxentiou is commemorated. EOKA commander Afxentiou, second in command after Grivas, perished on 3 March 1957 when the British Army uncovered his hiding place in the Machairas Mountains. After a number of skirmishes, the tiny dome-shaped hideout was doused in petrol and set alight, causing Afxentiou to be burned alive.

The monastery boasts a small Afxentiou Museum as well as a 7.5 metre tall statue of Afxentiou. On one of the nearby mountain peaks, a 7 metre high eagle by sculptor George Kyriacou has been erected next to a Greek flag. Just beneath the statue of the eagle stands Kyriacou's second statue: a charred and crumbled body on a threshing floor, an obvious reference to Digenes Akrites, the hero of a medieval epic who wrestled with death on a marble threshing floor. Digenes was also Grivas's "nom de guerre." Closer to the Machairas Monastery is Afxentiou's actual hiding place, the tiny cave where he was burned alive, now decorated with Greek flags.

Some memorials related to the Cypriot independence add victory and liberation to this discourse. One example is the Liberty Memorial that can be found in Nicosia, on the Venetian city walls.[3] At the top of this memorial is a female figure. Beneath her stand two armed EOKA fighters who are opening a barred fence with chains. The Cypriots are leaving their dungeon through this opened fence in blissful ecstasy.

1974: MATERIALIZATIONS OF A HEGEMONIC DISCOURSE

The statues and commemoration sites related to 1974 are, in the south of Cyprus, materializations of loss. They no longer celebrate victory but demonstrate and serve as reminders of the loss within the Greek Cypriot community, even when the notion of heroism remains present. The female figure plays a significant symbolic role but in a very different configuration than with the independence memorials, where she symbolizes freedom and victory. For 1974, the female figure has been transformed into a suffering mother;[4] she is a leitmotif that returns in a multitude of statues referring to this period.

One example is a sculpture by Vasilis Kattos from 1996 in Latsia.[5] The hexagonal base supports Doric columns and metopes which represent the (Greek) Cypriot tragedy. One of the metopes on the base carries the following script: "To you who did not die, to you who is no longer alive, to you who did not receive a real burial, to you who I am waiting for."[6] On top of the base, the four bent women carry a colossal metal platter with a burning fire. Their faces, even when half erased, still radiate pain and effort; they symbolize victimhood, absence and suffering, all catalyzed in the figure of the mother.

In addition to statues such as the Latsia sculpture, there are also a number of larger commemoration sites. The most important example is the Alexandros Papachristophorou foundation in Pyrga with the *House of the Missing* and the neighbouring Agios Alexandros church (see Sant Cassia 2005: 156ff). The church is named after the missing son of its founder, father Christophoros. One of the interior walls of the church is covered with small, black-and-white pictures of the Greek Cypriot missing, all framed in wood. In the forecourt and the inner court of the *House of the Missing*, several statues can be found, including a statue made by Michalis Papadakis,[7] where a desperate mother is shown crawling at the feet of a young man who is hanging from a pole. Inside the *House*, a series of paintings by Kostas and Hara Zouvelou are on display, including the *Long March* (Sant Cassia 2005: 156–57), which refers to the long way the family members had to travel to find out more about the fate of their loved ones. The paintings are explicit and leave little to the imagination – Sant Cassia (2005: 156–57) describes them as follows: "To refined aesthetic sensibilities these murals could be dismissed as kitsch" – but simultaneously they again portray suffering, sacrifice and absence.

In Dasaki Achnas, a new village built only a few hundreds of metres from the old one, the displaced villagers built the *Panagia Trachias Church Memorial*, which is partially shaped as a refugee tent and partially as a church (see Carpentier 2019). On one of its sides, we can find a window with about ten birds, tied up in stone ropes, symbolizing the trauma of the villagers, and their longing for freedom (and for their old village, now out of reach for them, as it is located in the Buffer Zone).

These statues and commemoration sites present 1974 as an inversion of the triumph of Cypriot independence. Whereas this independence was celebrated as a victory, 1974 represents for many Greek Cypriots a moment of traumatic loss. Yet both share a hegemonic emphasis on the justified acts of the Greek Cypriot community, in its resistance against the British colonizer and in its struggle against the Turkish Cypriot/Turkish alliance. By emphasizing their heroes, missing or dead (or both), the evilness of the enemy is implicated. Ironically, the absence of the missing also implies the presence of (the evilness of) the enemy. By the same token, this evilness of the enemy legitimizes the sacrifice of one's life, rendering one's death worthwhile as this victimhood is in the service of justice.

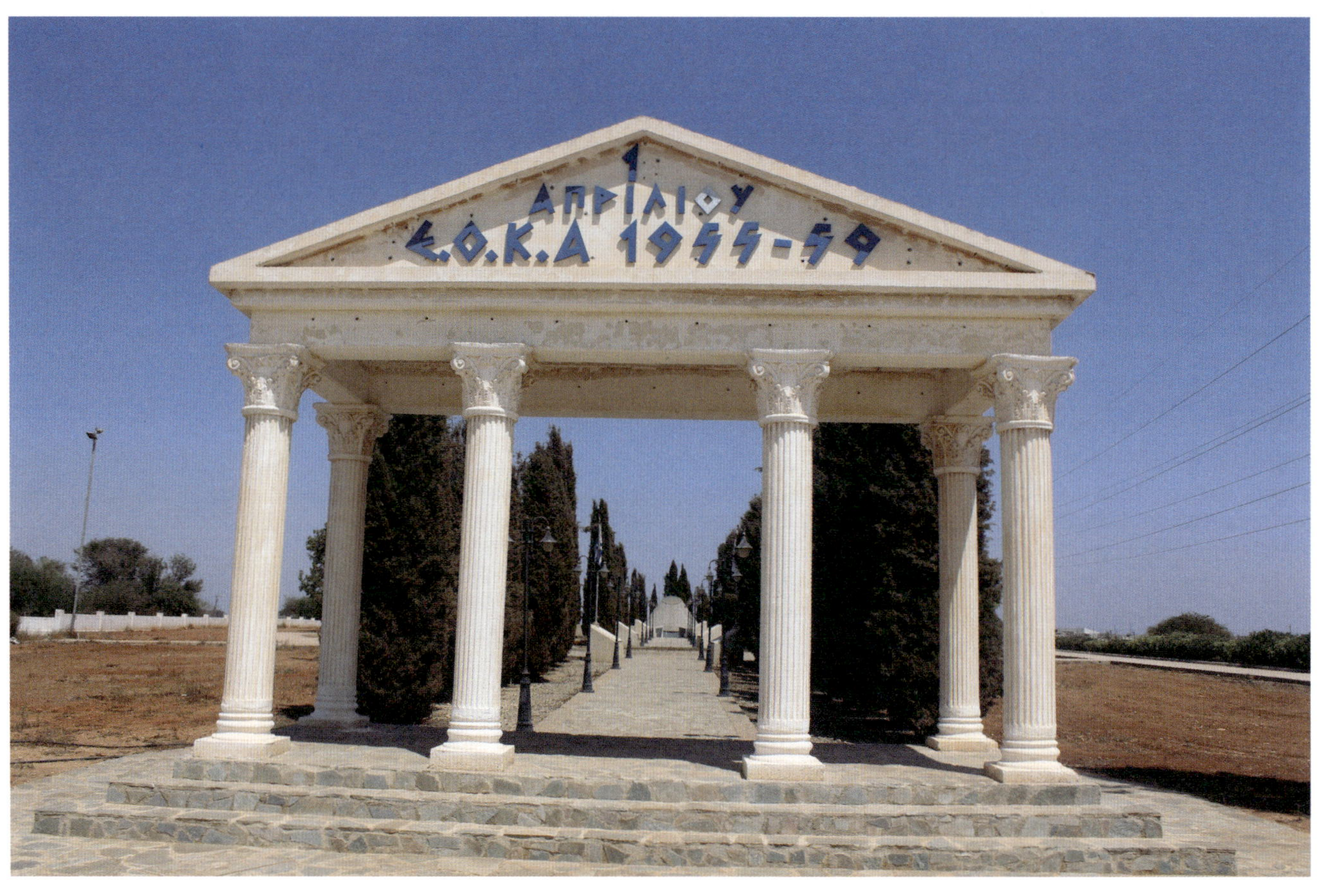

Down to memory lane

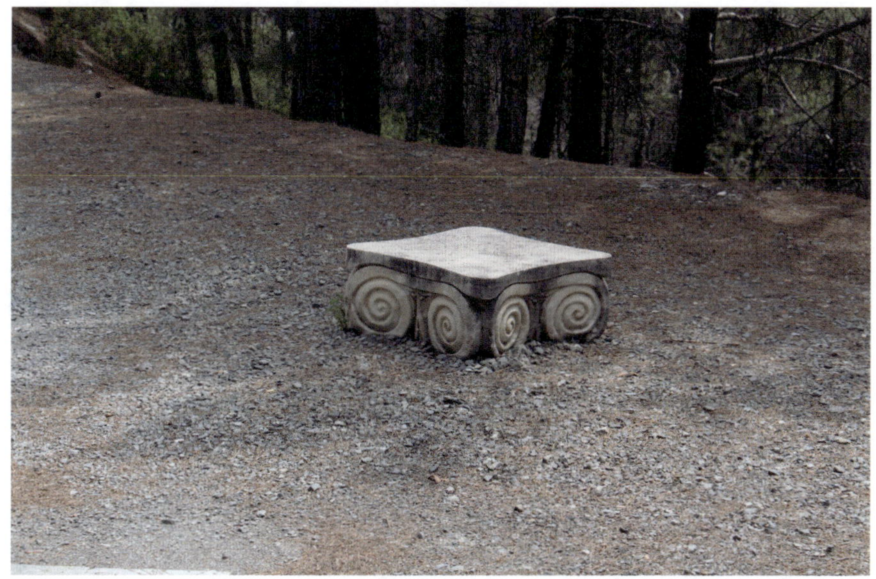

Sunken column

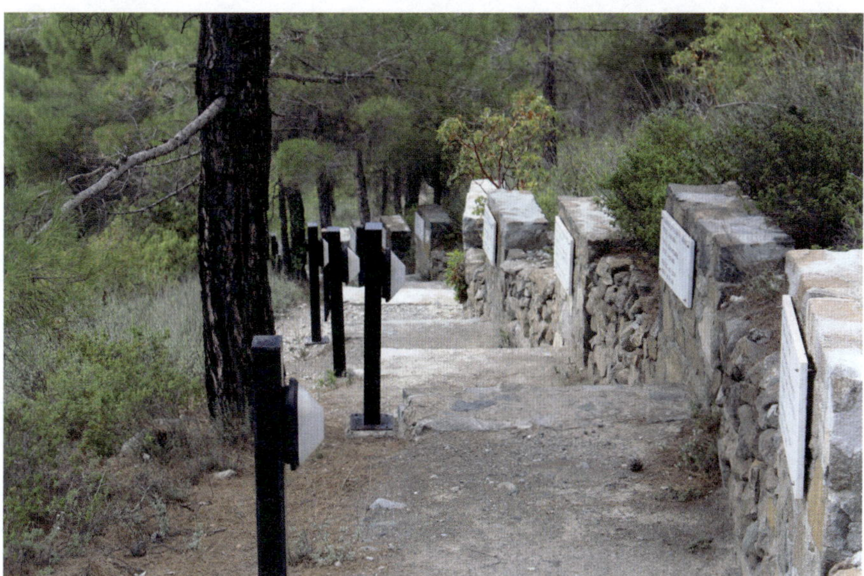

108 steps

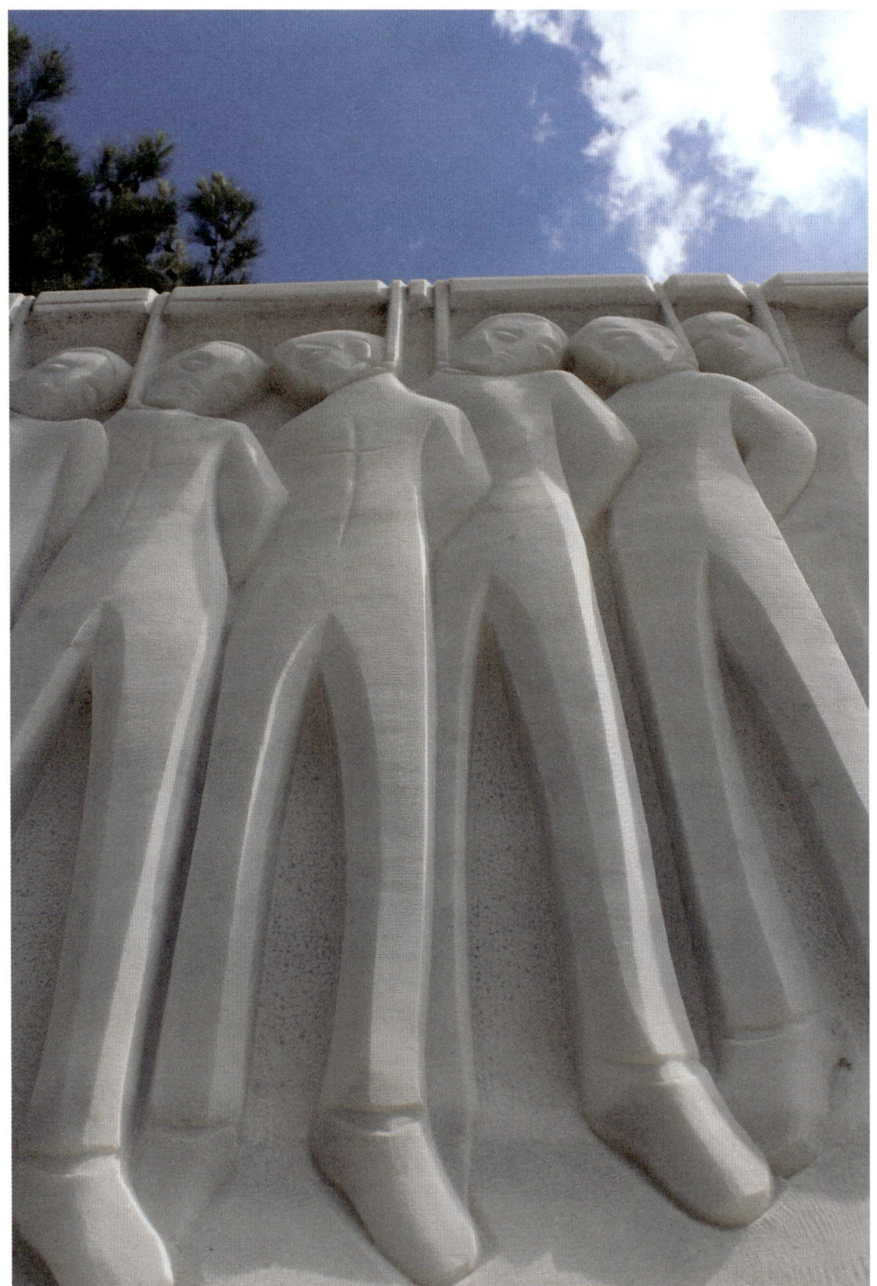

Colonial justice

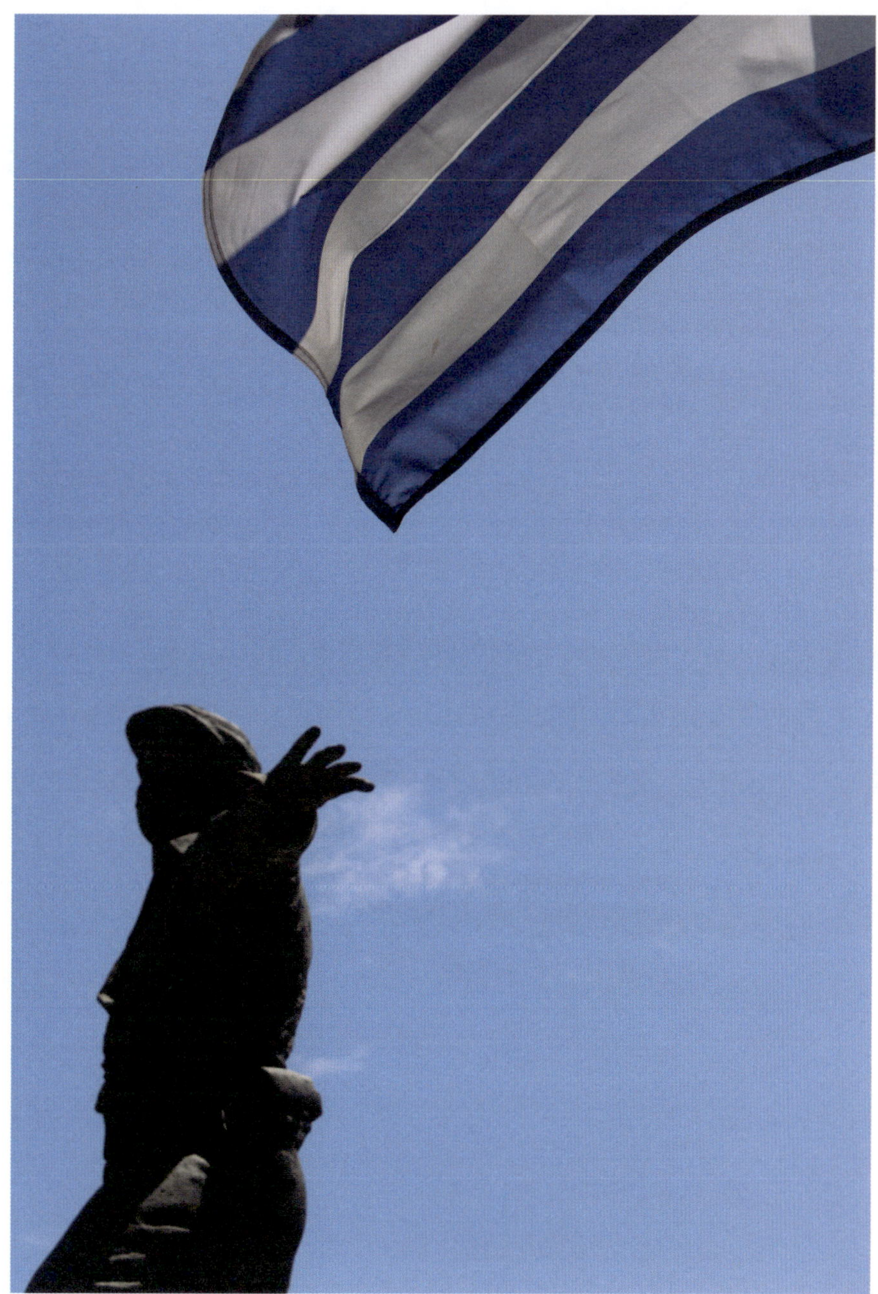

Out of reach

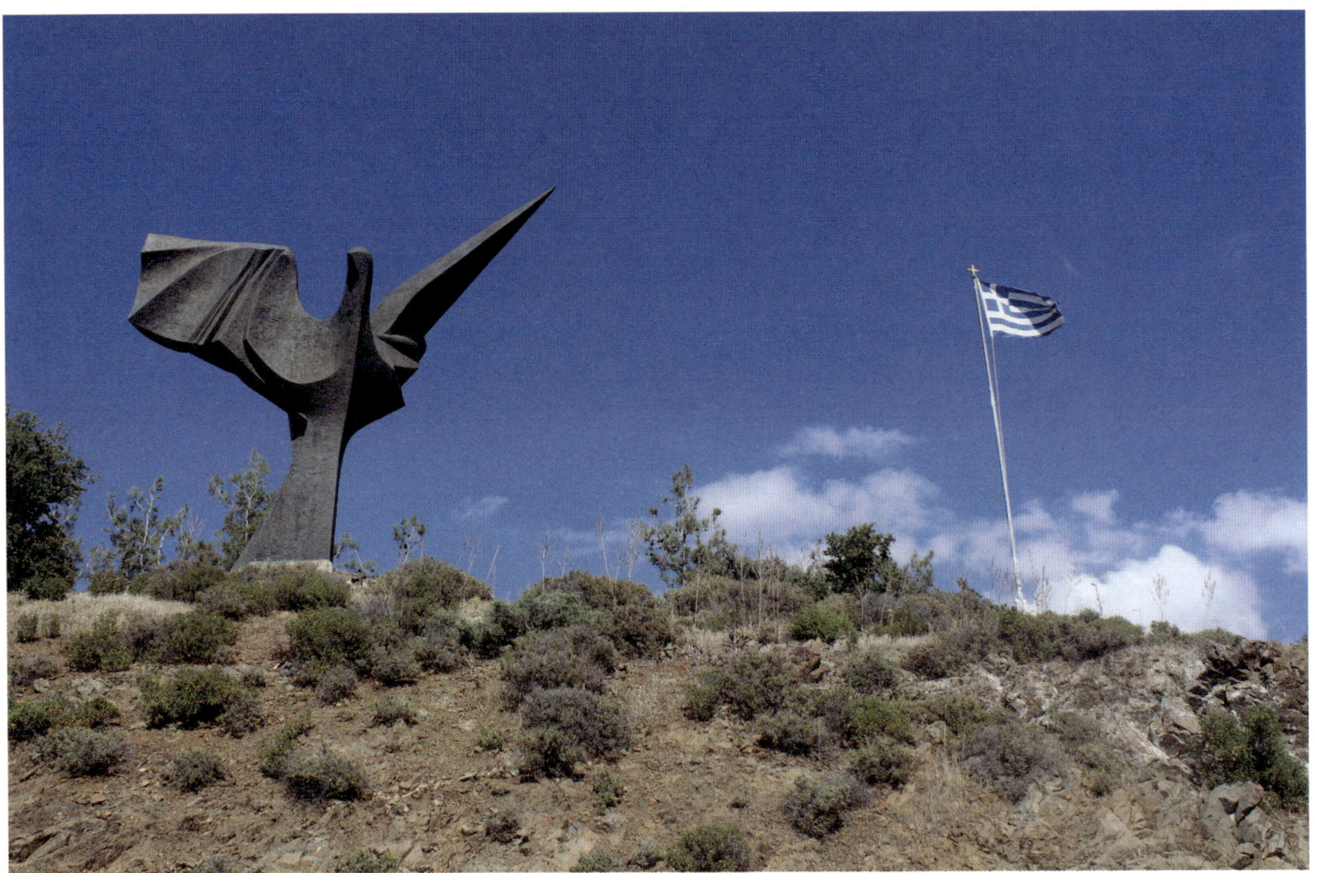

Flag-bird

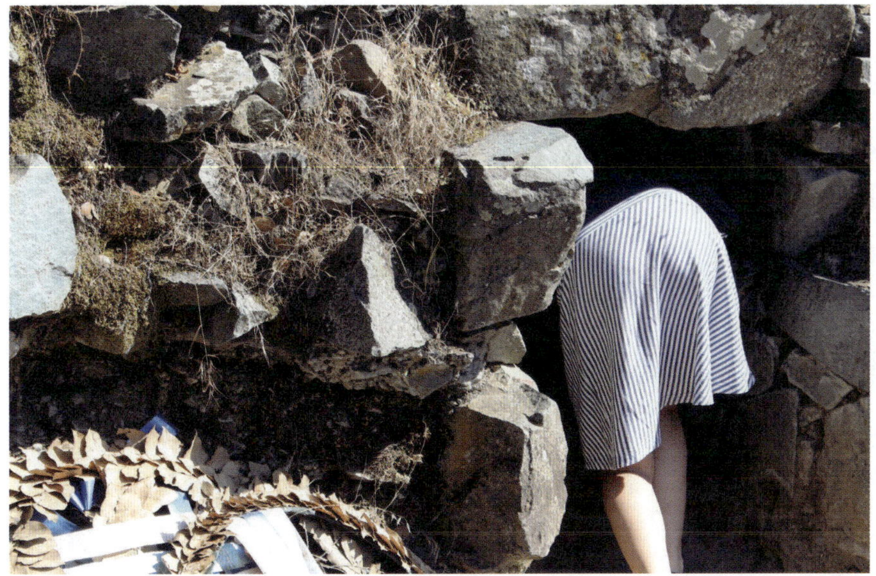

Gasoline

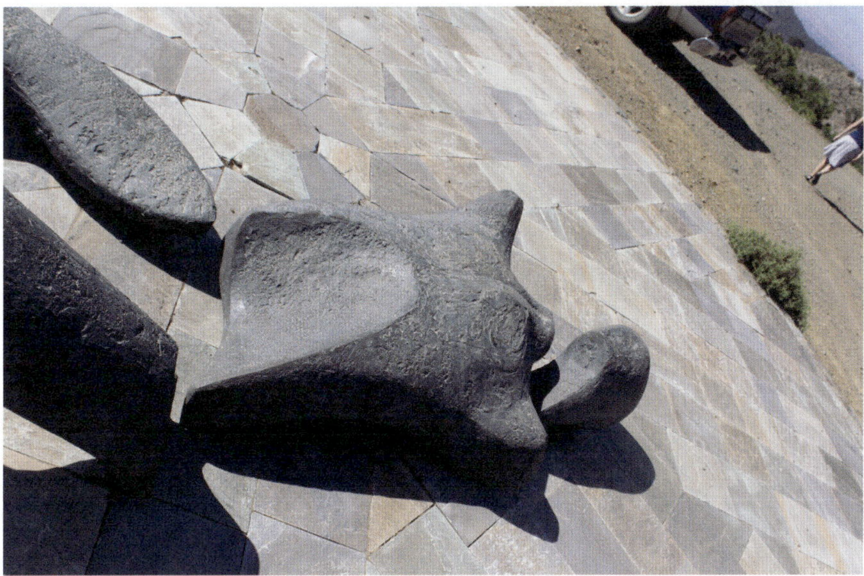

Threshing floor

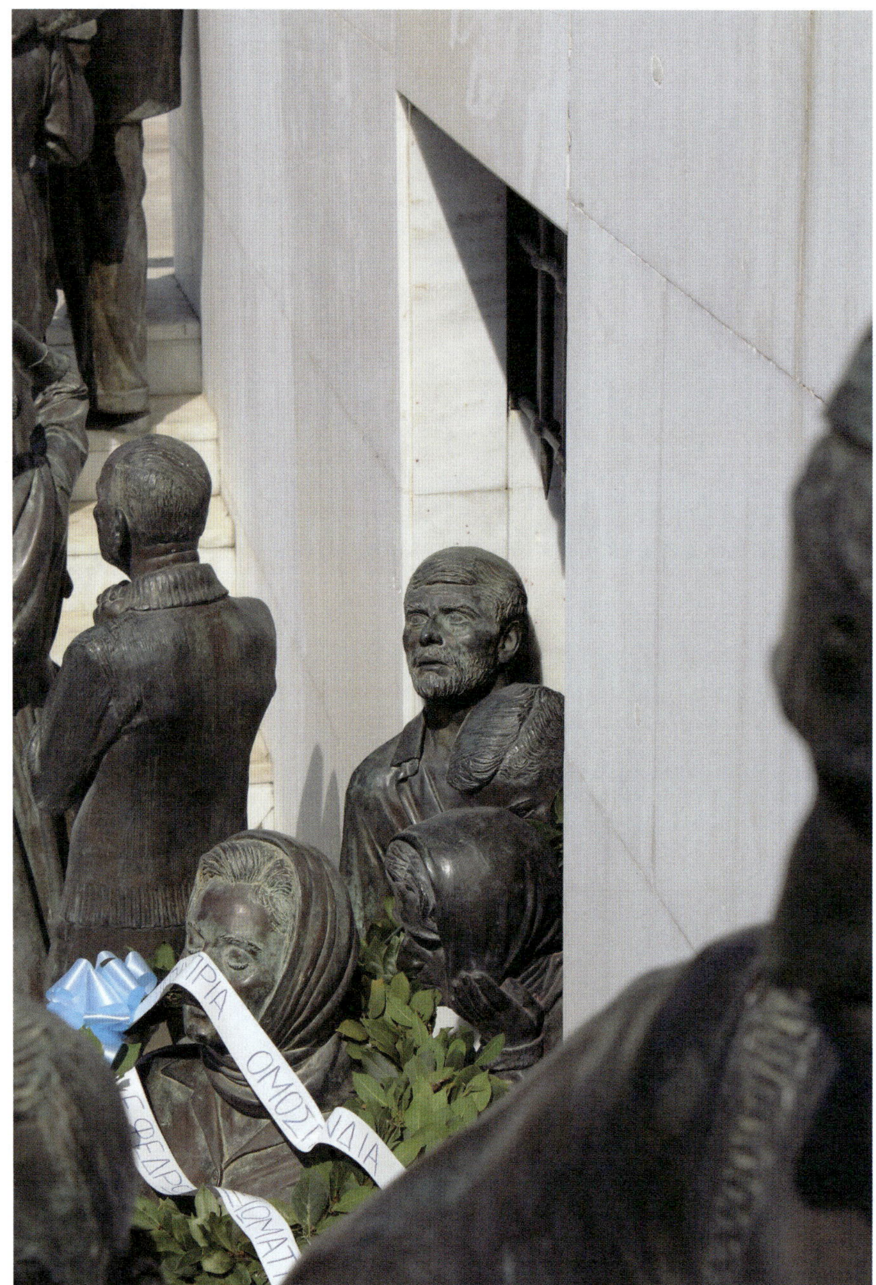

The ecstasy of freedom

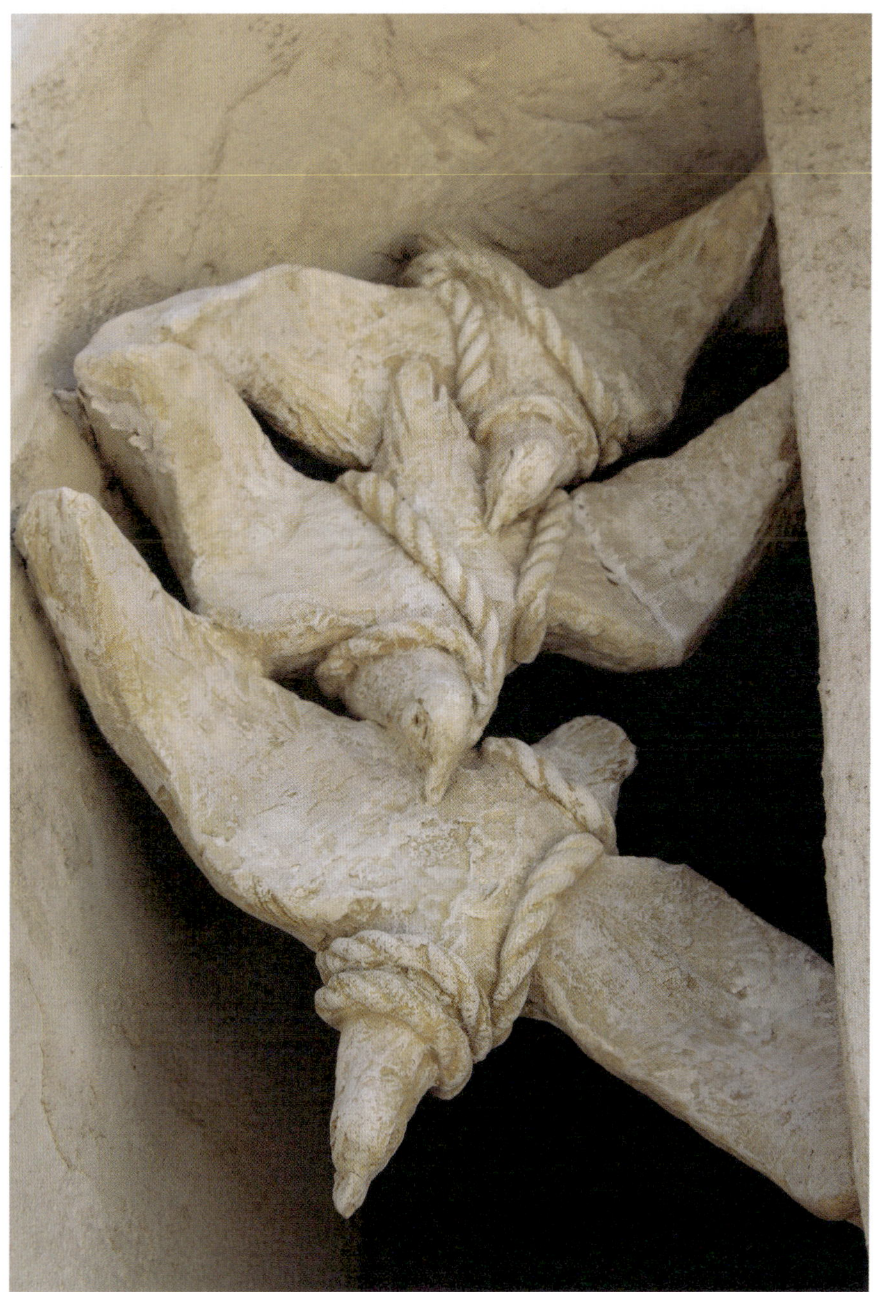

When the doves cry

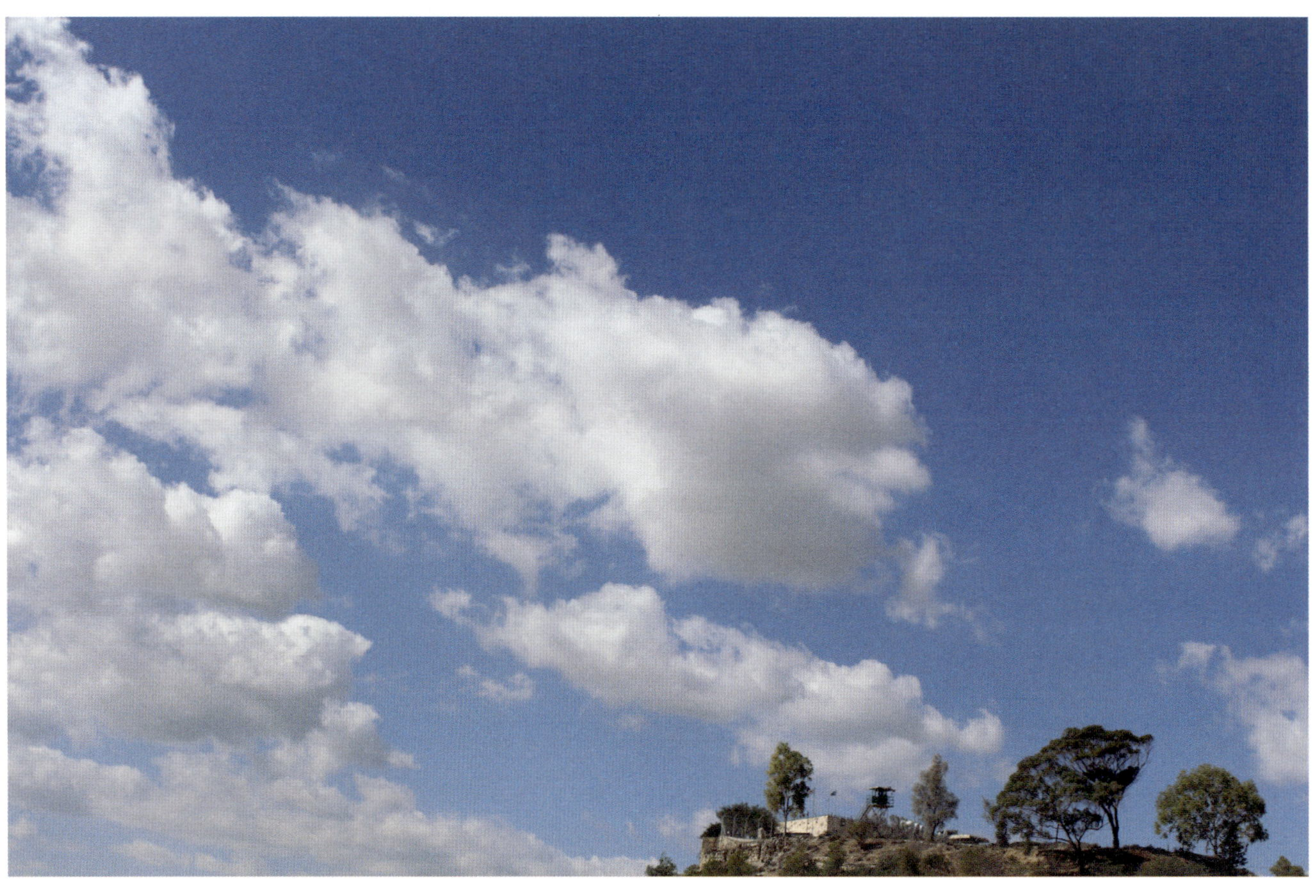

The Louroujina salient

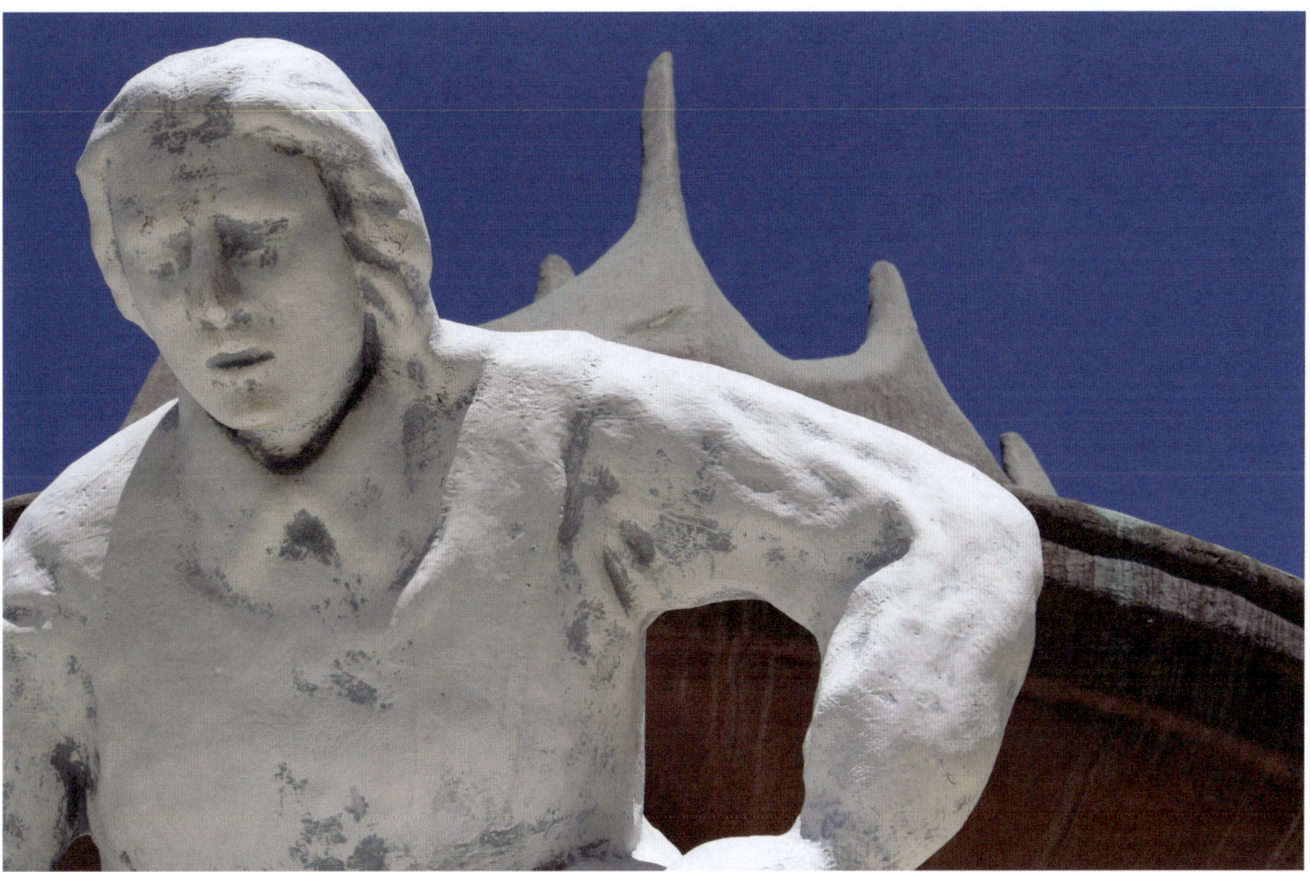

The weight of a nation

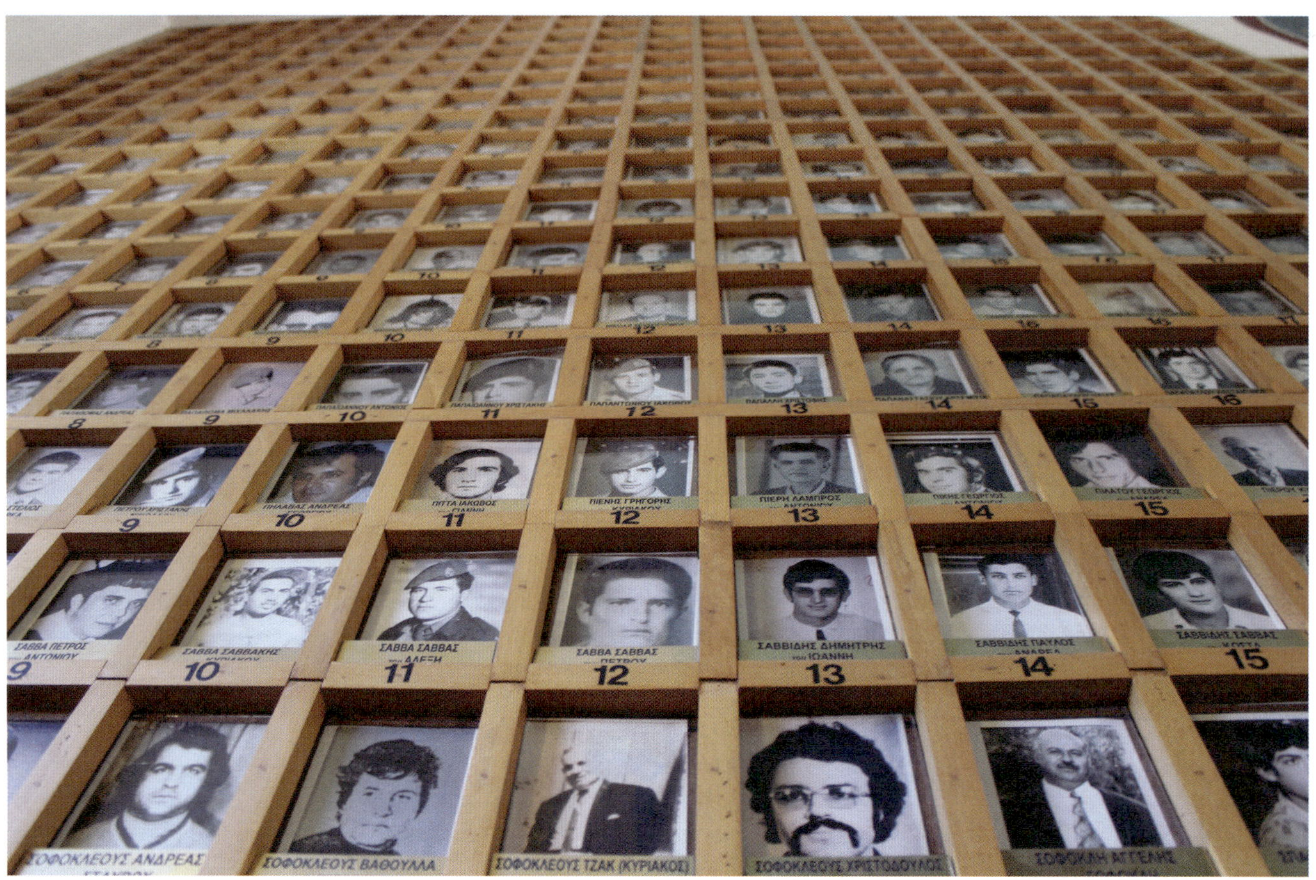

Church wall

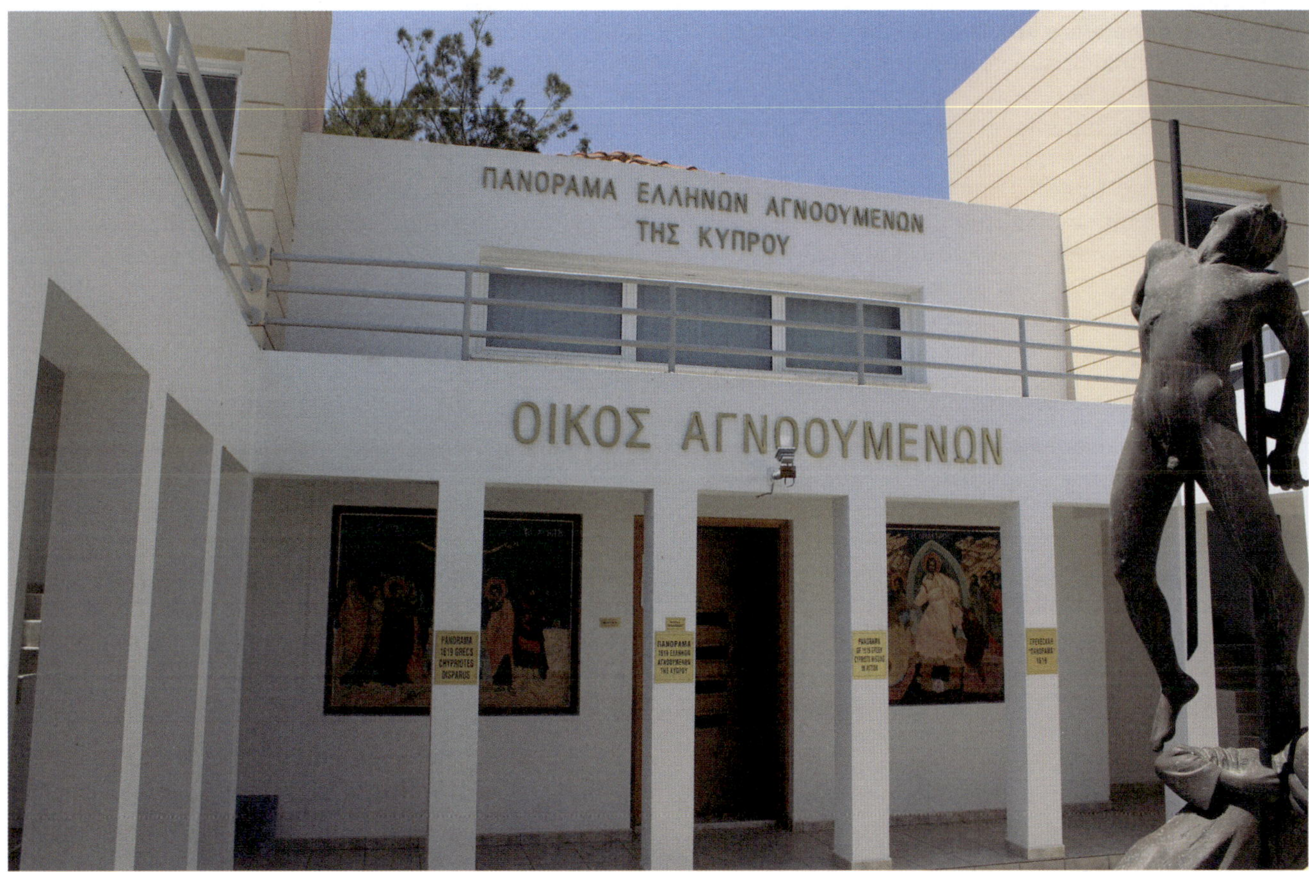

The present absent

INDEPENDENCE: EVERYDAY LIFE COMPLEXITIES

Nevertheless, there are crucial nuances to be made. With the last lethal upsurges of violence already dating from 1996, Cyprus has entered the stage of post-antagonistic nationalism, where, while elites (and part of the population) still identify with and communicate the nationalist discourses, the hegemonic force of antagonistic nationalism has severely been weakened, and its centrality in everyday life has decreased. This also translates into how these statues and monuments feature in everyday Greek Cypriot life, neutralized by the banality that surrounds them. As materializations of a hegemonic discourse, the statues as such invite (or even demand) to be viewed with attention and respect. Even though there are still rituals aimed at providing this attention and respect, the routines of everyday life do not always provide for this kind of attention.

This cold shouldering is reinforced even more by the tourist industry which exposes the statues to the often-disinterested looks of tourists. An example of this is the *Monument for Memory and Honour*, which includes a statue of Grivas, a memorial tower and a museum containing one of the smuggler ships used by EOKA (the *Saint George*). The monument is situated on the Chloraka coastline, just north of the tourist hotspot Paphos, and marks Grivas's landing on the island in 1954, when he arrived to prepare for the uprising. Once a deserted coastal strip, the area is now completely built up with hotels, restaurants and shops. Tourists avail themselves of the monument, which is wedged in between the seafront hotels, first and foremost as somewhere to leave behind their swimsuits, whereas children from all corners of the globe show little or no interest in Grivas's tough pose.

INTERNAL CONTRADICTIONS AND COMPLEXITIES

The hegemonic discourse about the Cyprus Problem is not undisputed, and sometimes there are tensions within this hegemonic discourse that undermine it. An example of the latter is the Tymvos Makedonitissa military cemetery in Nicosia. This is where the fallen, most of them killed in 1974, are buried. In the smaller left section of the cemetery, Greek and Greek Cypriot soldiers are buried in marked graves adorned with photographs, flowers and candles. The larger section on the right contains only unmarked graves, which offer a rather surreal sight. This relatively small military cemetery was extended in the 2000s to (re)bury newly identified bodies. The motivation for this decision rested on "the creation of more burial space and honour for the fallen soldiers," as the then Greek Cypriot secretary of defence, Costas Papacostas, declared at a press conference on 27 April 2009. However, the extra space remained partly unused. In some instances, the families refused to have their dead reburied at Tymvos cemetery, with some of these decisions motivated by the dissatisfaction of family members with the manner in which the Cyprus government dealt with the dead or how the missing were used in the hegemonic discourse on victimhood.

The cemetery thus represents the Greek Cypriot loss but at the same time this location has acquired a counter-hegemonic significance because of public discussions about how Greek Cypriot governments have used the missing dead (or the dead missing) and the suffering of their families to keep the hegemonic discourse of Greek Cypriot victimhood and Turkish(-Cypriot) offenderhood alive. In 2018, this part of the cemetery was changed again, adding even more complexity to its meanings. A large Noratlas aircraft replica was placed at the top of the slope, to commemorate the Greek commandos whose plane crashed here in 1974, after being shot down by Greek Cypriot friendly fire. As "Operation Niki" was a secret operation, the plane, with the bodies of fifteen soldiers still inside, was buried on the spot, while the remains of sixteen others were buried in graves. When the bodies of the latter were returned to Greece, some were misidentified. Moreover, the bodies inside the plane were only exhumed and returned to their families in 2016 (and after), in response to the decision of the families of two Greek killed soldiers to take the Republic of Cyprus to the European Court of Human Rights.[8]

In some cases, the everyday life complexities have more material causes. For instance, in the case of the Memorial to the Kontemenos dead and missing, in Nicosia, the wind intervened. This monument commemorates the 1974 victims of the Greek Cypriot village of Kontemenos, which is currently under control of the Turkish Republic of Northern Cyprus. The memorial consists of a series of metal figures that imitate the falling of a person in slow motion, lodged between two large stone elements. It is flanked by Greek, Republic of Cyprus and European Union flags. Exactly when the photograph published here was made, the Republic of Cyprus flag fell from its flagpole and landed in front of the memorial (leaving me, a rather surprised photographer, with the question what to do with it). Here, the materiality of the wind only left the Greek flag flying, supporting Greek(-Cypriot) nationalism.

RE-ARTICULATIONS AND CONTESTATIONS

A great number of statues and memorial sites support the hegemonic discourse, based on a definition of the other as the enemy and villain in combination with the heroism, self-sacrifice and victimhood of the Greek Cypriot community, so omnipresent in the (southern) Cypriot landscape. At the same time, however, this space cannot always be controlled, particularly in light of the role performed by local and private organizations in constructing statues and sites, so that alternative (and even counter-hegemonic) discourses have their part to play. In turn, these counter-hegemonic discourses do not remain uncontested, although they do offer a material presence for different ways of thinking.

Frequently, the statues that support an alternative discourse are equally based on a mimetic representational logic, although they do so by providing visibility to the Turkish Cypriots (and Turks) in the south of Cyprus instead. In Pyla, a mixed Greek Cypriot and Turkish Cypriot village in the middle of the Buffer Zone, the Turkish Cypriot school has a statue of Atatürk, the founding father of present-day Turkey, in its front courtyard. In Paphos, a city in the south of Cyprus, one can find the statue of Ihsan Ali, a Turkish Cypriot physician and politician who used to be advisor to the Cypriot president Makarios. From his pacifist point of view, Ihsan Ali used to defend the Cypriot identity and Cypriotism, as well as the Turkish Cypriot/Greek Cypriot friendship. He furthermore agitated against foreign interference, including intervention by Greece and Turkey. However, Ali's points of view brought him into conflict with radical nationalists from both communities (Özgür 1995: 5; Mirbagheri 2010: 8), and his life was frequently threatened (Sinclair 2006: 15). The statue, erected by the Ihsan Ali Foundation, bears the following lines, in Greek and in Turkish: "Pioneer of peaceful co-existence. Ihsan Ali Foundation."

A third example refers to the Kavazoğlu-Misiaoulis statues in Athienou, where the two busts stand side by side and look out over the Buffer Zone; they were inaugurated in 1997.[9] Beneath the busts of the two assassinated left-wing activists, a text is inscribed, which summons passers-by to remember the "heroic martyrs of the Greek-Turkish friendship." These statues not only commemorate the violent deaths of these two labour union activists (the first of whom was Turkish Cypriot and the second one Greek Cypriot) but also point out that the Turkish Cypriot/

Greek Cypriot collaboration was often located at the left-wing side of the political spectrum.

The statues in Pyla, Paphos and Athienou are important voices against the hegemonic discourse because they introduce representations of Turkish Cypriots (or Turks) into the Greek Cypriot community and its territory. For all that, they exhibit two more shared characteristics. First, they do not always occupy a central location within the landscape and are therefore quite difficult to trace (with the exception of the Atatürk statue in Pyla). The Kavazoğlu-Misiaoulis statues sit just outside the Buffer Zone, far outside of the village, whereas the statue of Ihsan Ali is situated at the back of a little square in the old quarter of Paphos.

Second, in all three cases, there have been desecrations, sometimes subtle, sometimes rather visible (given the disappearance of one of the busts). In the case of Ihsan Ali's statue, the desecration has been rather subtle – the dates of birth and death have been crossed out – the causes being uncertain. The paint and quicklime that have been thrown over the Atatürk statue in Pyla have been removed again. In the instance of the Kavazoğlu-Misiaoulis statues, the damage was more severe: the Kavazoğlu statue disappeared on 26 May 2014. Several days later, three Romanians were arrested on suspicion of metal theft.[10] Although there seems to be unanimous agreement that this is not a case of politically inspired vandalism and the statue has been replaced,[11] the period where the soccle of the Kavazoğlu statue was empty undermined its counter-hegemonic significance.

The complexity and vulnerability of this alternative representational logic is even more illustrated by the *Rainbow*, a lost work by Nikos Kouroussis. It used to stand in Agios Dometios, Nicosia, on the Kolokasidis roundabout on the way to the former international airport, close to the Buffer Zone. This artwork from 1975 consisted of a square column composed of a series of multicoloured rods, pointing skywards. It was an artwork that symbolized unity, diversity and reconciliation. After the *Rainbow* was damaged, and later removed, the present composition with five yellow diagonal and interconnecting rings was constructed, with next to it a statue of major general Tasos Markou. The presence of this war hero in a traditional pose fully reclaims this roundabout for the hegemonic discourse.

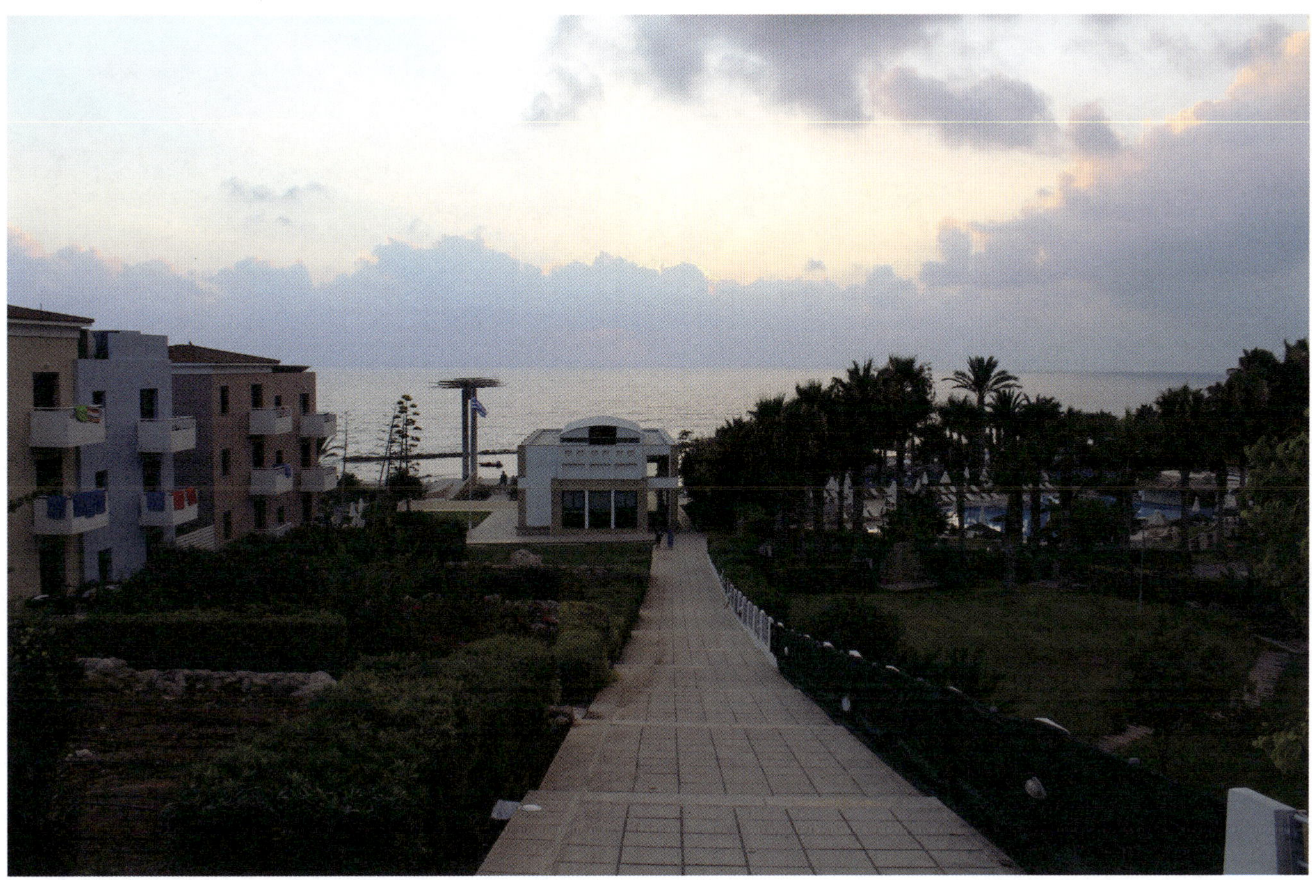

Tourist encirclement
(also entitled: *Finding Grivas*)

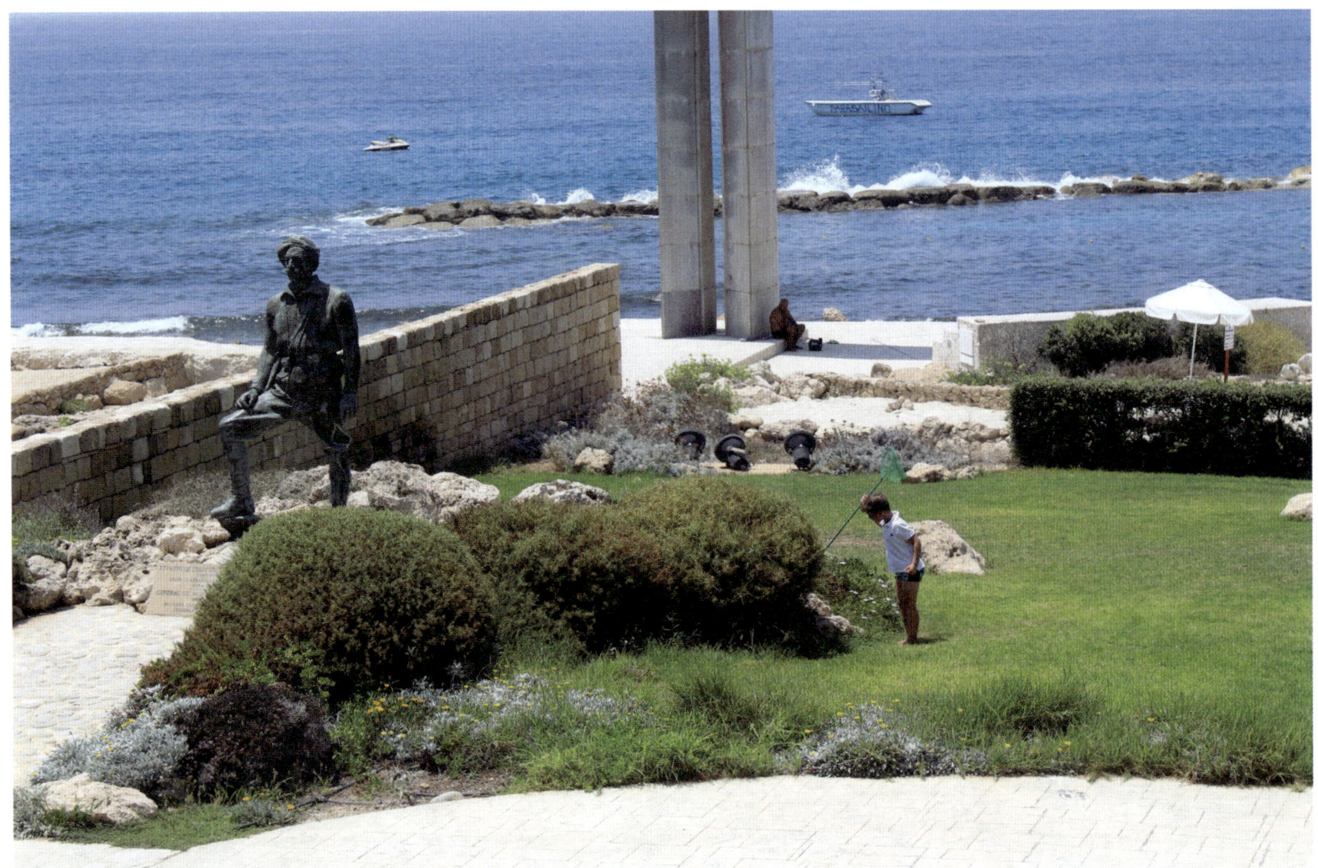

Grivas with child

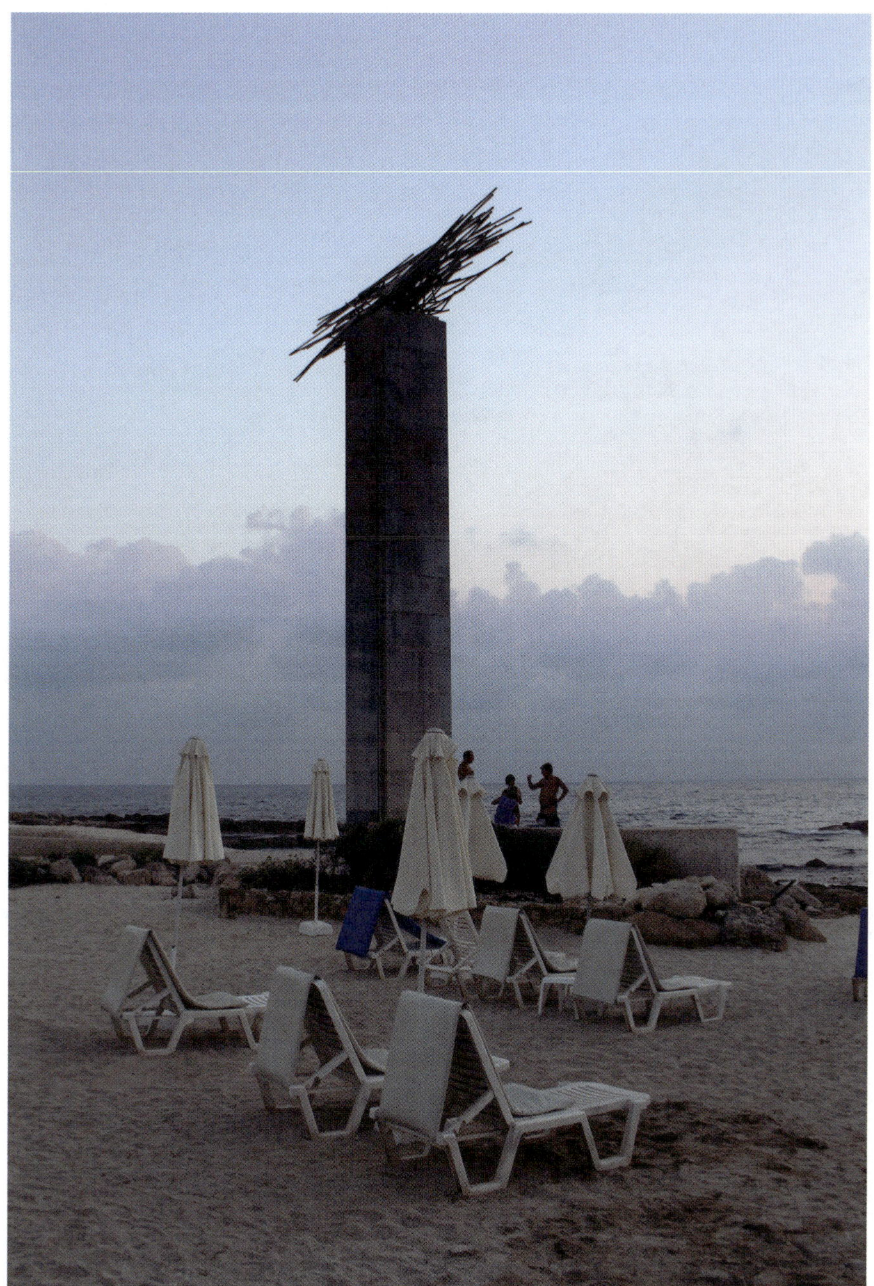

Going for a swim

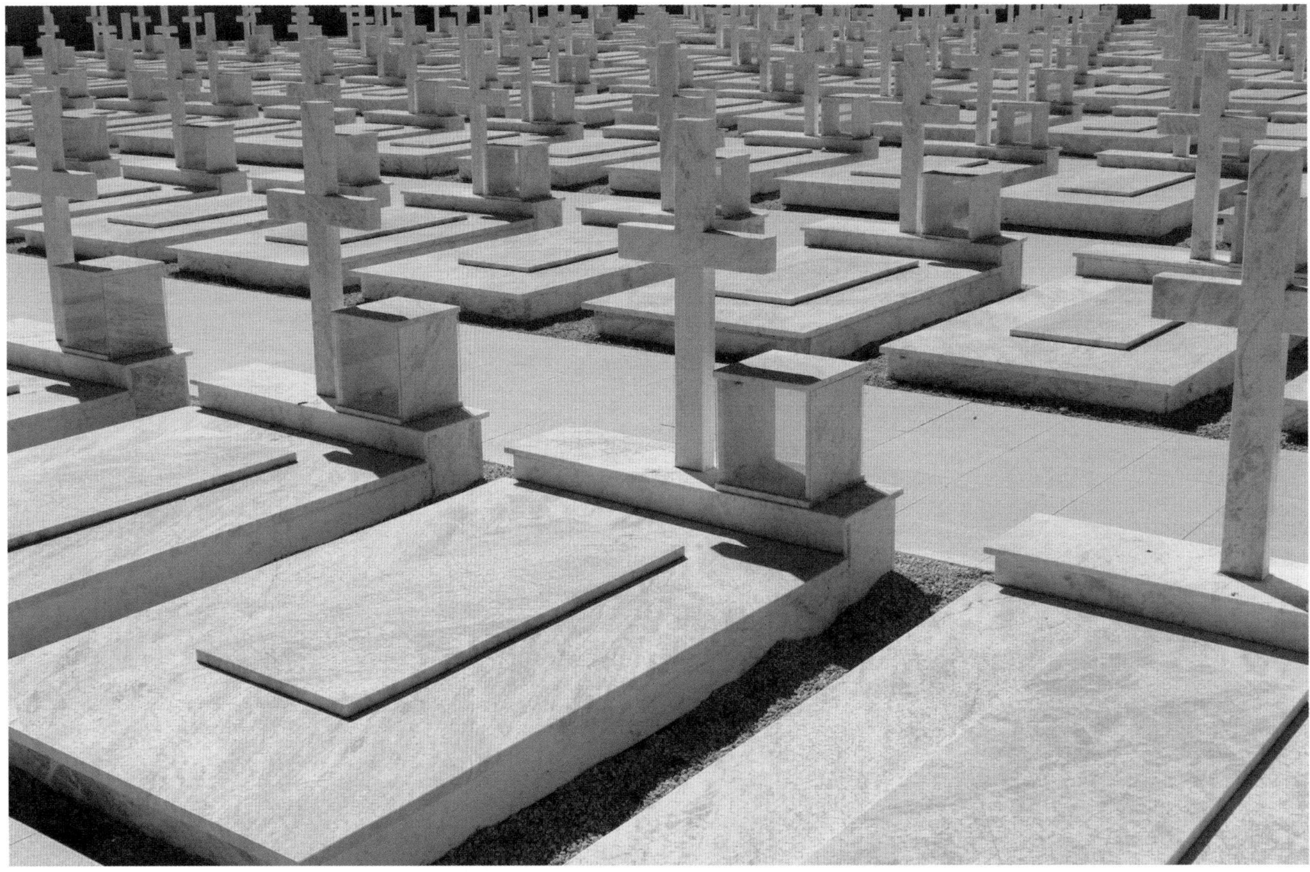

Waiting room

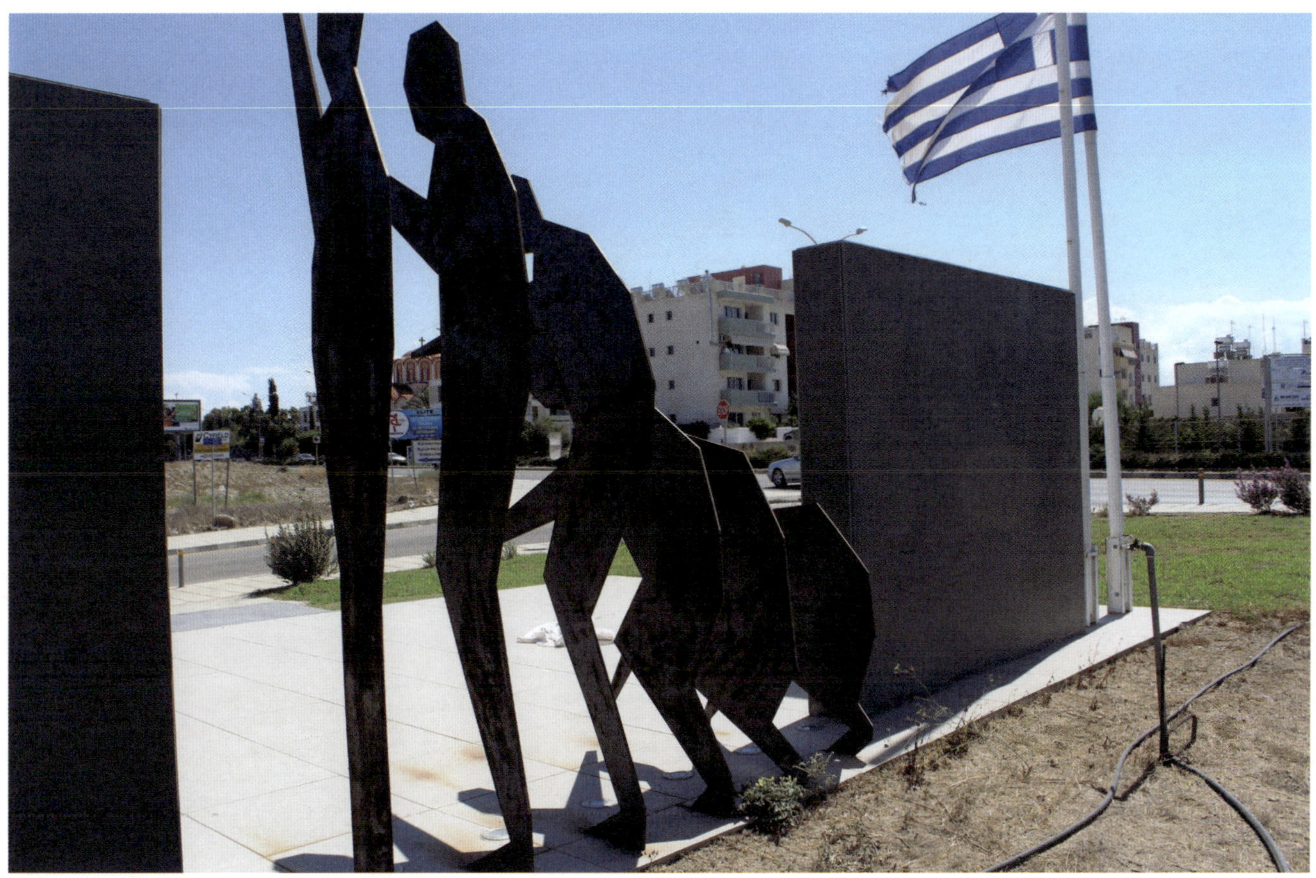

Losing the flag

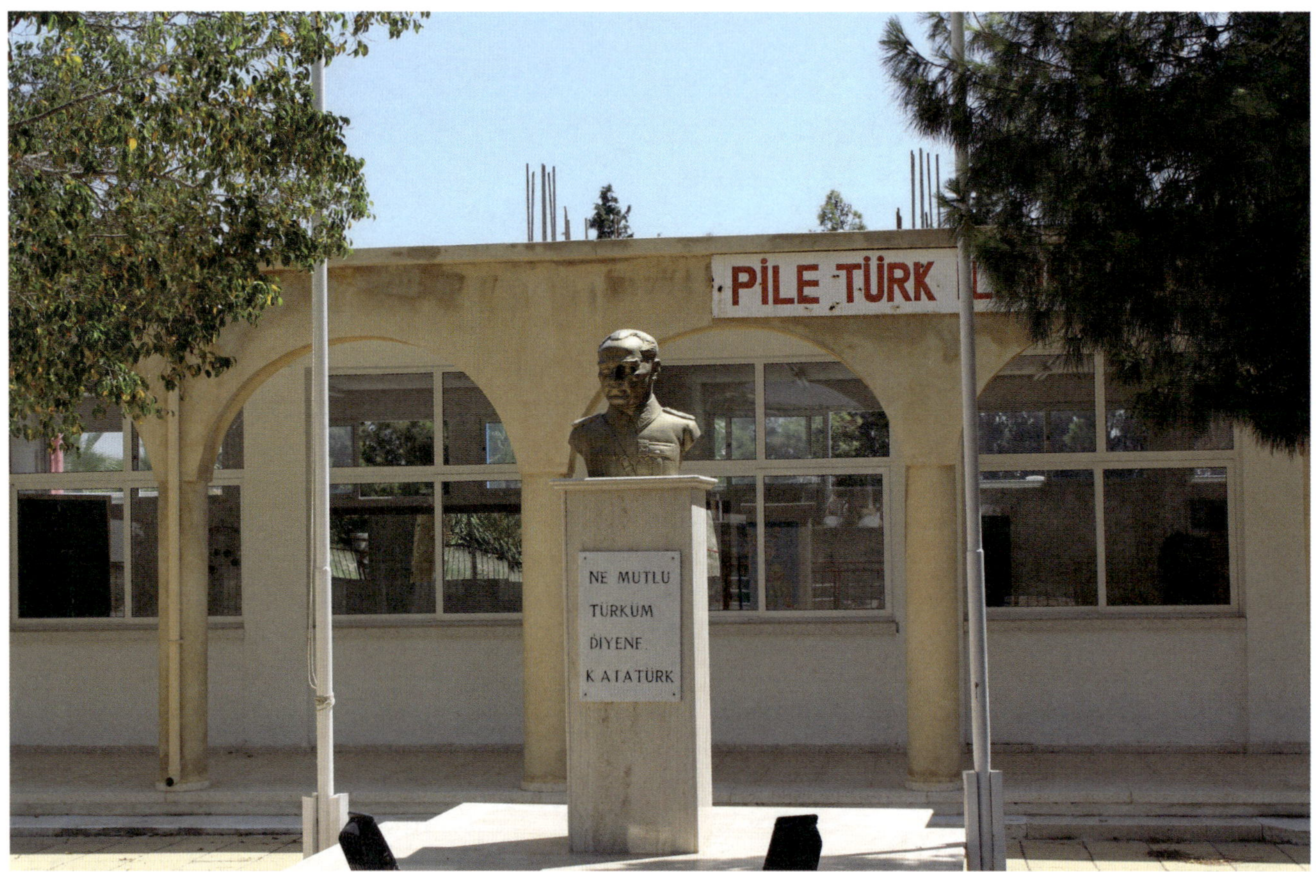

Atatürk in front of school

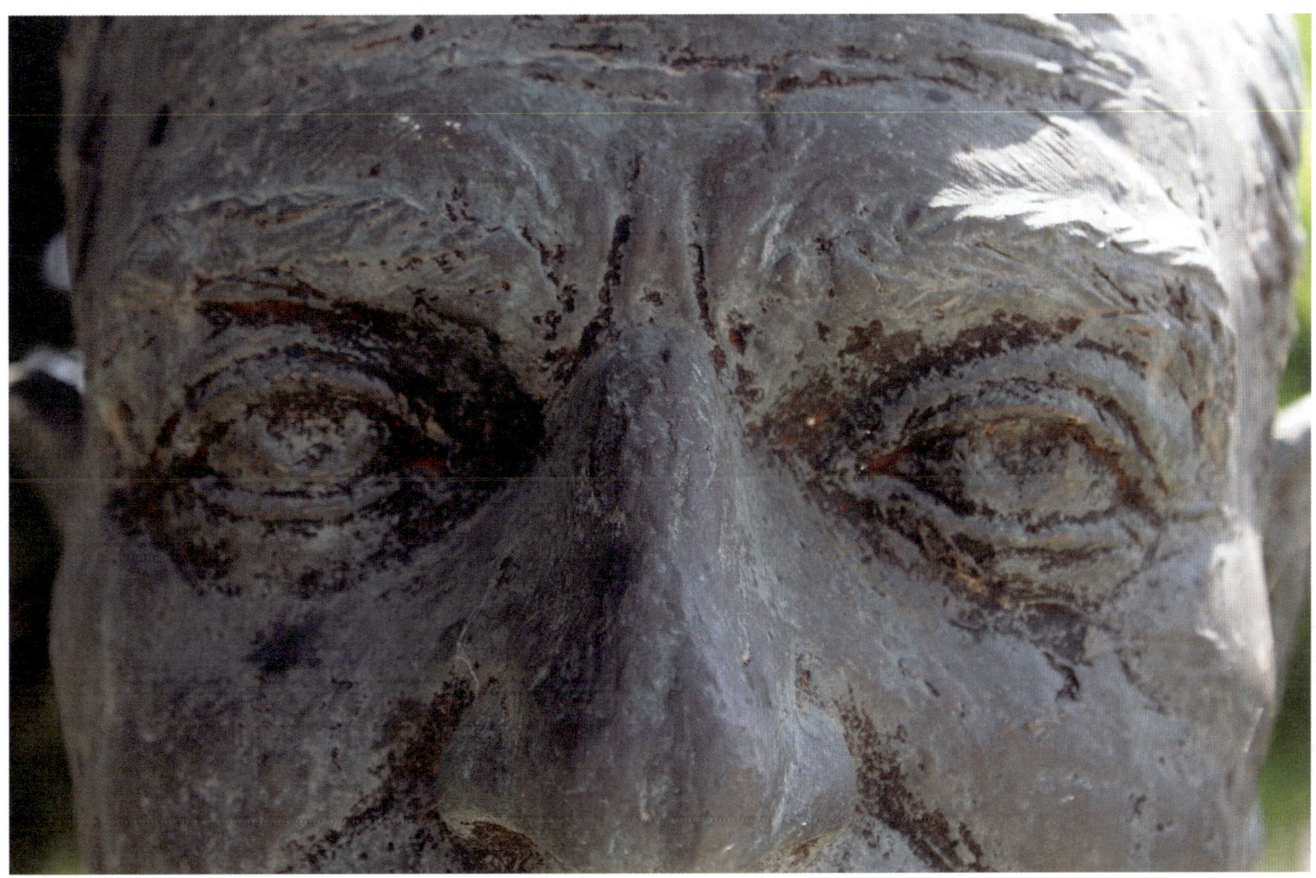

Ihsan Ali's gaze

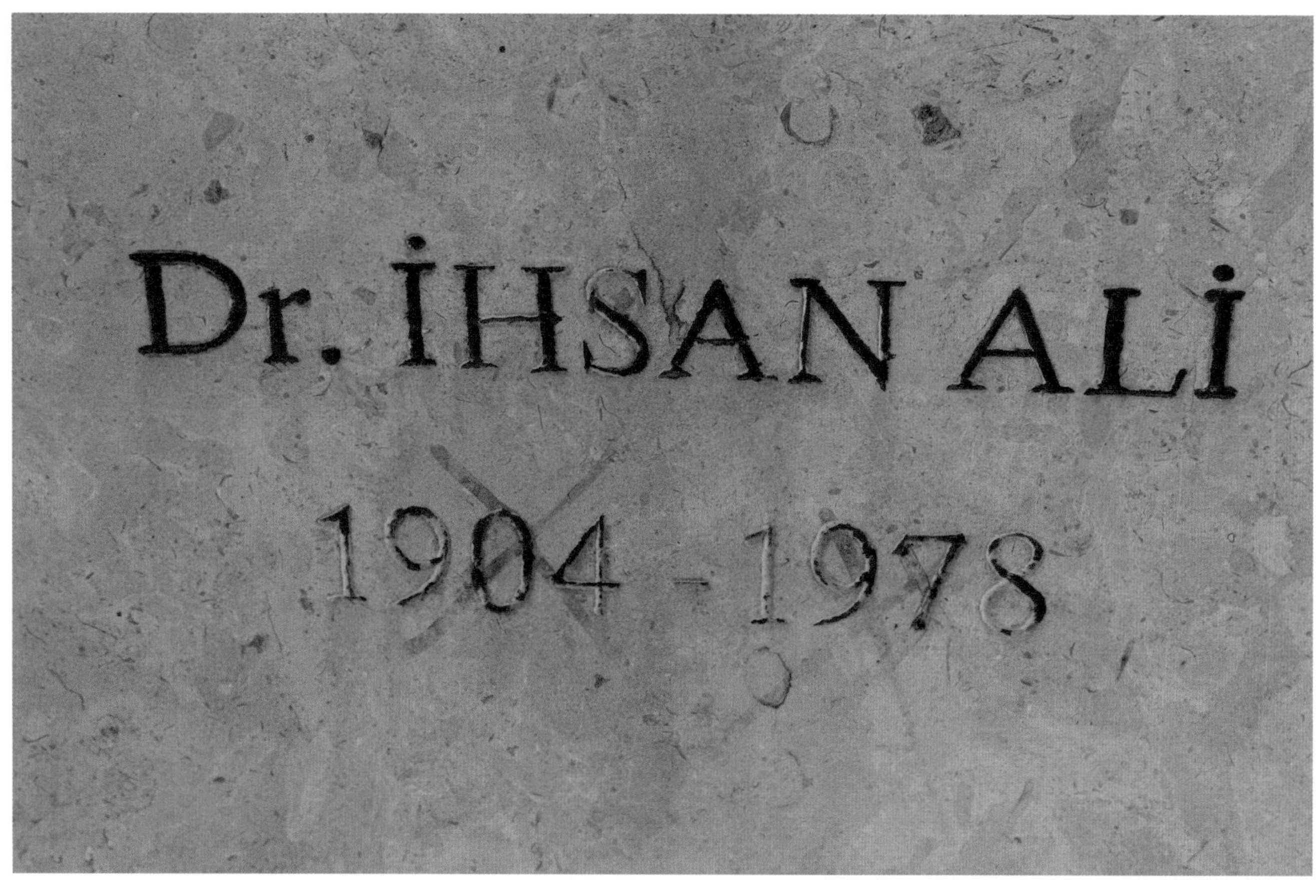

Scratches

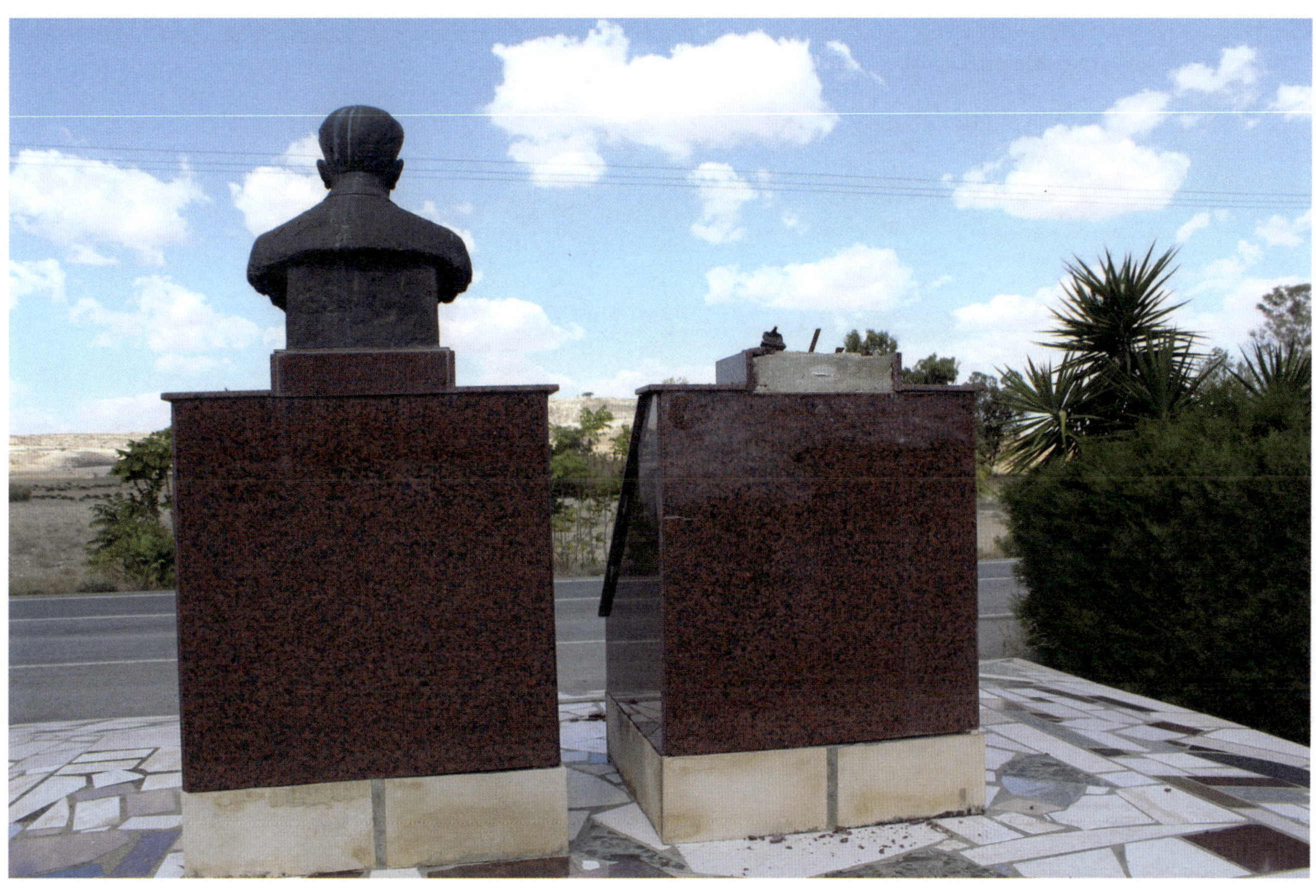

Companion in life and death (not just now)

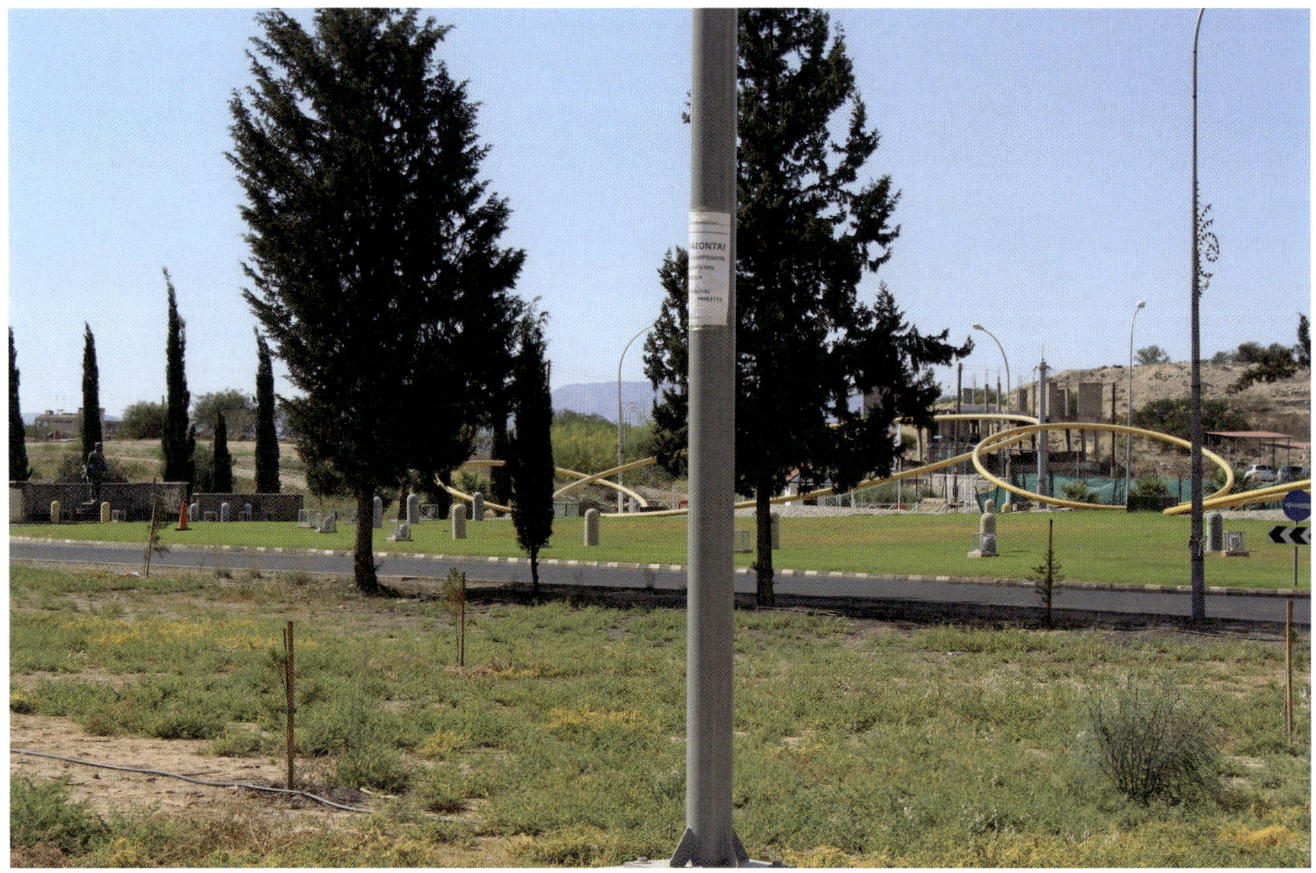

Vanished rainbow

A BRIEF CONCLUSION

Memorials and commemoration sites cannot be considered separately from the political-ideological projects that allowed for their creation and provide the framework for their interpretation. Iconoclastic Controversies shows how the protracted history of the conflict has equally been translated into memorials and commemoration sites, with the bulk of these statues telling a tale of the Greek Cypriot community and its heroism and sacrifice.

But these photographs also show that a hegemony is never complete or stable, and these (hegemonic) discourses are thus not without contestations. This analysis demonstrates the disruptability of hegemonic processes by alternative processes of signification. Simultaneously, this account is also about how material interventions in the landscape can permanently disturb the Greek Cypriot hegemonic discourse, so that the dominance of this discourse can never be complete or all-encompassing.

The presence of these alternative voices and counter-voices still remains rare. This merely confirms the difficulty of braving the complexity and ethical inconsistencies of this conflict, yet at the same time their presence stems one hopeful for the future of this currently still divided island.

NOTES

1. http://www.pelendri.org/english/propilaia.shtm.
2. http://www.pelendri.org/english/propilaia.shtm.
3. The Liberty Monument is one of the memorials where in October 2020 the Nicosia tourism board installed so-called smart info boards, with a short description and a QR and an NFC code linking to more information. See https://cyprus-mail.com/2020/10/19/smart-info-boards-installed-at-nicosia-sites/.
4. Very rarely do we see a grieving father figure, as in the *Memorial for the Missing* in Dali; in most cases, it is the mother who plays the central role.
5. http://publicart.ouc.ac.cy/?p=3186.
6. Translated from Greek.
7. http://publicart.ouc.ac.cy/?p=1777.
8. http://www.ekathimerini.com/212537/article/ekathimerini/news/cyprus-apologizes-to-greece-for-1974-friendly-fire-deaths.
9. http://publicart.ouc.ac.cy/?p=2083.
10. http://cyprus-mail.com/2014/05/28/three-remanded-suspects-could-be-bust-thieves/.
11. Stella Misiaoulis (Kostas Misiaoulis's daughter), interviewed by Stella Theocharous on 9 October 2014, and communication of Yiannis Christidis with Michalis Michael (responsible for the Misiaoulis and Kavazoğlu memorial events in the Athienou Municipality).

Chapter 6: The Reception of the Two Cypriot Exhibitions

(with Vaia Doudaki, Yiannis Christidis and Fatma Nazli Köksal)

If the *Iconoclastic Controversies* exhibitions aimed to de-normalize (post-)antagonistic nationalism, the question remains how these exhibitions were received in Cyprus.[1]

In order to analyse the exhibitions' reception, a case study method was used (Yin 1994), collecting different types of material: the exhibitions' press coverage, by Greek Cypriot and Turkish Cypriot news media (print and online); other online publications (e.g. blog postings) about the exhibitions; the texts generated during the exhibitions (the guest books, the recordings of the seminars and photographic documentation); the interviews and reportages that were produced and broadcast by MYCYradio and CUT-Radio; and finally, the (self-)ethnographic field notes (Ellis et al. 2010) and informal interviews that were collected before, during and after the exhibitions. An open textual analysis, closely related to grounded theory (Silverman 2006), was used for the analysis of all the material, focusing on evaluative statements, taking both positive and negative positions into account. This was complemented by a time dimension, incorporating also future-related practices that encompassed an evaluation. To enhance the quality of the analysis, a peer debriefing strategy was used, both internally (in the project team) and externally (outside the team). One important limitation to mention here is that the project team decided against organizing additional focus groups or interviews after the exhibitions, as these methods were difficult to reconcile with the interventionist nature of the exhibitions.

REACH

The (self-)ethnography produced data on the exhibition attendance, as at least one of the team members was present during the opening hours of the exhibitions and the events. Especially the receptions and seminars generated a considerable number of visitors, who in the case of the two seminars in 2015 at the Home for Cooperation directly entered the exhibition space, as this was the space where the seminars also took place. In the case of the NeMe-organized seminar, which took place before the exhibition opening, the majority of its participants walked to the exhibition venue for the opening. About 250 people attended these events (which could be established through their photographic documentation[2]). These numbers are contrasted by the scarce visitors during non-event times, although these visitors were often keen to engage in long conversations with the organizers. The conversations with the visitors showed their considerable diversity, even though these groups were still specific. They were, for instance, academics, students, NGO members, politicians or artists.

A second indicator of the exhibitions' reach is the media attention they provoked. In total 51 media publications were identified (excluding those created

TABLE 2: MEDIA PUBLICATIONS ON THE TWO EXHIBITIONS			
	#	# FIRST EXHIBITION	# SECOND EXHIBITION
Greek Cypriot	23	11	12
Turkish Cypriot	20	19	1
Cypriot	1	1	0
Other	7	3	4
Total	51	34	17

by the project partners – see Appendix 2). As Table 2 shows, while the attention from Greek Cypriot and Turkish Cypriot media was balanced, there was more attention from Turkish Cypriot media for the first exhibition, while the second exhibition (in Limassol, in the south) attracted mostly Greek Cypriot attention. This does not necessarily mean that the information about the exhibitions circulated throughout the island. As a matter of fact, informal discussions with visitors during the exhibitions indicated that many of them were informed on the events by the social media and not by news media.

Even though the majority of the media publications briefly announced the exhibition, or published (part of) the press releases (which were made available in Greek, Turkish and English), almost half of the media publications included one (or more) photographs of the exhibitions (see Table 3), which had been made available together with the press releases. This allowed for a considerable distribution, in particular of the photograph of one of the female figures of the Latsia monument, which was also used for the poster of the first exhibition (see Figure 1). While the media focused more on the announcement of the exhibitions, relying mostly on the promotional material, there are some differences that are worth mentioning. The Greek Cypriot media, when referring to the event, largely reprinted the female figure of the

Latsia monument, which is expressive of the suffering caused by the 1974 Turkish invasion. However, some of the Turkish Cypriot media did not focus on the content of the first exhibition, but rather on its Buffer Zone–based venue (the Home for Cooperation) or the related seminars, publishing photos of the venue or of the people attending the opening, and not of the "suffering mother."[3]

RECEPTION

When analysing the reception, or, in other words, the signifying practices of the visitors in relation to the exhibitions, three main clusters of signifying practices were identified, namely those of relevance, problematizations and triggers. In the first case, the visitors argued for the analytical and critical relevance of the exhibitions. Still, many of the visitors also problematized (part[s] of) the exhibitions, at a wide variety of levels, which will be discussed afterwards. Finally, the triggers refer to the moments where the exhibitions contributed to the generation of new signifying practices that built on the meanings communicated by the exhibitions.

Relevance

One example regarding the relevance of the exhibitions can be found during one of the MYCYradio broadcasts, where the guest says: "I think it is very important

TABLE 3: MEDIA PUBLICATIONS AND VISUAL ELEMENTS				
	TOTAL	GREEK CYPRIOT	TURKISH CYPRIOT	OTHER
Photo of "mother" included	19	15	0	4
Other photo of exhibition included (as well)	5	2	3	0
Other photo(s)	8	2	6	0
Other visual element (flyer, map, etc.)	5	3	0	2
No photo or visual element	14	1	11	2
Total	51	23	20	8

that a conversation emerges through this exhibition about the role of these monuments in our perception towards history, towards memory" (Andreas Papallas – MYCYradio broadcast, 22 December 2015). This relevance is grounded in two types of argumentation, namely the importance of analysis and the importance of critique. One of the entries in the guest books[4] illustrates the former: "Very interesting exhibition. Creating the language to things in a clear view. I would imagine it to be difficult. You manage to make it easy for us. Thanks" (Guest book exhibition 2). In many cases, Cypriot visitors expressed their surprise about their own lack of knowledge about the statues, explaining that they had never seen or noticed some (or many) of them. The latter type of argumentation, based on the importance of critique and de-naturalization, can be found in the following fragment from one of the MYCYradio broadcasts:

I remember one of the photographs of the exhibition. I think someone was entering the safe house, I'm not sure it was Afxentiou's, and it was a lady, and they took a picture [...] she was, she bent over to get in so that also you could see her butt. That was what you can see. And for me [laughs] that was an interesting aspect, I mean, choosing to take that photo and not some school or someone putting flowers or something. It could happen anywhere. I mean [...] and actually, it takes off that magic, let's say, and all that heroism, out of the picture. (Christos Mais, AHDR – MYCYradio broadcast, 22 December 2015)

The relevance of analysis and critique is also shown in the following example, again from one of the MYCYradio broadcasts, explicitly bringing the de-naturalization process to the fore:

Most of the people did not like the pictures themselves. What they [would] see in them. That for me was a positive reaction. I mean that: We're done with this. We have to move forward. The grand narratives of the past that lead us [...] gradually led us to the situation we are in today, the segregation of the island, belong to the past. And that was actually the main thing for me, I mean the positive, the reaction of most of the people that they didn't like what they saw, not because the pictures weren't nice, but because of what they saw in the pictures. (Christos Mais, AHDR – MYCYradio broadcast, 22 December 2015)

Problematizations

Nevertheless, the reception study does indicate a number of problematizations, which first of all concerned three specific areas of politicization, namely the exhibitions' relevance, the exhibitions' space and the use of specific "sensitive" signifiers. First, the signifying practice of critique towards the nationalist "grand narrative" (or discourse, as I prefer to call it here) is not shared by all visitors. When a group of Greek Cypriot students visited the second exhibition, a few of them, for instance, expressed their dissatisfaction and claimed that they expected "a different form of respect." Also, the (academic) analysis was labelled as "too political," as was the case with photographer Pavlos Vrionides, a guest in the CUT-Radio broadcast of 1 February 2016.

Moreover, we should also here keep in mind that the two exhibition spaces were specific, with the Home for Cooperation very clearly connected to the bi-communal (peace) movement and the NeMe Arts Centre affiliated with the (progressive) arts scene. This (most likely) produced its own exclusions, which disallowed some voices to be captured by the reception study. The politicization of space also creates another level of exclusions. For example, the only Turkish Cypriot newspaper that published an article on the second exhibition, which took place in Limassol, was *Afrika*[5] (a newspaper with a radical left-wing political ideology). Communication with newspapers in the north indicated that they usually do not cover cultural events in the south. Even if this does not concern a policy decision, it is an indication of their criteria of (geographical and cultural) relevance. On the other hand, the selection of the first exhibition's venue (the Home for Cooperation), being located within the Buffer Zone, not "belonging" to either side of the divide, was seen as an invitation to

both communities to attend. This space escapes from being politicized (at least with these visitors) (or can be related to an alternative type of politicization), functioning as a silent ambassador for reconciliation.

Particular signifiers, used in the signifying practices about the exhibitions, also become politicized, as words do matter in the Cyprus Problem (as they often do in conflicts). One example concerns which exact signifier is used to refer to the south of the island: the Republic of Cyprus, the Greek Cypriot part of Cyprus, South-Cyprus, south-Cyprus, the Southern part or southern parts of Cyprus. For a number of reasons, almost every label is potentially problematic, and the choices made by the curator (and the organizing teams) did lead to polite but critical inquiries from visitors. It also led to concerns expressed by one of the exhibition locations, eventually resulting in a change of the subtitle when the exhibition moved from the Buffer Zone to the south of the island (see Figure 4).

A second area of problematization is related to the articulation of the photographer as a (non-Cypriot) outsider. In some cases, this positioning was gentle and did not impede the acceptance of the exhibitions' analysis, as the following entry (using "us" in a particular way) in the second exhibition's guest book shows: "Life is what you make of it. Thanks for making it clearer for us" (Guest book exhibition 2). But in other cases, the outsider position is used to discredit the analysis, for instance, by equating it with colonialism: "it is as if someone says: 'hey guys, your monuments are rusty, you need someone to fix'em up?' This makes me feel awkward/as if we are being examined by our colonialists" (Pavlos Vrionides – CUT-Radio broadcast, 1 February 2016).

A third problematization relates to the aesthetics of the exhibition, which in some cases draws away the attention from the analysis. For example, one of the students visiting the exhibition referred to the "odd shots" that were used, and another visitor

A visual sociology of statues and commemoration sites in the southern part of Cyprus by Prof. Dr. Nico Carpentier

A visual sociology of statues and commemoration sites in the southern regions of Cyprus

Figure 4: Subtitles of the two exhibitions on the posters. Source: Author's analysis.

expressed concerns that the "use of specific shots, or just showing a part of the statues" would impact on the (other) visitors' reception. This call for a more "neutral" representation of the statues that implicitly rejected the (principle of the) analysis could also be found in one of the broadcasts, where the particular aesthetic choices (driven by the analysis) were critiqued. At the same time, the aesthetic dimension of the exhibition was structurally questioned, in the following terms: "there is not an aesthetic intention other than a 'snapshot' style" (Pavlos Vrionides – CUT-Radio broadcast, 1 February 2016).

Fourth, the issue of context also produced comments and critique. The twenty photographs on display at the first two *Iconoclastic Controversies* exhibitions were combined with seven title panels and fifteen text panels to provide more context and structure, and offer a second layer of academic analysis, without explicitly suggesting a particular reading of one photograph. This difficult balance between photographs and written text produced in some cases critiques, as could be observed in one of the guestbook entries: "I would prefer less texts and more photos! Nevertheless great concept and well executed. Keep going and good luck" (Guest book exhibition 1). But on the other hand, a number of visitors found the combination of text with the photographs to be effective. In one of the conversations with a visitor, the need for (even) more context was expressed, as she exclaimed to have "[n]ever seen emotion in Grivas's eyes," while the picture she was referring to did not portray the eyes of the EOKA (and EOKA-B) leader Grivas, but of the Turkish Cypriot pacifist Ihsan Ali.

The final problematization referred to the incompleteness of the exhibition and, from a broader perspective, to the impossibility of full representation. One of the most frequent recurring comments was about the focus on the south, and the absence of an analysis of the north,[6] as the following (still constructive) guest book annotation shows:

A challenging invitation for questioning, interpreting, analysing, reflecting on memory and forgetting (ΜΝΗΜΗ και ΛΗΘΗ) [MEMORY and MORE]! Thoughts and emotions raised through the photographs! I would love to be initiated in a 2nd part of this exhibition: A dialogue South-North Cyprus, representations and hegemony. A powerful challenge. (Guest book exhibition 2)

In other variations of this problematization, the choice behind the twenty photographs is questioned, and "missing" (photographs of) statues and commemoration sites were mentioned, with the suggestion that they should be included. A number of conversations with visitors were centred on the one (always different) "missing" picture that they thought should have been included. A more general comment in the guestbook of the first exhibition refers to this problematization and captures it nicely: "A small yet full of meaning exhibition [...] an extended version would be great" (Guest book exhibition 1). Relatedly, some visitors suggested that the existence of an exhibition catalogue would create space for additional photographs, while allowing for less written text being used in the exhibitions.

Triggers

Despite these problematizations, the photographs, the exhibitions and the organized discussions have acted as triggers for debate, or fed into existing debates, in relation to future commemoration practices in Cyprus, the educational role of statues and the Cyprus Problem in general. In response to the exhibitions, visitors reflect(ed) about how to deal with the statues and commemoration sites in contemporary Cyprus but also in a post-solution Cyprus, as, for instance, the Irish ambassador, interviewed at the opening of the first exhibition, refers to:

> It is important to keep the statues, not necessarily so that they would become a place of pilgrimage and be encouraging extremism or particular attitudes, but in a museum park, or somewhere else, where they can be acknowledged as a historical dimension [...] newer monuments will reflect reconciliation between conflicting parties. (Nicholas Twist, then Irish ambassador to Cyprus – MYCYradio broadcast, 22 December 2015)

A similar comment is made in a blog posting, by a Cypriot journalist, almost one year after the first exhibition:

> An exhibition entitled "Iconoclastic Controversies: A Visual Sociology of Statues and Commemoration Sites in the Southern Part of Cyprus" by Prof. Dr. Nico Carpentier at the Home for Cooperation, almost a year ago now, has had me thinking about monuments in Cyprus ever since. In a reunified Cyprus, should we erect new monuments? Should we get rid of the old ones? And what narrative should we attach to them? How we remember is important. (Natalie Hami, my Cyprus, my Κύπρος, my Kıbrıs blog – 2 September 2016[7])

Also the educational potential of the statues and commemoration sites is mentioned. The exhibition here allows for a discussion about the possible re-articulation and re-signification of these material components of the antagonistic nationalist discourse, embedding them in a different set of discourses, as this interview citation from an AHDR collaborator illustrates:

> It help[s] us [to] look at these monuments with different eyes. Sometimes, because we are used to see these monuments, or not even see them, because they are taken for granted, we don't have the chance to make them an instrument for learning. (Marios Epaminondas, AHDR – MYCYradio broadcast, 22 December 2015)

In other cases, the exhibition is incorporated to support existing counter-hegemonic discourses. One example is the article that Sevgül Uludağ, a Turkish Cypriot peace and gender activist (and also one of the speakers at one of the exhibition seminars), published in the Turkish Cypriot newspaper *Yenidüzen* (Figure 5). Here the exhibition becomes articulated with the

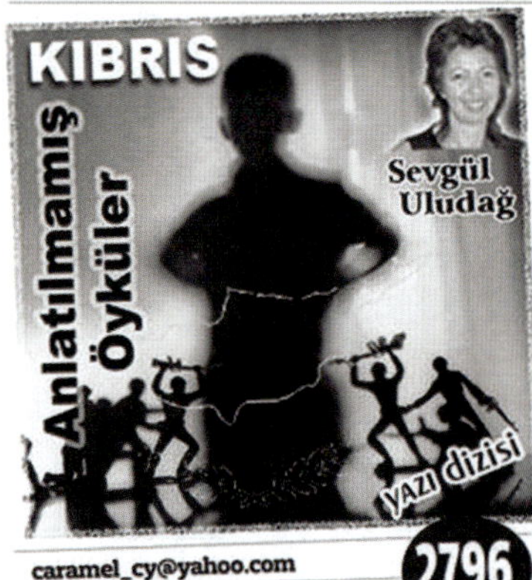

"Kıbrıs sorununu irdelerken" başlıklı medya tartışmasında "kayıplar" da ele alınacak...

"Kıbrıs'taki kayıpları araştırırken tarihle ilgili gerçekle yüzleşmek..."

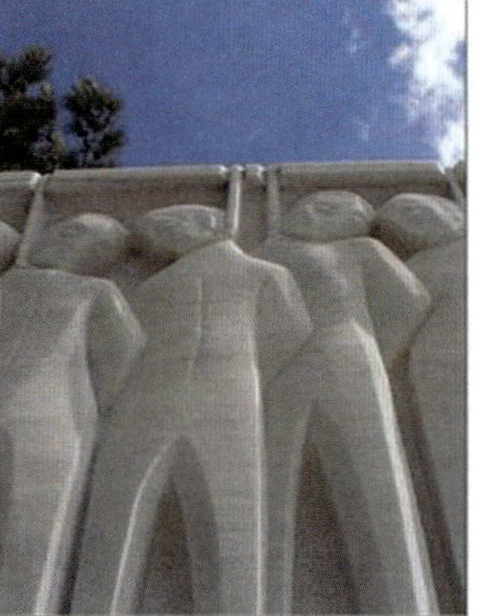

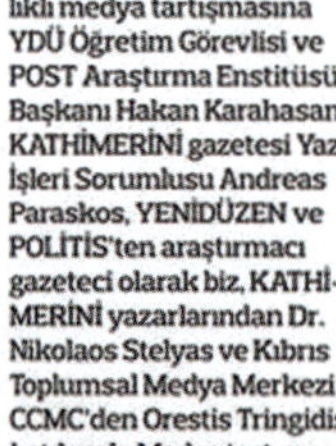

Belçika'dan Profesör Dr. Nico Carpentier'in Kıbrıs sorununa ilişkin Tarihsel Diyalog ve Araştırma Merkezi AHDR ve Kıbrıs Toplum Medya Merkezi'yle birlikte yürüttüğü görsel bir sosyoloji projesi çerçevesinde "Kıbrıs sorununu irdelerken" başlıklı bir de medya tartışması düzenleniyor ve bu tartışmada "kayıplar" konusu da ele alınıyor.

19 Kasım 2015 Perşembe akşamı 18.00-20.00 saatlerinde Lefkoşa'da, ara bölgedeki Dayanışma Evi'nde gerçekleştirilecek "Kıbrıs sorununu irdelerken" baş-

---

Bildiklerinizi paylaşmak istiyorsanız:

İsimli veya isimsiz olarak konuşmak isteyenler için telefonum:
0542 853 8436
Kıbrıslırum okurlarım için
CYTA telefonum:
99-966518
Elektronik postayla ulaşmak isteyenler için
e-mail adresim:
caramel_cy@yahoo.com
Normal posta yoluyla bana ulaşmak isteyen okurlarım için posta adresim:
19, Necmi Avkıran Sokak, Lefkoşa
Kayıplar Komitesi'ni aramak isteyenler 22-83607'den Mine Balman'ı arayabilirler.
Kıbrıslıtürk olsun, Kıbrıslırum olsun, çağrım herkesedir:
Bildiklerinizi paylaştıkça bu sorunların çözümüne katkı koyabileceğiz, "Kayıplar" ve "Toplu Mezarlar" konusunu temize havale edebileceğiz... Anlatılmamış öykülerinizi anlatmaya devam etmenizi bekliyorum...

---

lıklı medya tartışmasına YDÜ Öğretim Görevlisi ve POST Araştırma Enstitüsü Başkanı Hakan Karahasan, KATHİMERİNİ gazetesi Yazı İşleri Sorumlusu Andreas Paraskos, YENİDÜZEN ve POLİTİS'ten araştırmacı gazeteci olarak biz, KATHİMERİNİ yazarlarından Dr. Nikolaos Stelyas ve Kıbrıs Toplumsal Medya Merkezi CCMC'den Orestis Tringidis katılacak. Medya tartışmasını gazeteci Yorgos Kakuris yönetecek.

Andreas Paraskos "Kayıp şahıslar: Yarım yüzyıldır devam eden bir trajedi ve toplumumuzun kırılganlığı"nı anlatacak, biz ise "Kıbrıs'taki kayıpları araştırırken tarihle ilgili gerçekle yüzleşmek..." konusunu işleyeceğiz.

Hakan Karahasan "Annan Planı döneminde ve sonrasında Kıbrıs sorununa ilişkin Kıbrıslıtürk medya anlatımlarına bakış" konusunu işleyecek. Dr. Nikolaos Stelyas ise "Kıbrıs sorununda medyanın rolü: Çözüme bir engel mi yoksa iki toplumlu diyalog ve iletişim köprüleri kurucusu mu?" sorusuna yanıt arayacak. Orestis Tringidis ise "Kıbrıs sorununa alternatif medya anlatımları, programları ve yaklaşımları: Ne kadar etkili, neler yapılabilir? Kıbrıs toplum medyası CCMC ve MYCYradio örnekleri"ni anlatacak.

18 Kasım 2015 Çarşamba günü aynı yer ve aynı saatte ise "Heykeller konuşur mu?

Anıtlar bizim varlığımızı anlatır mı? Her gün yanlarından geçip giderken eksik olan ne?" başlığı altında "Tarihsel bellek ve anıtlar" konusu tartışılacak. Tartışmaya Mehmet Adil, Zehra Azizbeyli, Despo Paşa, Reyhan Sabri ve Teopisti Stilyanu-Lambert katılacak.

Brüksel'deki Vrije Üniversitesi öğretim üyesi Prof. Dr. Nico Carpentier'in Tarihsel Diyalog ve Araştırma Derneği (AHDR) ve Kıbrıs Toplumu Medya Merkezi (CCMC) işbirliği ile hazırlanan "İkonoklastik Uyuşmazlıklar" adlı fotoğraf sergisi, 13 Kasım'da saat 19.00'da Lefkoşa'da ara bölgedeki Dayanışma Evi'nde açılacak.

Sergide "Kıbrıs'ın güneyindeki heykel ve anıt alanlarının görsel sosyolojisini" konu alan, Eylül 2012-Eylül 2014 arasında çekilmiş 20 fotoğraf yer alacak. Sergi 21 Kasım'a kadar açık kalacak.

Devam edecek

Figure 5: Sevgül Uludağ's article on the exhibition in the *Yenidüzen* newspaper. Source: Author's analysis.

issue of the missing Turkish Cypriots and Greek Cypriots from 1963 to 1974, which is one of the main areas of Uludağ's activism.

Finally, the exhibition had also an impact on the project partners, who, in the case of CCMC, NeMe and CUT-Radio, translated the initial interest in particular actions (e.g. radio programmes and projects with relevant content and focus) or who, in the case of AHDR, became more attentive towards statues and commemoration sites as materializations of historical and political discourses, as the following citation from a MYCYradio broadcast shows: "it is still interesting to us, but like [...] the first feeling we had was like: Wow [...] We never thought of all this behind the statues we come by everyday" (Nadia Kornioti, AHDR – MYCYradio broadcast, 22 December 2015 – opening speech at exhibition 1).

CONCLUSION

It is important that research that is relevant for communities is also communicated to these communities, in ways that they can appreciate, relate to and interact with. The use of non-written texts to communicate this academic research project has – to some degree – enabled and facilitated this (as discussed in Chapter 2). It is equally important for society at large to be engaged in the analyses, discussions and debates generated by academic research, especially for issues that immediately concern these communities and that have an impact on the lives of their members, as it is the case with the Cyprus conflict. But even if there is little disagreement with this position in academia, academics often remain stuck in paying lip service to these ideas, limit themselves to an occasional op-ed in a mainstream newspaper or – if they are truly courageous – produce a short science communication video that can be uploaded on YouTube (or a similar platform).

Arguably, projects such as the one discussed in this book allow for more complex and intense forms of community engagement and, at least potentially, community empowerment, despite the limitations these projects undoubtedly always have. Even if audience attendance of the photo exhibitions was low during the non-event periods, the openings and the seminars generated substantial levels of interest. Visitors frequently confirmed the exhibitions' relevance, at both the analytical and the critical level, and there is material evidence that the exhibitions fed into broader debates in Cyprus. In this sense, the decision to organize an academic-artistic intervention, combining the logics of these two fields – inspired by, for instance, action research, arts-based research, visual sociology, multimodal academic communication and the work on the articulation of the arts with agonization – seems to have been fruitful.

Still, we should not remain blind to the problems encountered with Iconoclastic Controversies and its limitations. The project was both complex in nature, as it used a broad variety of analytical and communicative methods, and sensitive, because it was addressing issues of antagonistic conflict and the Greek Cypriot nationalist assemblage, connecting them to the everyday environment of the Cypriot landscape. The reception analysis of the *Iconoclastic Controversies* exhibitions clearly shows these complexities and sensitivities, with the different visitor problematizations discussed in this chapter. The Cyprus conflict often works like a vortex, pulling all academic analyses into it, rendering them part of the politics of conflict. This process makes them significantly easier to reject it as "just" one of the many political signifying practices that circulate on the island or as the perspective of an ignorant outsider. But also the genres of photography and exhibition generated (signifying practices about the) problematizations, with, for instance, the aesthetics sometimes covering the analysis instead of carrying it forward.

But these challenges and limitations should not be univocally problematized. They can also be seen as creative translations of the confusion and discomfort that some visitors experienced. This has a positive side to it (at least from my perspective), because these affects indicate a certain degree of success of our de-naturalization and empowerment strategies (even if there is a need for more research into this). Showing the repetition and pervasiveness of hegemony, also in its materializations, shedding light on the counter-hegemonic assemblage through the statues that invite for agonistic readings of the Cypriot histories and showing the first signs of the re-articulation of antagonist nationalism through everyday life practices (which aligns well with the current post-antagonist setting) matter very much. The photograph of the mother of the Latsia monument, which early on in the Iconoclastic Controversies project became its icon, exemplifies these changing times, as her stone face is slowly fading away, because of environmental exposure. In a way, the process of erosion signifies her pain even more, but it also heralds the new times that await Cyprus.

Even if *times are a changin'* for Cyprus, there is still much work to be done, and the de-naturalization of antagonist nationalism remains a crucial activity for critical academics that are committed to the transformation of this antagonistic conflict into one of its agonistic versions.

NOTES

1. This reception study did not include the third *Iconoclastic Controversies* exhibition in Brazil, as the first two exhibitions in Cyprus received priority, given the scarcity of resources.
2. Corroborative information is provided by the count on the Facebook page of the first exhibition, which had 879 people, 93 indicated interest and 168 were under the category "went" (count on 20 July 2016).
3. As in the Cypriot (antagonistic) nationalist discourses, the emphasis is often on the "own" casualties and suffering; the Greek Cypriot mother was an obvious (and simultaneously problematic) choice for (many of) the Greek Cypriot media and a less desired choice for (many of) the Turkish Cypriot media.
4. Guest book entries and interview citations are rendered ad verbatim in this chapter.
5. In June 2020, the newspaper reverted to its original name, *Avrupa*, after accusations of racism. See http://www.t-vine.com/turkish-cypriot-newspaper-afrika-changes-its-name-and-logo-after-being-accused-of-racism/.
6. This was also interpreted as one of the reasons for the poor level of attention by the media in the north.
7. http://mcmkmk.org/index.php/2016/09/02/talking-statues-how-do-monuments-speak-to-us-part-3/. This blog posting was not included in the analysis of the media publications, discussed before, as it was published much later.

Chapter 7: The Interviews

Iconoclastic Controversies website interview

Interview: Eva Giannoukou
Transcription: Eirini Avraam
Interview on: 8 October 2015

Eva Giannoukou: Can you explain what the exhibition is about? How did the idea take root?

Nico Carpentier: There are actually two components to it and these are different stories. One is the visual sociology part, which is an old interest of mine. That is based on the question, how to communicate academic research in a way that is not only text-based. So how to tell a story in an academic way that is not an article, or a book, or a book chapter but that uses other technologies to communicate research outcomes, or theoretical frameworks. That is a question that has been with me for a very long time. This is actually a question which is connected to what is called science communication. How do we communicate our academic results to the outside world? That is why photography became important to me. Because in visual sociology the image is used as a tool not only for analysis. Of course, analysing the visual is what we often do in Communication and Media Studies. But in visual sociology the question also becomes how can we use the visual – whether this is photography, video, audio – to communicate research in itself. And that, I think, is a very important and a very difficult question.

This idea is not entirely new – nothing is [*smiles*]: A number of people have been working with photography within academia. There is a genre which is called the visual essay. Here, photography is used in article form, as an essay, using images to tell the story and not just to illustrate it. I used some of these ideas for this exhibition. Instead of simply saying, "Let us publish the photos in an article form, in an essay form," I said, "Let us display them in their original photographic mode. Let us use photography and let us combine them with an exhibition." So that is the first part of the story, which goes back to a number of other projects that I have been doing in order to try to find this other language.

Eva: Is this a very common practice in your field?

Nico: It is a small group of academics that use it, because, you know, academics like to write. Academia is very much about writing. And it is very important part of our work; I am not saying that writing is not important, but a lot of weight is being put on writing. These other media, these other ways of communicating, are not very present. They are not a part of our training, they are not part of our usual academic practices. There are not part of our teaching practices either. But there is a small group of people working with these ideas, trying to find other ways of telling their academic story. And the real challenge is that we need to find ways of doing this in a way that is still academic. Because anybody can (more or less) make a video, but to make a video that follows the principles of academic storytelling, of academic narration, is not that easy. To make an exhibition that still stays within the logics of academic storytelling is definitely not an easy thing to do. Moreover, there are not too many examples to build on. Of course, there are always other people that have done that. But I think it is still new in the sense that it is hardly been used and it is definitely not the "normal" way of doing it. It is still experimental.

In the case of the exhibition, and many other projects, there is a reversal. What is happening with the exhibition is that it is turning things around. It is like when you are sitting at the table and all of a sudden you say, "Let us change seats. Let us go and sit somewhere else." Photography changes places, it does not become the object of study, it becomes the tool of communicating the study. It [the exhibition] just gives to photography a wholly different role, a new role I could say. But different for sure. And it also changes my position as researcher because I communicate differently. So I also take a different seat. And, finally, it changes the role of the spectator. It is not the reader of the academic article but now s/he can go to an exhibition and see academic work.

Eva: Is this new – the researcher being part of the research instrument?

Nico: I would say that it is always the case. It is very difficult to be outside the topic and that is a general comment again. We ourselves, as researchers, are always research instruments at the same time. We are part of our research. I mean, our personality, who we are, what we see, how our ontologies and epistemologies work,…

This also brings to the second component. I was living in Cyprus for one year – this island was also my environment and my home. Well, I am not Cypriot, or at least not entirely [*laughing*] but I am still there, I am still doing the research and when you are using photography it makes you more part of the research, it involves you more. But this has many different aspects. The being-there part has lots of different components. Photography is only one of them.

Presence matters, unless you go for more experimental photography, but even then … I think you have to be there. You also show that you have been there. In the history of anthropology, there is a very old and very problematic way of doing anthropology, which is called "armchair anthropology." Some of the early anthropologists were writing about faraway countries, without being there, from their homes in the West. That is not what I want to do. I wanted to be there to do the research on the island itself and not to be one of these "armchair sociologists" but immerse myself in this research topic and the culture that was surrounding it. Of course, you are never totally inside, but who is? You remain an observer, something which has advantages and disadvantages as well.

It is very difficult to balance these roles, because, on the one hand, you have to be a part of this world, you have to immerse yourself, you have to participate in a particular culture and, on the other hand, you have to be detached; as academic you need your critical distance. Looking at the social reality and not telling the way that you want it to be but the way it is, mediated through your methodologies, procedures and theories. And finding that balance, between being part and being detached, is both very important and very difficult.

Eva: We were talking about one of the two components of the exhibition – the method of visual sociology – the second one, is it that the project is about Cyprus?

Nico: Yes. I came to Cyprus in September 2013 and I stayed for a year until September 2014. So in that period I was almost full-time on the island. But I came here to do research on Cypriot community media, and, of course I was writing about that. This community media research project is still going on – I was (and am) interested in community and alternative media, and in the way that they play a role within conflict transformation in Cyprus. That was the reason for being here… in 2013 and 2014 as a sabbatical project.

Because I have been working on community media and conflict for quite some time, this was an important research project for me. I think that Cyprus is a place where the entire world can learn from, for instance, about the way that media function, the way that conflict functions, how diverse these ways of dealing with conflict are and maybe even how the transformation of conflict functions. That was the main reason for being here in Cyprus. Of course, doing this kind of nomadic research is always a bit complicated. In this case, it required an understanding of how Cypriot society functioned, and in particular how the Cyprus Problem functioned. And very quickly I came to see that history is crucial for understanding the Cyprus Problem; not only the history of the Cyprus Problem itself but the history of Cyprus. There is no escape to the historical dimension. You have to understand at least 300 years of history; possibly more. Particularly the twentieth century is very important with, for instance, the crucial role of the British period and EOKA's independence war. I started focusing on that independence war, in combination with the events of the 1960s and 1970s. As historical events are endless, I started doing small projects to better understand the Cypriot history in a more contained way. One of these

projects was based on the statues and commemoration sites in the south of Cyprus. And that actually brings me to the content of this exhibition.

What I should emphasize is that this was originally a spinoff project. It was not planned, it happened almost accidentally, with me being here and becoming fascinated by the language of statues. Their way of representing reality triggered my interest. It was one of these moments where you looked at a social reality, and then you realize: This is something, it is important and relevant. There is something to be said about this here. And it transformed from a spinoff project into something important, because of what it allowed me to say. But, at the same time, it allowed me to better understand Cypriot society. It also helped me with the community media project because it provided me with much more context and a better understanding of how things worked. And I think it also gave me a better understanding of how conflict works and how materiality, the objects, plays a role. Conflict is not just about how people think, how they talk and act. It is also about these objects are there, in the cities and villages, and how these statues also communicate to us. We often think that material objects are silent. But they are not. They speak to us. And they tell us a story. Analysing these stories, through their materiality, is important.

Eva: The exhibition focuses on statues and commemorative sites. You are a professor in Communication and Media Studies. How do you connect them?

Nico: The statues are about communication. I should add that it is often figurative art. There is not too much public art in Cyprus that is abstract. Most of the statues are very figurative, so the communicational act is often also rather straightforward. What is selected to be displayed is communication. Who is selected is also communication. How the person is displayed is communication. Statues have a material presence through which they communicate their importance. I have always had a very broad definition of communication, and of media. I enjoy arguing that, for instance, a museum is a location and act of communication. It is a medium. And these statues are also media. They tell us something, they are vehicles of ideology, etc. It is not only the explanatory text that matters, but it is the entire object that becomes a medium.

Eva: Are the ways statues are used in Cyprus different from those of other countries?

Nico: Yes and no. I think there are two answers to your question. One is that the logics of what statues are telling us are very often quite similar. In that sense, Cyprus is not special but it is special. [*Laughing*] You will find the different types of communication through statues also in other countries. Statues are acts of ideology in many countries. If you take Belgium, my home country, as an example: Quite a lot of the Belgian kings have their statues there. It serves a political-ideological purpose, that is to legitimate the monarchy, and to propagate a particular perspective on history, leadership and democracy. All these political components are very often invoked. But at the same time – and that is my second answer – I think that in Cyprus there is a very strong emphasis on the political, linked to the military and the heroic. What you often see, in other countries, is that there is, for instance, a stronger emphasis on the artistic. You will find more of mix of these different types of statues. Well, in Cyprus, the political statue is very dominant. And that is different and special.

Eva: Are you now saying that abstract art is not communicational or political?

Nico: On the contrary. It is very clear that abstract statues can communicate political messages. There is a long tradition in intentionally doing this, by the way. But abstract art requires more interpretation and contextualization. It is much more complicated to communicate through the abstract. If you use the figurative, you say, in a very mimetic way: look, this person is our hero and we are showing you the hero in a very heroic pose. Then things are very clear and easy. That is one of the reasons why the figurative, and especially the mimetic representation of the person, is so important in the Cyprus landscape of statues.

One should also not forget that, as communicational acts, statues have audiences. They are sometimes addressing a large community, for instance, the Greek Cypriot community as a whole. But sometimes they talk to a very local community. Then they are saying, "This is our hero, this is our fellow citizen, our fellow villager, fellow towns(wo)man, who died for this cause, or who did this…" So a statue also talks to the people from that very local community. This is our district, this is our hero. That is also what they are saying.

Eva: Are these statues then community media? Are they participatory?

Nico: Oh, this is a tricky question. On the one hand, a lot of these statues were actually created by the community for the community. Because often particular foundations were financing and building them, so it was not always the city council that initiated the construction of these statues. Still, the city had to approve it, but the initiative and the funding came from individuals and/or these foundations. So, this process was not always centralized – it was actually often very bottom-up. So, it is by the community and it is also for the community. It was for that district, for that village, for them. So in that sense you are right, this is exactly the definition of community media.

But things are not that simple. There are a few reasons why they are not community media. Community media are organizations, which aim at communicating quite regularly. More importantly, community media have a tendency towards the alternative, the non-dominant ways of thinking, and the counter-hegemonic. They move away from dominant mainstream culture. In contrast, these statues are very much part of the dominant culture. They tell us a dominant story, a story about nationalism and heroism which is – I think – the dominant way of looking at the past. In other words, maybe community media would create a different kind of statue. One that is more open, one that is more asking for different interpretations and maybe one that is more geared towards peace.

Eva: What about the statues in the north?

Nico: This exhibition is not about the Turkish Cypriot part of Cyprus and about the statues that can be found there. I think that is important to stress. If you do research, you always have to make choices. It would be wonderful to do this sort of analysis on both parts of the island. Because the communicational structures are very similar, while the content is different. To put it in other words: the heroes are different. But I did do some work there, on the statues in the north and there are, of course, lots of differences, but also similarities.

Eva: I would like to come back to an earlier question. Why are the political statues so present in Cyprus?

Nico: I think the Cyprus statues show a number of things. They show how important and how dramatic the Cyprus Problem actually is. I do not want to be too poetic but I think that the Cyprus Problem has scratched the Cypriot soul. It was (and still is) really traumatic. The trauma went very deep. And the statues are ways of dealing with that. Trauma is a word that is often used for individuals, to describe a situation where an individual suffers, after having gone through terrible things. At an individual level, it is called trauma. But you can also use the word *trauma* for a culture, or for a community, and that is the way I am now using it here, as a cultural trauma or a collective trauma. The trauma spans the entire island, both the north and south. It is something that they share and that unites them. The entire island went through terrible events, in so many different ways, in so many variations. These were very traumatic experiences. And that needs, that requires communication. It also produces it. It is like you open up a box and all these things start pouring out. And that is partially triggered by the need to protect oneself. It is also a form of working through the trauma, of coping with it. It is a part of a healing process. I am not sure if the healing process is over, to be honest. But communicating the pain and communicating the loss is really important in case of trauma. That is what I think has happened and is still happening.

At the same time, if you are traumatized, it is very difficult to see the complexity of the context that caused the trauma. You become partially blinded through the pain. Of course, there are many ways how individuals deal with this kind of collective trauma, but there are dominant ways of doing this, and they get used and repeated more than others. We can see that with the statues – they have a very similar way of looking at the past, and of looking at the trauma. And that is why they are focusing so much on a nationalist discourse, and on a discourse of heroism, that support the construction of the Greek Cypriot nation as a people.

And then you could raise the question, are there then no alternatives? This takes time. Time to see that events are complicated and that there are many sides to a traumatic event. A lot of terrible things happened and a lot of terrible things have been done by very different people, on both sides. And I think that the statues show that how difficult it is to develop alternative ways of thinking about the Cyprus Problem. That was one of the reasons why I went to look for these exceptions, for these alternatives, in the project and in the exhibition. One-third of the exhibition's photographs are about statues that tell a different story, that are in some way counter-hegemonic. This is not to ignore the dominant way of representing the Cyprus Problem through the use of statues. No, the thing is that I really had to go and look for these alternatives. These statues are hidden, they are very difficult to find, their existence is not well-documented… They are still publicly displayed, but in places that are not easy to find and to reach. I was lucky to be able to use the Public Art of Cyprus database for this, otherwise it might have been impossible.

But what is important to stress is that these alternative statues are there. They exist and they are very much showing us that it is possible to have alternatives. That it does not have to be only that one way which comes out of the traumatized way of looking at the past. There are also other ways of looking at the past than looking at the Other (with capital O) which is seen as the Enemy (with capital E). There are different ways. My research project was, on the one hand, about documenting and analysing the very dominant way of thinking, as it was materialized in the statues. But on the other hand, it was also about finding these exceptions, finding these alternatives that are so important if you want to understand a culture and a conflict.

Eva: They coexist within the same community?

Nico: The thing is that a community can produce very dominant ways of thinking and a community can produce at the same time very alternative ways of thinking. It does both. There are both from the community. Also the dominant ones that are produced within the Greek Cypriot community. They are part of the Greek Cypriotness, part of the history, part of the urban spaces. Most of them are from and by the community, but they are like two sides of a coin. They show both, they show what the Greek Cypriot community is about, but in very very different ways. And this shows that a community is a contradictory space, characterized by diversity. There is not one Cypriot community, there is not one Greek Cypriot community.

The ideological model of war imposes the idea that there is a homogeneous community, with all constituent groups included in a chain of equivalence. That is something that is actually part of the problem. In this case, all are seen as Greek Cypriots, united in their being threatened by Turkey. This feeds into a homogeneous collectivity. Conflict transformation consists of making these internal differences, within the community itself, more visible, bringing them out more clearly. And that was one of the reasons why I have been emphasizing these two sides of the coin. The nationalist homogenizing discourse and the alternative diversity-based discourse coexist. And you will find both of them in the Cypriot landscape, even if the statues that materialize the diversity-based discourse are more difficult to find. Sometimes they are in the outskirts of a village. But sometimes they are in the city. One example is the Ihsan Ali statue, which is in Paphos. It is interesting to describe where it is located. It is on a square, but at the back. It is not facing the main street, which is the Grivas Digenis Avenue. You have to first find that little square but then you also have to cross it and look behind the trees. And the Ali statue is there, at the end, looking away from the main street. True, it is not in the outskirts of a village but it is not exactly in the centre of the city either.

Eva: You mentioned before the similarities in how the enemy is seen. Does that also apply to Cyprus?

Nico: I have done quite some research on conflict and it is always incredibly striking how similar the structures of thinking about the Other-Enemy are. It is like a mirror image. It is like looking in the mirror and seeing the other which is another, but so much the same at the same time. This is how conflict works. The mirror is the barrier and the other is on the other side. But the other is a reflection of the self at the same time. And I think that is the best description I can give you on what the similarities and what the differences are. It is a combination of radical otherness and radical similarity all at the same time.

This is obviously a very paradoxical situation, but if you start looking closer at conflict and study it, then what you often see is this mirror image. There is a very silly proverb, it takes two to tango, but that is the reality of it. It is like locking these two communities together but in a very conflicted and sometimes a very violent way. What I am saying is that the ways the representation of the other is structured are very similar. This structure is, of course, filled with always particular people and events, but the structure is similar. The way that there is a focus on the suffering of the self and the way that suffering of the other is ignored (or legitimated), that is extremely similar.

Eva: Can the exhibition then escape this structure that creates the other?

Nico: Of course, if you go to an exhibition like this, there are two ways of handling it. You can see the confirmation of the evilness of the enemy in it. So there is a danger with an exhibition like this, only covering the Greek Cypriots materialized discourses. (From a Turkish Cypriot position) you can say, "Look, they are all nationalists." It might allow people not

to see themselves as being part of the same kinds of dynamics. The other way to look at the exhibition is to reflect about how both communities have been representing themselves and the other. I definitely hope that people from the north that visit the exhibition feel invited to analyse how the Turkish Cypriot community has been dealing with the conflict. I think there are many similarities in the structure. There are, of course, a considerable number of differences. I think that, for instance, one of the big differences is how the missing were defined and remembered, but discussing that would now take us too far.

The place of the first exhibition, in the Buffer Zone close to Ledra Palace, is a very conscious choice for a number of reasons. It also wants to show the need for analyses that bridge and connect. But actually the risk, the risk of misinterpretation, always exists. And it is not only Turkish Cypriots that might be affected, of course. It is also Greek Cypriots and others that can be offended. A critical analysis showing how a dominant nationalist discourse is among us in Cyprus is important, but also showing that diversity may be a way out is equally important. But visitors might disagree. People sometimes feel very strongly about nationalism and national identity and that is their good right, even if we might need to think about how to tame that force more. Also because it feeds the risk of misinterpretation.

That was one of the reasons why I started working with different NGOs, including the AHDR. Whatever written text has been produced for the accompanying panels, it was discussed with them to see whether I was not unconsciously or accidentally saying things that would be insulting or humiliating. We thus created a mechanism to at least limit the risk of misinterpretation. The other thing we did was to decide to have two seminars during the [first] exhibition. It is not a coincidence, it is not to just entertain people. Having these two seminars invites people to reflect on the results of this research project, to work with them and to take it further, to use these results. It is not about putting some pictures that aestheticize statues on display and then to go away. This is also an invitation for dialogue. An invitation for analysis, an invitation for self-reflection and an invitation for conversation.

Eva: Was this project something you did on your own?

Nico: When you start looking back at the project and the exhibition, it is bigger than you would say. The original research stay was funded by the VUB, the [Dutch-speaking] Free University of Brussels. They allowed me to be here. More funding came from the north Belgian scientific funds, which is called FWO. There are also a number of Cypriot partners, including a number of NGOs. I already mentioned AHDR earlier, who provided great support, but there were also the CCMC people. They have been extremely supportive during the entire project. Their former coordinator, Michael Simopoulos, was one of the core partners, not only in relation to helping me with my research at CCMC but also in helping me to understand Cypriot history and society. CCMC has remained a very helpful partner throughout the years. Then, there was also the organizing team of the [first] exhibition, with Eva Giannoukou, Yiannis Christidis, Fatma Nazli Köksal, Stella Theocharous and Vaia Doudaki, some of whom were involved before the exhibition. Stella, for instance, helped with the research in relation to some of the commemoration sites. And there was collaboration with CUT [the Cyprus University of Technology], with Vaia Doudaki, who was my guide through the rather complicated Cypriot landscape. But she was also helping me with translations and contextualizations; she played a really important role in the entire project. But sometimes there were also more anonymous helpers. At one point, we went to look for Kyriacou's eagle statue on a mountain top close to the Machairas convent. Our car broke down, as the mountains were too much for it. In the village where we got stuck, a friendly man decided to help us and he brought us to the eagle. I do not know his name by heart to be honest – it is probably somewhere in my notes [it was Nicolas] – but this story shows that these people were just as important. I would never have made it there if our wonderful guide had not helped us so generously. So, there was institutional support, yes, but there were also many people that were "just" telling me stories, sharing their knowledge with me.

Eva: Will you continue this project? What about the north?

Nico: I would love to do this analysis in the north, to be honest. I have done some work there, but there is much more to do. I would like to find something like two months and a good guide to show me round, and to look for the statues... There are some practical difficulties. I have not found an accessible public art database in the north. Maybe it exists, but a database like this has turned out to be a key instrument in enabling me to do this kind of research in the south. It would be more difficult in the north, but I would definitely love to. Or maybe somebody else should do it? Maybe we should have other analysts/photographers tell their story about the statues in the north, and maybe others should analyse and re-analyse the statues in the south. It should not be only me doing these things, I think. Maybe we should start a photographic conversation about this, and I would like to hear other voices.

Eva: Thank you for the interview.

Nico: And thank you for all your work.

CUT-Radio interview[1]

Interview: Yiannis Christidis
Transcription: Eirini Avraam
Editing: Nico Carpentier
Broadcasted on: 23 January 2016

Yiannis Christidis: Today I have here Professor Nico Carpentier in the studio. We are going to talk about the [second] exhibition which is now taking place in Limassol, at the NeMe Arts Centre. The exhibition is called *Iconoclastic Controversies: A visual sociology of statues and commemoration sites in the southern regions of Cyprus*, and I would like to start the interview by asking you: How do you explain the concept of the exhibition to a 6-year old child?

Nico Carpentier: That is a quite challenging opening question. I should think about an answer for a couple of hours. No, more seriously, first of all, thanks for having me here to talk about this baby of mine; it is not a 6-year-old but just a baby of mine.

Let me try to explain the concept of the exhibition: An exhibition is a medium, and it tries to tell a story. In this case, it tries to tell the story that a statue is not just a statue. That is actually the simple version, the simplest version I can give you. If I can add another couple of sentences, obviously, I mean: a statue is made in stone or bronze – it has this materiality. It is there. It is placed in a particular setting, in the streets of a city or village. It orients your gaze, it invites you to look at it. The way that it is positioned is often at a central place where the entire landscape is geared towards attracting your attention. There are lots of things to be said about this material positioning.

But, there is another layer – we give meaning to it. Moreover, different people give different meanings to it. We look at it in different ways. If you know the historical context, you will look at it differently. For instance, tourists do not always know that historical context. And if you do know the historical context, then you look at a statue differently, you might understand more. So, a statue is not just this piece of stone, or a bronze object; it is actually inviting you to interpret it in a particular way, on the basis of contextual knowledge that you may, or may not, have.

Now, I am not talking to the 6-year-old anymore [*laughing*]. After this answer, one might actually wonder about my capacity to talk to a 6-year-old. To reassure you, I do know that one does not talk with a 6-year-old like this. And I am not positioning anyone that is listening to this as a 6-year-old either.

The idea is that they communicate something to us. They invite us to think in particular ways. But the "Controversies" part is making things more complicated. What I am adding (to the idea that statues are communicating to us) is a very simple thing: there are different meanings. Not everybody agrees on these meanings. You can interpret the statues in different ways. Meanings are not stable; they are not given and fixed in eternity. The statue is an invitation to think about something in a particular way. But an invitation is something that you can ignore. It is something that you can actually deflect. You can think about it in different ways. It is something that is negotiated and not fixed. People have different opinions about what the statues mean. In some cases, they provoke really very strong emotions. But they also provoke different emotions, which are based on different readings. What the exhibition wants to show is that diversity – the diversity of meanings and interpretations – is also present in the Cypriot context. Here too, there are different interpretations at work. The statues sometimes create different invitations. All of them try to communicate something but you can still always reject it. You can refuse.

Some of the photographs in the exhibition are actually about this refusal. They are about the refusal to follow the invitation of dominant (nationalist) ideologies. There is one picture, if I can give you one example; there is a picture of a Grivas statue. It is set at the Grivas landing site memorial, on the Chloraka coast. It portrays a child playing there; it's a Russian child, poking a stick in the bushes at the feet of the Grivas statue. The young child is clearly not in full admiration for whatever the Grivas statue is inviting us to admire in relation to the independence war and for the sacrifice that is linked to that independence war. The child is not accepting the invitation of the statue. The photograph that I made is analysing that rejection of the invitation to pay tribute to Grivas. What the exhibition is trying to explain is this very complex interplay between communicational invitations, acceptances and rejections of dominant meanings.

Yiannis: One can wonder whether this invitation is a kind invitation, or not. Because, I mean, when the state is constructing these statues, when they are ordering a sculpture from an artist, referencing to national pride, or whatever it may be called, it is kind of an intervention in which other people are not involved. This sort of invitation might be kind of rude. Actually, to me, it is a rude invitation. And maybe it is rude to more than one person?

But what I want to find out with my comment is: How do you photographically translate this public intervention? How do you transfer the whole experience, which is located in public space, to an exhibition? How do you take these statues and move them to another medium – photography – and then after this, to an exhibition space. This transition of the public space to photography, and then from photography to a printed version in an exhibition space, is quite a route to take.

Nico: Yes, it is a trajectory, which is well considered. Of course, it affects the meanings. Let me start with the invitation part of your question. I agree with you that the invitation can be rude, but it does not mean that it is not an invitation. It does not mean that you necessarily have to accept the discursive constructions that are embedded in the statue, sometimes created by the state, sometimes also by particular groups in society, for example foundations, etc. Some invitations are more open and kinder than others. I fully agree with you. What I want to emphasize with using the concept of "the invitation" is that the communication originating from the statues is not that strong, and its meaning is definitely not a given. It can never be that strong that it cannot be resisted.

Their invitations do try to seduce you into accepting particular meanings. Heroism is one meaning which is very present in the Cypriot statues, but it is still possible to use irony and just see a pompous object. Some gaze in admiration at a statue and others see something ridiculous, which does not speak to their life worlds. That is what the invitation does. It does try to push you to see heroism, but you might not accept the invitation. Actually a lot of people do not (any more).

The landscape of statues in Cyprus – each with its own invitations – is also characterized by the different (and sometimes contradictory) discursive positions that they embody. If you take one step back and start looking at the Cypriot public space, you see that there are also interventions in this public space that are not driven by the state. That are not even driven by dominant ideologies. That are actually trying to resist the dominant ideology. Public space is not something that the state can totally control. Individuals and foundations can buy pieces of land, get permissions and then use it. But these usages are not necessarily in accordance with government policies or aligned with dominant ideologies. There is also a more participatory-democratic control over these spaces, even if the government can be a very imposing actor on how we can use public space.

That actually brings me to your question about the translation of public space into photography and then into an exhibition, and its particularities. I think that that trajectory is driven by an analytical perspective. That perspective is what is allowing me to transgress these spheres and to move from one sphere to another, from the public space where the statues are situated, to photography where they are represented, and then to an exhibition space where they are contextualized (more). It is the analysis that drives the translation, that made these statues travel through this trajectory. The statues and commemoration sites have been selected for particular reasons, and they are represented in particular ways and for particular reasons. The reasons why they are represented as they are represented through photography is the analysis. It is an academic reflection about the role of meaning through statues in Cyprus. That makes the exhibition specific – it is not a mimetic or exclusively aesthetic representation of statues, it is an analytical exercise in trying to understand what these invitations are about and how they work. And that is an analytical process. And, of course, I am not ignoring that artistic interventions are also analytical and reflexive. But I think that in the case of this exhibition, the balance is different, in the sense that the analysis is much more present. And we should not

forget that I am still an academic who uses photography, which renders the analysis more present than usual. Although I hope that the aesthetics have not completely disappeared from my work, but that is up to people to come and see.

Yiannis: How does the genre of photography influence the analysis, of what you want to say about the monuments? What effort did you make during the shooting to exactly capture what you wanted to say? What about angles and perspectives? How did they influence your analysis and how did you use them to analyse?

Nico: This question moves us into the back office of both photography and academic analysis. The answer lies in a complicated (and hopefully sophisticated) mixture of all these different components, of the analysis, the technology (the camera), the setting, the light, the angle, the framing, etc. I find it still difficult to get it right, to be honest. But talking as an academic, I think that writing an article is also pretty difficult, as you are also combining very different elements. What I am doing here is applying a slightly less common communicational technology in combination with an aesthetic framework to convey the results of an academic analysis. It is just a different language that I am trying to use, in contrast to what academics usually use.

Still, I think that there were a few basic guiding principles that I used. I wanted to stay away from the purely documenting approach. Because that would still be the common thing to do. Most academics, when they write articles and use photography in them, they use it in an illustrative way. I believe that we can use aesthetics, we can use form, we can use emotions, to convey a message, to communicate analysis. And we can use humour.

Yiannis: Yes, humour, I wanted to ask you about that.

Nico: Yes, of course. You can use humour for that. Humour is a legitimate communicational tool for analysis, although it is an incredibly difficult one, as one also needs to avoid that things become tacky or disrespectful. But in particular, I think that staying away from the documenting approach was important to me. I wanted to also allow the form, the way you actually capture the statue, the light, the angle, to play a role, but in alignment with the analysis. That made it slightly challenging for me, because I did not want to work with contradictions. That would have been a totally different project. I wanted to tell one story about this complexity of meaning (in relation to the statues) and I wanted to show the diversity of meanings, but I still wanted to tell that one story. I did not want to go for internal contradictions in my story. That would be different analysis and a different format.

What I was trying to do is to align the analysis with some of the formal components of photography. Trying, in some cases, to enhance some elements by using a close-up, or a particular framing... There is the photograph of the memorial to the missing in the Agios Alexandros church, with its many little wooden frames where the horizon is used as a formal method. You do not see the end of this dreadful list and collage of faces, it is endless. This photograph does not only show the way the pictures of the missing are displayed in a church in Pyrga, it also represents the societal debate – and comments on that debate – of the missing here in Cyprus. It is again an analysis communicated through that very formal aspect. The photograph refers to the fact that, sadly, these people are no longer there, they are beyond our horizon, but it also comments on the endlessness of the debate about them. Apparently, it has no end. Or better, it seems to have no closure, which is exactly one of the problems of this debate. This formal component

interacts with the more textual analysis, supported by other academic publications on this debate. But I try to symbolize my analysis. I think this is the best way I can summarize my work, as I am using these formal elements to symbolize an analysis and to symbolize societal processes through that analysis. I think that is what the exhibition tries to do.

Yiannis: It is important to know how to combine these photographs with the textual analysis and what meanings you want the visitors to understand, in a second reading or maybe in the first reading. Let me ask you this one thing, before we go to the second topic which is more sociology related. Having done the first exhibition in Nicosia and having received all the feedback from this exhibition... From the set-up in that space, in the Home for Cooperation in Nicosia, and the space you have created here in Limassol... How were the photographs organized and how is this different now?

Nico: One very quick comment is that there have been two exhibitions and that these are two totally different exhibitions. The spaces are completely different and I was... Actually you guessed what I was thinking about yesterday, I was looking at the main set-up and I was simply taken aback by the differences, generated by different lighting, a different way of organizing the pictures and the huge contextual difference between the two spaces, one in the Buffer Zone at the Ledra Palace crossing in Nicosia, and one in Limassol. And, again it is important to emphasize how the particular exhibition space influences the story that one tells. After all, it becomes a part of the medium. Actually, more correctly, the exhibition is a medium in itself. One of the things I have learned from this experience is how spectacular the impact of the exhibition space can be, and how you can use exhibition spaces in different ways to communicate your work.

One substantial difference, obviously, is that in the Limassol exhibition we are using the basement of the exhibition space as an opportunity to bring in the voices of others. What we have done in the basement of the NeMe Arts Centre is that we have created a series of listening posts. There, people can sit down on a bean bag, or at a table, and they can listen to different voices, discussing different dimensions of the exhibition, giving different perspectives on the object of the exhibition. Some of the debates that we organized in Nicosia in November 2015 have been recorded by the Cyprus Community Media Centre, and they are now being made available on the site of the exhibition. Also the seminar organized by NeMe in January 2016, recorded in by CUT-Radio, is being played in the basement. The idea behind that set-up – and I think that this is most important – is that it is not my voice only that matters. First of all, an exhibition is a collaboration. There are many wonderful people that worked with me, and that I worked with, in creating these exhibitions. But what the basement set-up is now communicating is that there are many voices to speak about the exhibition and its objects of analysis. There are many interpretations possible, also of the exhibition. What I do not want to do is to close off meanings. That is actually the last thing that I want to do. The space here, at the NeMe Arts Centre, is allowing me to emphasize that openness of interpretation much more than before. The interpretatory openness, not just of accepting or rejecting the invitations embodied by the statues in always particular ways but also of the photographs and the exhibition. The process of interpretation is something that I could emphasize much more by using the basement space at the NeMe Arts Centre.

At the same time, there are similarities between the two exhibitions. The set-up is still fairly linear, which is a debatable choice I made. The exhibition's narration is highly structured, probably because that is how I work and think. And it is actually translated into the exhibition. There is a linearity present in the exhibition that combines the textual (through the use of text panels) with photographs and that tries to create a trajectory within the exhibition space. A visitor goes through the different stages of the analysis. Both exhibitions had this idea of a clear starting point and ending point. Now, I do not think that a visitor is obliged to respect this built-in order. It is one of these debates in any kind of museum or exhibition set-up. How much do you expect visitors to follow a particular trajectory? There is often the tendency of museums and exhibitions to have signs like: "Start Here," "Walk This Way," "Exit," "Exhibition Continues Here,"… All these rather authoritarian signs force people to follow a particular trajectory. At least I was trying hard, to be a bit more open, and used the logics of the invitation here as well. But I am not going to claim that I was using the logic of the "1000 plateaus," allowing visitors to enter the exhibition at a thousand different entry point.[2] I would not have the audacity to make that claim. This exhibition does have different entry points, but it is still a fairly linear narration at the same time.

This raises all sorts of questions when we want to talk about which medium is actually more important. Is it the textual linearity that still matters most, in the end? Of course, the photographs are still involved, but what is dominant? Is it the multi-dimensionality of the photographs, that is actually dominating, where the picture literally attracts all the attention and where the written text on the panels, and the order of things, is just secondary? That I find a difficult debate, and I am not sure if I have clear answer to that question. It also depends on the visitor. Some like to be invited into that trajectory, to take the steps as I created them. But still, there is the back door, there are the different entry points, which I see as gates, into the exhibition. But I think that the exhibition's linearity is still pretty strongly present.

Yiannis: And at the same time you are creating an invitation which is more polite than the other invitations we were talking about before.

Nico: I definitely hope so. I think that any kind of project created by academics (as academics) has to be respectful. They can (and I would say: should) be critical but I believe they have to remain respectful. I do not think I would defend any kind of communicational activity that is disrespectful. I think that is for others, for other people, or for other roles. It definitely makes sense in some cases, but I would not be comfortable with using disrespect in an academic setting, which I think the exhibition is still part of.

Yiannis: Just to make a small comment, or two, about the monuments. From what I have seen, because I have had a sneak preview [*laughs*] ... You see the monuments as generators of audience satisfaction. That is your perspective, and that is your photography. Analysing this tendency of people to follow ideas, in order to get satisfied by certain values as these ideas can, for example, be called by the creators of these statues, by the state or by whoever has intervened to build and create these monuments.

Nico: That is a good comment. It is not an easy one to reply to. I would now be inclined to revert to some French theorists, which is maybe not the most polite thing to do [*laughs*].

Yiannis: The 6-year-old is already gone.

Nico: He ran away after the first sentence. [*Laughing*] There is the notion of interpellation, and that is what I think that different discourses actually do. They try to seduce us, they console us, they give us ways of being part of something. Discourses are very strong

forces because of that. They offer commonality and togetherness, they sometimes drive us to war because others have other commonalities. There is Sam Keen's quote: "In the beginning we create the enemy"; "We think others to death and then invent the battle-axe or the ballistic missiles with which to actually kill them." It shows us how strong these forces, these ideas, can be. We often forget the importance of ideas, not only (by the way) as lethal destructive forces but also as forces of goodness. "Values" is an old term; I prefer to use "discourses," but basically values are a sub-category of discourses, so let us stick to "values." These values can create togetherness, they can create solidarity, they can create equality, they can create democracy. But they can also create war and death. They can instigate them. They do have a key role to play in our societies, for the better or for the worse.

And yes, you are right, I was actually playing with these ideas in the photography and in the analysis, because what often happens in this kind of discursive struggles is that one particular idea, one particular perspective, gets privileged. And other perspectives therefore become eliminated. I feel uncomfortable with that, in particular when dealing with history. I like the diversity of ideas, and I do not like to have one particular mind-set, or one particular set of values to be imposed, becoming the dominant and only one. If we look at history because this is an exhibition about history, there is often this emphasis on glorification: On the glorification of the self, on the heroization of the self, where one party sees itself as good, where its (national) identity becomes articulated as an intrinsically good thing to have. This essentialist identity can then never be questioned, or even critiqued. I think it should be questioned and critiqued. Because the logics of glorification and heroization is concealing a lot of things. This is something that needs to be discussed more, and to be theorized much more.

That identity discourse is one reason why I am using photography to talk about these issues, as I want to show the restrictive workings of dominant nationalist identities. But there is more: we need to be careful not to enter into the glorification of war itself. This is something with which I am even more uncomfortable. I am open to discussions about diversity and about the ways that national identity tends to contradict diversity. But I am upset and troubled by the creation of military heroes, which supports the moral acceptance of war (or worse, its celebration). We should not go there.

There are a lot of question marks to be placed with these kinds of twentieth-century (and also nineteenth-, eighteenth-, seventeenth-century) memorials as they might convey an undesirable message. Should we not construct a different interpretation, allowing us to rethink these memorials, reconsidering and re-contextualizing them, because they literally celebrate death and destruction? There is a lot of academic and artistic work on this topic, all over the world. Obviously, Cyprus is not the only country that has issues with this. There is the wonderful analysis of Krzysztof Wodiczko, a Canadian-Polish artist, on the *Arc de Triomphe* (the Triumphal Arch) in Paris (France). If you start analysing what this particular memorial is actually convening, it turns out to be horrific. It is the purest celebration of militarism you can think of. Maybe we should not be doing these things. Maybe we should raise questions about these memorials, and maybe we should start looking at some of these statues and memorials as problematic, and in dire need of re-contextualization, exactly because of that.

Yiannis: And just to connect what you say with the whole spirit of this interview, it is all about the children that grow older and that become established members of society. It is they who are creating new images and ideas that construct a new reality. They have never lived through the times that these monuments refer to, even if the monuments that your photographs are referring to in this exhibition are quite recent. But children who are being raised today have not witnessed these events. Still, they cannot escape from seeing the statues every day, outside of the schools, going to honour the war heroes on every anniversary. Today should be about them. About their vision. And your photographs show that older generations are trying to push them in a particular direction...

Nico: And in that sense, these statues are pedagogical, to use a more neutral term. Or even better, they have a pedagogical dimension. The invitation is also pedagogical in the sense that what is typical for any kind of project like this is that it wants to transgress time. It does not want to speak about the now only. Memorials want to speak to the future. They want to convince you that the way of looking they embody is the right way. Not just now but also when you are looking at them in a later stage, looking back at the past. So, they play with time, in very particular ways, and sometimes in very troubling ways. We should not forget the very materiality of these statues. They are set in stone, in bronze. They are fixed. And they also try to fix the meaning of a particular time, through this logic of the invitation. At the same time, their context has changed. People changed, the times have changed. The interpretations have changed and will change even more. And, at some point in time, the invitation will no longer be accepted. It might not even be recognized anymore.

We can see this if you go back to the previous centuries, and I have been doing some research on older conflicts if you go back to, for instance, the seventeenth century. A few weeks ago, I was visiting a memorial in Prague (in the Czech Republic), with a group of university students. The memorial was commemorating a battle from the seventeenth century. Even if people have some knowledge about it, it is hard for them to contextualize it, and nobody has a strong emotional response to it anymore. It refers to the Thirty Years' War, which was one of the bloodiest wars in that period of our history. However lethal it was, it does not provoke much response anymore, because it is situated in the distant past. Its cruelty has been forgotten. There are other memorials where people are simply ignorant about their meaning and even their existence. They do not have the knowledge frameworks anymore to interpret them. The invitation is gone. It just disappeared, evaporated over time.

Even if this can sometimes be reassuring, it is not always a good thing either. Maybe we should not forget, after all, memorials are memories. But I do think that the pedagogical dimension is important if you talk about new generations of citizens. We have to think about what we want to communicate to them and what we want statues and commemoration sites to communicate to them. And this is not a question that stops. It is something that we need to revisit over and over again. As any pedagogical project, we need to think about what kind of story we want them to tell to us. Obviously, this is a very difficult thing to do and it requires a rather intensive reflection.

Yiannis: This also applies to the role of public space as a whole, if we connect what you now say with what we have discussed before.

Nico: We have this sort of hierarchy in our minds, which I find troubling. We believe that media (and nowadays the internet in particular) are the centre of our society. We watch television, we surf or we go on different social networks, and that is how we see and learn about our world. That is of course a myth. Discourses and ideologies work through the interactions of different spheres in our societies. But we

seem to cling to this hierarchy. Media are seen to be the top level of the work of discursive construction, and then, maybe, the role of the school, and maybe of religion, and then possibly public space is acknowledged. Public space dangles somewhere at the very end of this hierarchy. I think that this is wrong. We need to look at different communicational environments, not in hierarchy but in interaction. They work onto each other, they strengthen each other, they contradict each other but they still work with each other. Public space is crucial in that process of signification. We tend to forget this, because, of course, exactly the strength of public space is that it so naturalized. It is normal and unquestioned. If there is a statue there, it is normal that it is there, we do not even see it. If it disappears, we might notice that it is gone. But at the same time, it is a form of continuous communication. Even if you do not notice it, you notice.

Yiannis: A form of passive knowledge?

Nico: And a form that matters, I mean, in the sense that the public space can be a very strong communicational and pedagogical instrument of power. Again, in our hierarchy of the most important centres of discursive power, we tend to put the media first and forget about the rest. I think that this needs reconsidering. We have to be more careful and acknowledge that public space matters.

Yiannis: I want to end this conversation with one more question. How would you explain the concept of the exhibition to a 75-year-old Cypriot patriot? Someone with very patriotic feelings?

Nico: It is a rather good question, because it is a very difficult question. I am not sure if I can answer you, but let me try. Earlier, I talked about the need to be respectful and I want to use this idea as a starting point. There is a need to be respectful for the heroism of people. I definitely do not want to reject suffering, and I also do not want to reject courage and sacrifice.

Mind you, I have studied war, but I have not been in a war. Still, I might have a vague idea of the intensity of emotions, about the horrific things that happen in war, but also of the most wonderful things that sometimes happen. We should try to understand them in a respectful way. At the same time we need to think critically about the past. That would also be part of my response: Maybe some things from the past need to be revisited and rethought – with respect for the emotions of all involved, with respect for all sacrifices and losses, because war is about loss. But we should also use other values, like humanity, to look back at wars. Maybe also the value of togetherness. Maybe also the value of respect for diversity. I like to see the exhibition as an invitation to go back into the past and see that precious things were lost there. I also see the exhibition as an invitation to think about the future, to create a better and safer future. These losses do not have to occur again.

We should keep in mind that the experience of war changes people. War can create traumatized people that continue to live in the past for as long as they live. For understandable reasons – who am I to critique that? But war can also create visionaries for the future. Here, my cultural heritage matters, as I am a Belgian that knows about the impact of the First World War. War can create visionaries that say: "Never again." "Never again" is an incredibly important lesson that people have learned from the First World War (and from other wars) but that in Europe has been forgotten still too quickly, unfortunately. But the trauma of war can feed into different ways of thinking about conflict and war. Looking at the future, finding realistic ways to prevent this from ever happening again and maybe even helping others in other places in the world to prevent this from happening again should still be the most important focal point in our thinking about war, I think. That would be my answer to the patriot.

Communication, democracy and participation: An interview on *Diálogos*[3]

Interview: Fernando Oliveira Paulino
Transcription: Kirill Filimonov

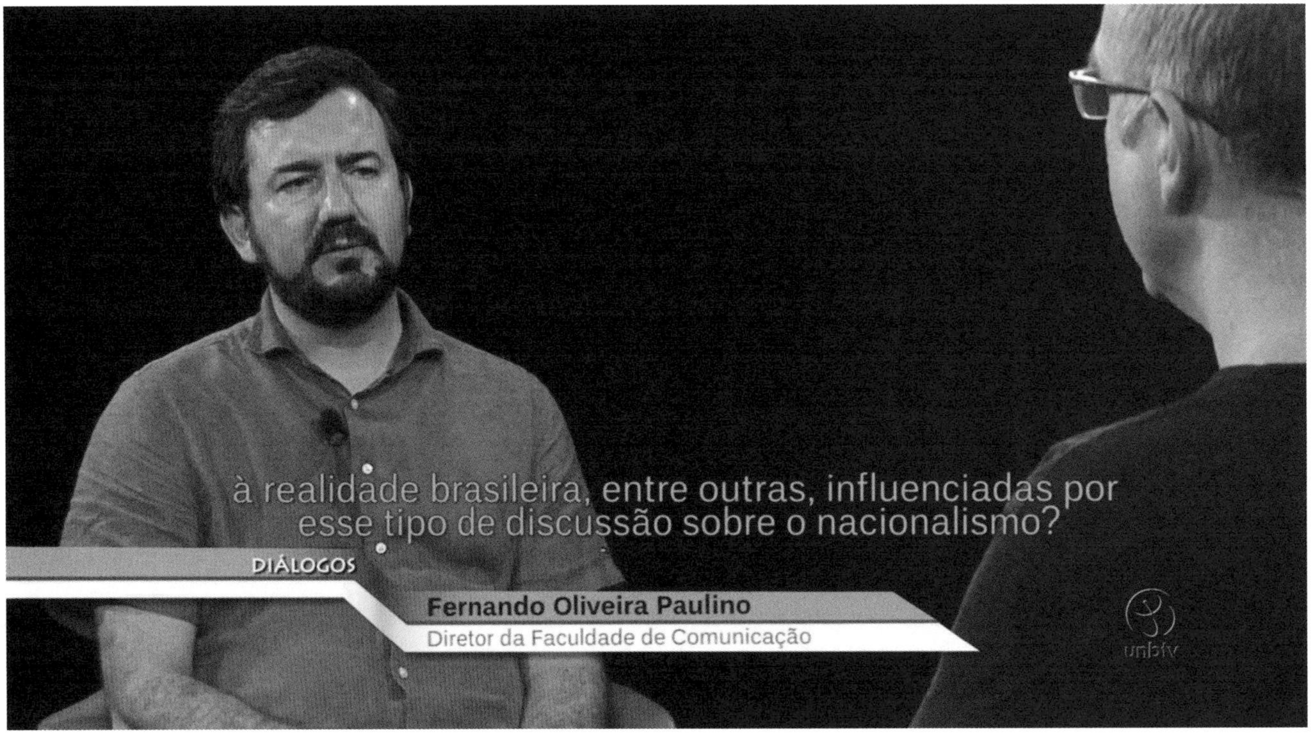

à realidade brasileira, entre outras, influenciadas por esse tipo de discussão sobre o nacionalismo?
DIÁLOGOS
Fernando Oliveira Paulino
Diretor da Faculdade de Comunicação
unbtv

Fernando Oliveira Paulino: Hi, we begin our program *Diálogos* here at the University of Brasilia TV. We are receiving today professor Nico Carpentier... with a career dedicated to themes like communication, participation and democracy. Nico is in Brasilia organizing an exhibition about Cyprus. Nico is [also] offering in this period here in Brazil three workshops related to this kind of discussions. Nico, could you please tell us about your exhibition and the research that you produced to organize the exhibition here?

Nico Carpentier: The exhibition, in a way, is about Cyprus, and in another way, it is not. And let me start with the last part: I think the exhibition deals with the role of nationalism and the role of antagonism in society. Actually, in different societies in the world. And what I try to do is to look at how nationalism and antagonism, the logics of conflict, the logics of the enemy, go into commemoration sites, go into statues... How these statues actually communicate nationalism, communicate the logics of heroism, the logics of war... And at the same time, I am also interested in how things sometimes go wrong with these statues, how the discourse does not come across, how there are contradictions... And sometimes, how there are counterhegemonic logics. How some statues tell very different stories. A story of peace. A story of tolerance. A story of diversity. And I think that that is a fairly universal story. But at the same time, it is about Cyprus. Every conflict is contextualized. So in the exhibition, you will find a lot of references to Cyprus, simply because the research is done in Cyprus, and it tells us a story about Cyprus, making it, on the one hand, a very global narrative but also a very local narrative. That is the very short version of the exhibition.

Fernando: Before talk[ing] more intensely about nationalism, could you please contextualize the Cyprus conflict and try to explain to Brazilian people the reality there?

Nico: If we have a few days, I will be happy to talk you through that, but I can also give you the very short version. It is a terribly complicated conflict which basically, at this point, boils down to the island being divided in two parts. In between is a Buffer Zone, which is a militarized/demilitarized area protected by the United Nations. In the north, we find Turkish Cypriots in non-recognized state, the Turkish Republic of Northern Cyprus. In the south, we find Greek Cypriots with the Republic of Cyprus, which is officially recognized. Now, the question "how did we get there?," how did the island get divided, is a very difficult question and the answer is very long. It has to do with different periods: the Ottoman period, it has to do with the British colonial period, it also has to do with the independence war in the 1950s, it has to do with the Turkish invasion in 1974. There is this immense series of conflicts that have driven the Cypriots to the divided island that we see now. But behind that, I would argue, we find two nationalisms: we find the Turkish nationalism and we find the Greek nationalism that is very much at the cause and at the core of what is called the Cyprus Problem.

Fernando: The importance of nationalism in its impacts, its subject related to conflicts around the world, not just in Cyprus. Right now we have [presidential] elections in Brazil. How is it possible to use the conclusions of your research in terms of Brazilian reality and in other realities influenced by this kind of discussions on nationalism?

Nico: We see nationalism on the rise in many different parts of the world, including Brazil, of course. And it is fascinating to see because I am not necessarily that much into this ideology myself, being a Belgian, having grown up in a very complicated country that has a very difficult relationship to nationalism. I have my own perspectives. But it is also important to say that there is not necessarily something terribly wrong with nationalism in itself. It becomes deeply problematic, though, if it becomes antagonistic nationalism, if it becomes a violent form of nationalism. Nationalism is always based on the idea that there is an Other, that there is somebody outside the nation that is different from us, from the self. But if we want to destroy that Other, if we want to use violence to expel the Other, to remove the Other, then we go into a very tricky area. My sense with nationalism is that it is like a sleeping dragon. If it sleeps, if it is calm, there is no issue, but if the dragon wakes up, it is a terribly destructive force. And I think that, also in Brazil, is a key idea to keep in mind.

Cyprus is a very grim warning sign. It is a terrible story about loss, about destruction, about suffering that has been going on for decades. People lost their lives, they lost their houses, some of their family members went missing for decades. It is a terrible story that was driven by these two nationalisms, that turned out to be [forms of] antagonistic nationalism. And that is a warning, and in that sense the Cypriot case is a very, very sad story. There is lots of sympathy with me with Cypriots for having been put through this. But at the same time, it is like a sign that we need to understand and that we need to learn about, also to bring it to our own countries and to avoid falling into these traps. Once you go on to the road of destructive nationalism, of antagonistic nationalism, it is very hard to turn back. That is also something that the Cypriot case teaches us. They have been stuck in this Cyprus Problem for decades, for 60–70 years, and they have been negotiating for 60–70 years, just simply unable to overcome this nationalism. And that is a lesson to remember, right? Once you go into these violent logics, you create scars, you create traumas. They are very difficult to heal. They do not stop when people die; they are being passed on to their children. And it is a process that will take several decades more to heal, if it will heal at all. And that is something I think that we all need to remember.

Fernando: The exhibition you have created is not just to register but also to discuss the celebrations of war and the possible celebrations of a culture of peace. How is it possible to create a space to celebrate, discuss and stimulate this culture of peace?

Nico: There are different ways of doing that. Actually organizing these kind of critiques – because the exhibition is still a critique towards antagonistic nationalism – organizing these critiques is one strategy; I think it is an important strategy. Rethinking how, for instance, conflict is memorialized, how it is condensed into statues, into commemoration sites, is a very, very important thing. We need to reflect about these things. And we will continuously need to reflect about them. That is one thing.

The second is a reinterpretation. It is not just critique; it is actually giving new meanings to these statues. Sometimes you need to say, "This person was actually not a hero, it was actually somebody that did awful things. And maybe we should re-contextualize and reinterpret that." So having these statues there is also a wonderful opportunity to start thinking about your past. And the Belgian example – outside the exhibition – Leopold the Second who did terrible things in the Belgian Congo has lots of statues in Belgium. And it is actually a way that allows Belgians to reflect about this and to critique it and sometimes to ask for them to be demolished. That is a second strategy.

But I think that the third strategy is not used enough, and that is the creation of these heroes of peace. We always think about heroes, actually, in very negative terms: in terms of war, in terms of achievements that were not always that civil. And we need to rethink what the hero is and how we commemorate the hero. And I think having more attention for people that did wonderful things, that in very difficult circumstances were very courageous by *not* joining the people that called for death and destruction, but by trying to resist that, trying to show the humanity in the Other. I think we need to celebrate these people more, and these organizations more, and these phases much more. And I think there we need to do a lot of work, not just in Cyprus, but I think this is, again, the global and the universal need to bring out more attention for these heroes of peace.

Fernando: The exhibition reflects your research about communication, history and memory in Cyprus. One of your workshops here has this theme: How is it possible to construct exhibitions, to communicate academic research? How is it possible for the Brazilian [academic] community to organize exhibitions using your methodology, what kind of tips [would] you offer to the university community here to make this kind of exhibition?

Nico: It is a difficult question, because as academics – and actually we also teach that to our students – we like to write, we like the written text so much. It is very much at the heart of what academia is about, and it should be. I am not going to argue against the importance of writing; I think this is an achievement and we should protect it at all cost.

What I am arguing for is that we need to complement that with other ways of communicating research. And the visual is one, the exhibition is another. There have been quite a number of people that have been working in the area of what is called arts-based research. And that refers to research that uses the arts to organize reflection, to organize knowledge production. It is not just a way of communicating, It is actually a way of integrating artistic practice in knowledge production itself. And you can do that with poetry, you can do that with dance. There are really interesting examples of people that try to push the limits of what academic knowledge production and the condensation in text actually means. I think there are two lessons and two hints, or two ideas. One is creativity. Academics can be

extremely creative. We are actually creative in writing and in doing research. We can also be creative in using other repertoires, like an artistic repertoire in communicating our knowledge. And actually using that communication to further reflect on our knowledge at the same time. So allowing us to be creative and not becoming too rigidly locked into academic tradition is one thing that I think we need to do.

The other is to maintain control. And this brings us to the discussion on science communication. In a lot of cases we will find discussions about outreach. And then often people tell us, "Oh you need to write an opinion piece, that is really important." What the exhibition actually does, it allows me to communicate to an outside world, to reach audiences that with academic written texts I could never reach. But it also allows me to maintain control. I am not giving this to somebody else to edit. It is my own project, and it is my writing. Writing with an exhibition, as an exhibition. So finding this balance of maintaining control and allowing yourself to be creative, I think that is the road. A lot of people – I am not the only one – a lot of people have been doing that, have been writing about that and have been developing strategies and ideas about that, so I do not want to claim in any way that I am the first to do that. But it is an incredible liberating and a wonderful experience to try, so my basic piece of advice can be summarized in three letters: try.

Fernando: In terms of the academic production, Nico, there is discussion in Brazil and around the world about parameters to evaluate the academic production. One exhibition, like our exhibition, sometimes does not have the same recognition as a paper or a lot of papers. And you follow the movement nowadays related to slow science. In your opinion, how is it possible to improve the evaluation system in terms of recognizing this kind of academic productions, not just in papers and written texts?

Nico: This is an uphill battle, as they call it; it is a very difficult struggle. If you focus on the first part of your question, the idea of having these kinds of experiments recognized as academic work, to be entered into the databases is one part, and that has been a very difficult thing. But actually in the three universities where I am involved – in Uppsala, but also in Brussels and in Charles University in the Czech Republic – at least the databases have been adjusted to allow for the simple input, the registration of these events. So we have achieved quite something there. At least it can be counted.

But then – and that is the second part of the question – we have to ask ourselves: But should these things be counted? The quantitative, Is that the way to talk about our work? Is it just by saying, "Wonderful, I did three exhibitions, five books, three papers and possibly 25 articles, I have a wonderful career"? That does not make sense. Because it could be a terrible paper. It could actually be a terrible paper that everybody quotes, so that your citation index goes up, but it does not mean anything. It is the content that has meaning, and if we are going to evaluate and be evaluated, we should look at content. And then we go to slow science. Because what is that evaluation? Are we going to force people to publish more and more and more? More and more brilliant work or more and more mediocre work? Is it really about more or do we need to put a threshold? Do we need to say, "If you have done this in a year, it is really okay"? Then you have done your best. So slow science is very much about that. Also when it comes to these evaluations, it is about saying, "Let us stop here." If you have reached that level, you are good. You do not have to do more. If you want to, fine. But *that* is sufficient. I think as academics, we need to be excellent. I think that is crucial. But there is a difference between excellence and perfection. And sometimes we are being pushed over this edge of excellence into areas that are incredibly destructive. That

actually also works against the quality of our own work. And saying, "Stop, this is enough, this is good enough," is something we need to learn – because we are our own worst enemies – but also that our management needs to learn and the political responsibilities need to be adjusted also to deal with that.

So there is a lot to be said on academic reform in the long term and how we evaluate our work. The quantity and the quality of our work is a crucial component. But what is maybe even more important – and that brings me back to the exhibition – we need to find pleasure in our work. Because what I see with a lot of academics is that they become machines. They produce. They are like *Modern Times*, the famous Charlie Chaplin film where the hammer just hits the object at the regular interval, because you are working for – and being incorporated in – a capitalist industry. That is not what we want and that is what we should resist at all time. The answer to that is to find pleasure in what we do, but pleasure that is not destructive, pleasure that is also not destructive towards others that work with us, but pleasure that is genuine. And that also relates to organizing an exhibition and just taking time to talk to visitors about your work. And if that is one person coming there, that is fine. If it is twenty, that is fine too. But it is a matter of pleasure, I think. For me, slow science is about the rediscovery of pleasure.

Fernando: Nico, we have just [a bit of] time to listen to you talk about the next steps about communication and participation research, developed by you or other colleagues. What is your opinion about the future of this kind of histories?

Nico: I think at this stage there are a couple of weird things happening. Because honestly, I think the logics of participation itself is under threat. We see a lot of emphasis on the dangers of participation. Fake news discussions, for instance, are very much about these ordinary people that are not trustworthy in producing news. So we should be very careful now to avoid that this entire debate actually backfires and starts labelling participation, in the media field at least, as something problematic.

We also see in the world a much more authoritarian tendency. Knowing some of Brazilian candidates [for the Brazilian presidential elections], I think there is also quite some concern here. We need to be careful to protect this field of participation and we need to argue much better why participation matters. We have always… In participation studies, we have taken for granted that participation is relevant and important and desirable, but we have never taken the time, at least not sufficiently, to argue why it is relevant, why it is desirable. And as a defence of these new tendencies, I think that it is our job now to be very explicit: participation matters, yes, but for a series of reasons, because it generates public happiness, I would say, in a nutshell. But we need to find a ground, and much better normative ground, to talk about participation in the future.

Controvérsias Iconoclásticas em Brasilia[4]

A film by Nico Carpentier

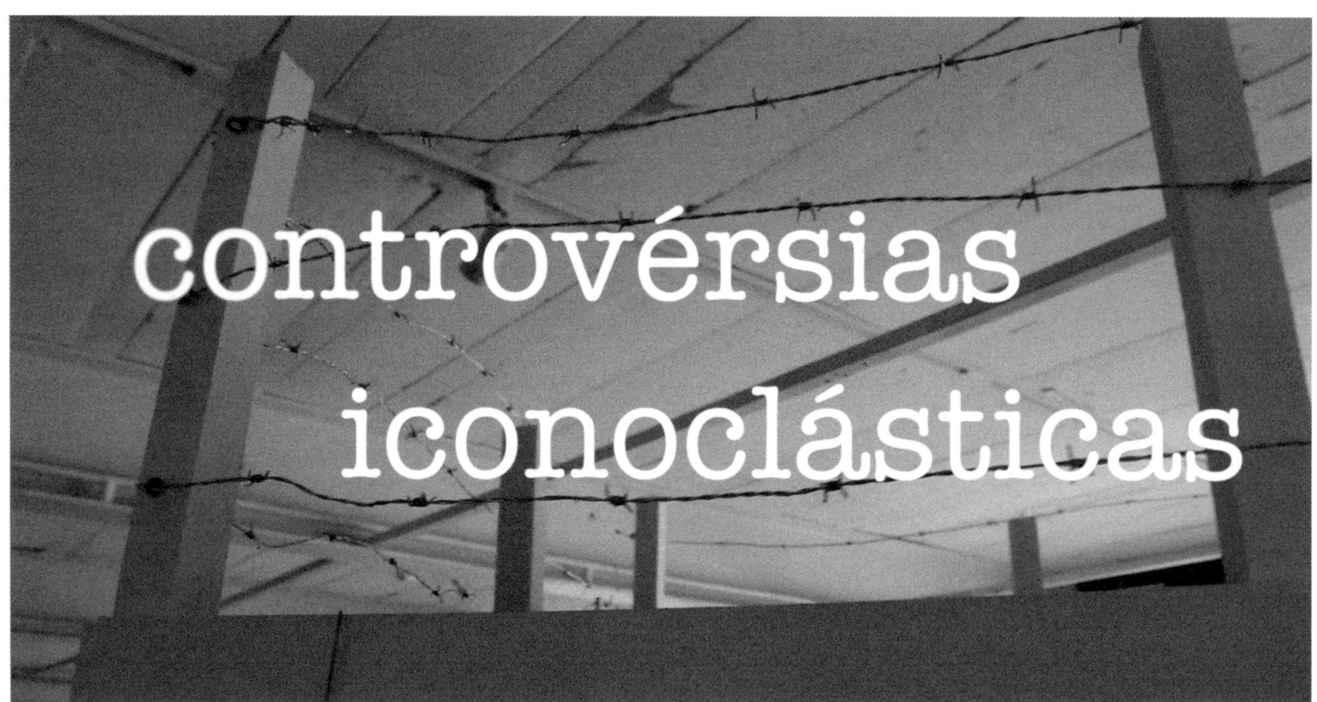

Nico Carpentier: The Art and Science of Peace[5]

A film by Fernando Molina
Transcription: Nico Carpentier

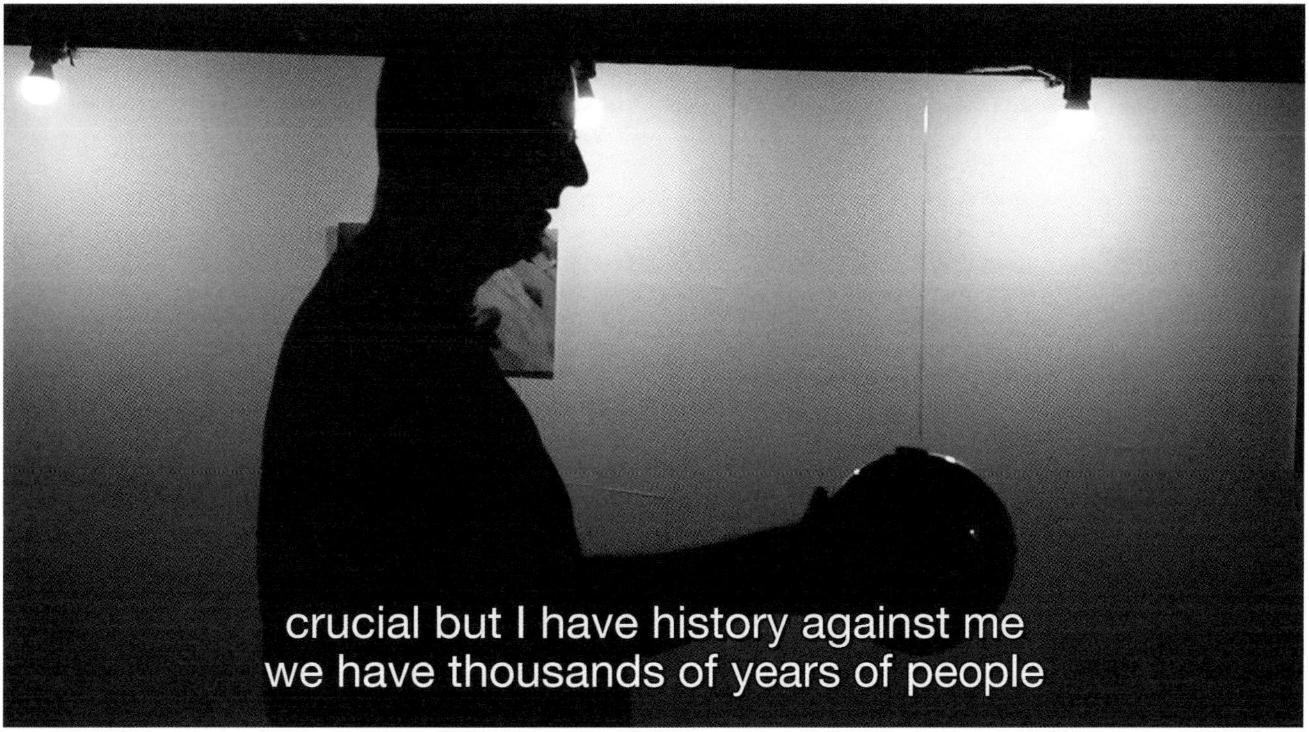

We need to find pleasure in our work. Because what I see with a lot of academics is that they become machines. As academics, and actually we also teach that to our students, we like the written text so much. It is very much at the heart of what academia is about. And it should be. What I am arguing for is that we have to complement that with other ways of communication research. And the visual is one. The exhibition is another.

There have been quite a number of people that have been working in the area of what is called arts-based research. That is research that uses the arts to organize reflection, to organize knowledge production... It is not just a way of communicating; it is actually a way of integrating artistic practice in knowledge production. We are actually creative in writing and doing research. We can also be creative in using other repertoires, such as an artistic repertoire, in communicating our knowledge, and actually using that communication to further reflect on our knowledge at the same time. What the exhibition actually does is that it allows me to communicate to an outside world, to reach audiences that, with academic research, I could never reach.

The exhibition, in a way, is about Cyprus, and in another way, it is not. And let me start with the last part: I think the exhibition deals with the role of nationalism, and the role of antagonism in society. Actually, in different societies in the world. And what I try to do, is to look at how nationalism and antagonism, the logics of conflict, the logics of the enemy, go into commemoration sites, go into statues... How these statues actually communicate nationalism, communicate the logics of heroism, the logics of war... (footage from *Diálogos*)

And at the same time, I am also interested in how things sometimes go wrong with these statues, how the discourse does not come across, how there are contradictions... And sometimes,

how there are counterhegemonic logics. How some statues tell very different stories. A story of peace. A story of tolerance. A story of diversity. And I think that that is a fairly universal story. But at the same time, it is about Cyprus. Every conflict is contextualized. So in the exhibition, you will find a lot of references to Cyprus, simply because the research is done in Cyprus, and it tells us a story about Cyprus, making it on the one hand a very global narrative, but also a very local narrative. (footage from *Diálogos*)

The exhibition is called *Iconoclastic Controversies* because it is exactly referring to these – literally – struggles over our memory. Memory is not stable. Memory is something that is constructed.

When we talk about war, we talk about the enemy, we talk about destroying the other, we talk about defining the other as radically different, through various antagonisms. But there are other ways of thinking about the other; for instance, there are ways of thinking about the other as being part of conflict, but not as the enemy, but as the adversary. Thinking about the other as other, but still respecting the political space that both parties are embedded in, and that is called agonism.

And we need to rethink what the hero is and how we commemorate the hero. And I think that having more attention for people that did wonderful things, that in very difficult circumstances were very courageous, not by joining the people that called for death and destruction, but by trying to resist that. Trying to show the humanity in the other. I think we need to celebrate these people more, and these organizations more.

We can do things differently; there are other ways of dealing with conflict: Agonistic ways, ways that are based on brotherhood, sisterhood, friendship... There are many different ways of dealing with conflict, and we need to move away from, on the one hand, violence, war, enemies, and we need to move towards respecting diversity, dealing with adversaries, but in a democratic and peaceful way. I think we can get there by changing the way we think, which is quite ambitious. We get there by trying to redefine what conflict is.

One of the mistakes we have made in the past, I think, is that we created a dichotomy. Either you have peace, or you have conflict. And what I argue is: We need to understand that we can have conflict and peace together. But not violent conflict. But still conflict. And I think that understanding that, learning from that, is crucial. But... I have history against me. We have thousands of years of people selecting options that are based in violent conflict. So, I can say whatever I say, but history works against me.

NOTES

1. https://www.mixcloud.com/cutradio952/iconoclastic-controversies-nico-carpentier-interview/.
2. In the case of the third *Iconoclastic Controversies* exhibition, much more care was spent on providing multiple entry points and trajectories for the visitors.
3. https://www.youtube.com/watch?v=iDyOq_0GLyI.
4. https://player.vimeo.com/video/290606097.
5. https://youtu.be/COXCZ5sbzN8.

Acknowledgements

The Iconoclastic Controversies project and publication benefitted from the support of a wide variety of people and organizations. First, there were the three exhibition-organizing teams, which consisted of Vaia Doudaki, Yiannis Christidis, Fatma Nazli Köksal, Eva Giannoukou, Stella Theocharous, Helene Black, Yiannis Colakides, Marina Simon, Jairo Faria, Fernando Oliveira Paulino, Liziane Guazina and Rose May Carneiro.

The key exhibition partners were the Association for Historical Dialogue and Research (AHDR), the Home for Cooperation (H4C), the Cyprus Community Media Centre (CCMC), NeMe and the University of Brasília (with the Faculties of Communication and Architecture). Further institutional support, in different stages of the project and publication, came from the Vrije Universiteit Brussel, Uppsala University, Charles University, the Research Foundation – Flanders (FWO), the Fundacao Universidade de Brasília, the Public Art of Cyprus database, Cost Action 18136, the NGO SQRIDGE and Mistra, the Swedish Foundation for Strategic Environmental Research, through the research programme Mistra Environmental Communication.

Also, the editorial teams of the journals (*Comunicazioni Sociali* and the *International Journal of Communication*) and publishers (Peter Lang, Berghahn, Vita e Pensiero and Intellect) merit my gratitude.

Special thanks go out to the members of the organizing teams (and in particular to Vaia, Helene, the two Yiannis (Christidis and Colakides), Jairo and Fernando), Orestis Tringides (CCMC and much more) and Fernando Molina. In addition, thanks to: 6x6 Centre for Photography, Adamylson Madeira, Alex Calheiros, Ana Beatriz Lemos, Andreas Paraschos, Angeliki Gazi, Aysu Arsoy, Bruno Bernardes, Carol Calmon, Chris Santos, Christiana Voniati, Christophoros Christophorou, Christos Mais, Chrystalleni Loizidou, Cora Chaibub Paulino, Daniel Caixeta, Derya Yüksek, Despo Pasia, Dimitra Milioni, Duda Bentes, Edielton Paulo, Eirini Avraam, Elton Bruno Pinheiro, Fábio Henrique Pereira, Fabíola Calazans, Fernanda Martinelli, Frank Lopes, Gabriella Negreiros, Galeria Ponto, Guilherme Strozi, Hakan Karahasan, Hazal Yolga, Herllon Novais, Ivoneide Brito, João Curvello, José Manoel Morales Sánchez, Josianne Diniz, Juliana Rochet, Julio, Kanali 6, Karin Nys, Kirill Filimonov, Laura Martínez Águila, Lilian Fernanda Souza Silva, Lorena Costa, Luana Melo, Lucas Moraes, Luma Poletti Dutra, M. P. L. Modern Productions LTD, Marcelo Feijó, Maria Conceição, Mariana Santos, Marios Shakides, Marisa Sanches Faria, Mehmet Adil, Michael Simopoulos, Monsieur Doumani, Nadia Kornioti, Neuza Meller, Nicolas (our one-day driver when our car broke down on a field trip in the Machairas Mountains), Nicolas Tsapatsoulis, Nikolaos Stelya, Nicoletta Demetriou, Panarod Management LTD, Pedro Russi, Raimundo Nonato Araújo Nascimento, Raimundo Pereira Lima, Regina Lúcia Oliveira, Renata Gomes, Reyhan Sabri, Rosa Helena Santos, Sevgül Uludağ, Shirin Jetha, Sivaldo Pereira, Soemes Barbosa, Stavros Anastasiou, Stelios Pellaras, Stelios Stylianou, Tao Papaioannou, Thaïs de Mendonça Jorge, the Camassa Touch LTD, Theopisti Stylianou-Lambert, Tony Maslic, Vasiliki Triga, Vassos Stylianou, Veerle De Pooter, Venetia Papa, Vicky Karaiskou, Wagner Rizzo, Yorgos Zotos, Zehra Azizbeyli, Wallas Silva and whoever I may have forgotten to include in this list.

Appendix 1: Overview of Interviews and Broadcasts by Project Partners about the Two Exhibitions in Cyprus

- Interview with Nico Carpentier, by Eva Giannoukou on 8 October 2015

- Interview with Nico Carpentier and Vaia Doudaki, by Orestis Tringides on 12 November 2015 in Downtown Choris Bakira on MYCYradio

- Interview with Nico Carpentier and Andreas Papallas, by Orestis Tringides on 16 November 2015 in Downtown Choris Bakira on MYCYradio

- Interview with Yiorgos Kakouris, by Orestis Tringides on 18 November 2015 in Downtown Choris Bakira on MYCYradio

- Exhibition report, by Orestis Tringides on 22 December 2015 in Downtown Choris Bakira on MYCYradio. Rebroadcasts on 29 December 2015 and on 5 January 2016

- Seminar 1, "Monuments and Memories," organized by AHDR. Recording by Orestis Tringides, broadcast on 23 December 2015 in Downtown Choris Bakira on MYCYradio. Rebroadcasts on 30 December 2015 and on 6 January 2016

- Seminar 2, "Covering the Cyprus Conflict," organized by CCMC. Recording by Orestis Tringides, broadcast on 24 December 2015 in Downtown Choris Bakira on MYCYradio. Rebroadcasts on 31 December 2015 and on 7 January 2016

- Exhibition review, by Orestis Tringides on 28 December 2015 in Downtown Choris Bakira on MYCYradio. Rebroadcasts on 4 January 2016 and on 12 January 2016

- Seminar, "Monuments and Memorials as Rhetoric/ Objectivity as Male," organized by NeMe on 23 January 2016. Recording by Yiannis Christidis and CUT-Radio

- Interview with Nico Carpentier, by Yiannis Christidis on 23 January 2016 on CUT-Radio

- Interview with Pavlos Vrionides, by Yiannis Christidis on 1 February 2016 on CUT-Radio

Appendix 2: Media That Covered the Two Exhibitions in Cyprus

Arts website
www.rhizome.org

Blog
www.allonan.com
www.michalbrzezinski.org

Events website
AngloInfo Cyprus
www.callupcontact.com
www.cyprusevents.net
www.roundtown.com
www.timeoutcyprus.com

Facebook
Embassy of Belgium in Greece and Cyprus
Open University of Cyprus

LinkedIn
Open University of Cyprus

Newspaper
Afrika
Halkin Sesi
Haravgi
Havadis
I Mahi
Kibris
Phileleftheros

Politis
Star Kibris
Yenidüzen

Online medium
I foni tis Lemesou
www.betweencut.com
www.cyprus-mail.com
www.dialogos.com.cy
www.gazete360.com
www.gundemkibris.com
www.haberalkibrisli.net
www.in-cyprus.com
www.paideia-news.com
www.parathyro.com
www.turkajansikibris.net

Online newspaper
www.philenews.com
www.politis.com.cy
www.yeniduzen.com

Political website
www.thecypriotpuzzle.org

Professional association website
www.euroclio.eu

References

Abousnnouga, Gill and Machin, David (2013), *The Language of War Monuments*, London: Bloomsbury.

Akgün, Mensur, Gürel, Ayla, Hatay, Mete and Tiryaki, Sylvia (2005), *Quo Vadis Cyprus?*, Istanbul: Tesev.

Akgün, Sibel (2012), "The manner of implementation of Britain's colonial administration policy in Cyprus: The Legislative Council," *TODAIE's Review of Public Administration*, 6:4, pp. 99–128.

Alter, Nora M. (2018), "Introduction," in Nora M. Alter (ed.), *The Essay Film after Fact and Fiction*, New York: Columbia University Press, pp. 1–29.

Anastasiou, Harry (2008a), *The Broken Olive Branch: Nationalism, Ethnic Conflict, and the Quest for Peace in Cyprus. Volume 1: The Impasse of Ethnonationalism*, Syracuse: Syracuse University Press.

Anastasiou, Harry (2008b), *The Broken Olive Branch: Nationalism, Ethnic Conflict, and the Quest for Peace in Cyprus. Volume 2: Nationalism Versus Europeanization*, Syracuse: Syracuse University Press.

Anastasiou, Maria (2007), "The institutionalization of protracted ethnic conflicts. A discourse analysis of 'the Cyprus Problem,'" unpublished Ph.D. thesis, Columbia: University of South Carolina.

Anderson, Benedict (2006), *Imagined Communities: Reflections on the Origin and Spread of Nationalism*, London: Verso.

Anthias, Floya and Ayres, Ron (1983), "Ethnicity and class in Cyprus," *Race & Class*, 25:1, pp. 59–76.

Asmussen, Jan (2006), "Dark-skinned Cypriots will not be accepted! Cypriots in the British army (1939–1945)," in Hubert Faustman and Nicos Peristianis (eds), *Britain in Cyprus. Colonialism and Post-Colonialism 1878–2006*, Mannheim and Möhnsee: Bibliopolis, pp. 167–85.

Asmussen, Jan (2011), "Conspiracy theory and Cypriot history: The comfort of commonly perceived enemies," *Cyprus Review*, 23:2, pp. 127–45.

Aspers, Patrik and Corte, Ugo (2019), "What is qualitative in qualitative research," *Qualitative Sociology*, 42:2, pp. 139–60.

Attfield, Judith (2000), *Wild Things: The Material Cultures of Everyday Life*, Oxford: Berg.

Barone, Tom (2008), "Creative nonfiction and social research," in J. Gary Knowles and Ardra L. Cole (eds), *Handbook of the Arts in Qualitative Research*, London: Sage, pp. 105–15.

Barthes, Roland (1974), *S/Z*, Malden, MA: Blackwell.

Baruh, Lemi and Popescu, Mihaela (2008), "Guiding metaphors of nationalism: The Cyprus issue and the construction of Turkish national identity in online discussions," *Discourse & Communication*, 2:1, pp. 79–96.

Bateson, Gregory and Mead, Margaret (1942), *Balinese Character: A Photographic Analysis*, New York: New York Academy of Sciences.

Bazerman, Charles (1988), *Shaping Written Knowledge: The Genre and Activity of the Experimental Article in Science*, Madison, WI: University of Wisconsin Press.

Bergh, Arild and Sloboda, John (2010), "Music and art in conflict transformation: A review," *Music and Arts in Action*, 2:2, pp. 2–17, http://musicandartsinaction.net/index.php/maia/article/view/conflicttransformation. Accessed 1 November 2020.

Billig, Michael (1995), *Banal Nationalism*, London: Sage.

Bishop, Claire (2005), *Installation Art: A Critical History*, London: Tate.

Blundell, Tom (2017), "Protein crystallography and drug discovery: Recollections of knowledge exchange between academia and industry," *IUCrJ*, 4, pp. 308–21.

Borgman, Jessie C. (2019), "Dissipating hesitation: Why online instructors fear multimodal assignments and how to overcome the fear," in Santosh Khadka and J. C. Lee (eds), *Bridging the Multimodal Gap: From Theory to Practice*, Louisville: Utah State University Press, pp. 43–65.

Breton, Albert (1964), "The economics of nationalism," *Journal of Political Economy*, 72:4, pp. 376–86.

Brewer, David (2010), *Greece. The Hidden Centuries. Turkish Rule from the Fall of Constantinople to Greek Independence*, London: I. B. Tauris.

Broome, Benjamin J. (2005), *Building Bridges across the Green Line. A Guide to Intercultural Communication in Cyprus*, Nicosia: United Nations Development Programme.

Bryant, Chris (2003), "Does Australia need a more effective policy of science communication?," *International Journal of Parasitology*, 33, pp. 357–61.

Bryant, Rebecca (2004), *Imagining the Modern. The Cultures of Nationalism in Cyprus*, London and New York: I. B. Tauris.

Bryant, Rebecca (2007), "Disciplining ethnicity and citizenship in colonial Cyprus," in Veronique Benei (ed.), *Manufacturing Citizenship: Education and Nationalism in Europe, South Asia and China*, London: Routledge, pp. 104–25.

Bryant, Rebecca (2012), "The fractures of a struggle? Remembering and forgetting Erenköy," in Rebecca Bryant and Yiannis Papadakis (eds), *Cyprus and the Politics of Memory. History, Community and Conflict*, London: I. B. Tauris, pp. 168–94.

Burns, Terry W., O'Connor, D. John and Stocklmayer, Susan M. (2003), "Science communication: A contemporary definition," *Public Understanding of Science*, 12, pp. 183–202.

Byford-Jones, Wilfred (1959), *Grivas and the Story of EOKA*, London: Robert Hale.

Calame, Jon and Charlesworth, Esther (2011), *Divided Cities: Belfast, Beirut, Jerusalem, Mostar, and Nicosia*, Philadelphia: University of Pennsylvania Press.

Canan-Sokullu, Ebru (2013), *Debating Security in Turkey: Challenges and Changes in the Twenty-First Century*, Boulder: Rowman and Littlefield.

Capous-Desyllas, Moshoula and Morgaine, Karen (2018), "Preface," in Moshoula Capous-Desyllas and Karen Morgaine (eds), *Creating Social Change through Creativity: Anti-Oppressive Arts-Based Research Methodologies*, Basingstoke: Palgrave Macmillan, pp. vii–xix.

Carpentier, Nico (2014), "Beeldenstrijd in Cyprus: Het problematische herdenken van een conflictueus verleden" ("Iconoclastic controversies in Cyprus: The problematic rethinking of a conflicteous past"), *nY*, 24, pp. 129–68.

Carpentier, Nico (2017), *The Discursive-Material Knot: Cyprus in Conflict and Community Media Participation*, New York: Peter Lang.

Carpentier, Nico (2018a), "Deconstructing nationalist assemblages. A visual essay on the Greek Cypriot memorials related to two violent conflicts in 20th century Cyprus," *Comunicazioni Sociali*, 1, pp. 33–49.

Carpentier, Nico (2018b), "Iconoclastic Controversy in Cyprus. The problematic rethinking of a conflicted past," in Vaia Doudaki and Nico Carpentier (eds), *Cyprus and Its Conflicts: Representations, Materialities and Cultures*, New York: Berghahn, pp. 25–54.

Carpentier, Nico (2019), "Memorialization, participation and self-representation: Remembering refugeedom in the Cypriot village of Dasaki Achnas," in Tanja Thomas, Merle-Marie Kruse and Miriam Stehling (eds), *Media and Participation in Post-Migrant Societies*, Lanham: Rowman and Littlefield, pp. 197–219.

Carpentier, Nico (ed.) (2019), *Respublika! Experiments in the Performance of Participation and Democracy*, Limassol, Cyprus: NeMe.

Carpentier, Nico (2020), "Communicating academic

knowledge beyond the written academic text: An autoethnographic analysis of the mirror palace of democracy installation experiment," *International Journal of Communication*, 14, pp. 2120–43.

Carpentier, Nico, Doudaki, Vaia, Christidis, Yiannis and Köksal, Fatma Nazli (2018), "De-naturalizing antagonistic nationalism through an academic intervention: The reception of two photography exhibitions on the memorialization of the Cyprus Problem," *Comunicazioni Sociali*, 1, pp. 50–67.

Chaplin, Elizabeth (1994), *Sociology and Visual Representation*, London: Routledge.

Chapman, Owen and Sawchuk, Kim (2015), "Creation-as-research: Critical making in complex environments," *RACAR: Revue d'art Canadienne/Canadian Art Review*, 40:1, pp. 49–52.

Charalambous, Giorgos and Ioannou, Gregoris (2015), "No bridge over troubled waters: The Cypriot left in government, 2008–2013," *Capital & Class*, 39:2, pp. 265–86.

Christophorou, Christophoros, Şahin, Sanem and Pavlou, Synthia (2010), *Media Narratives, Politics and the Cyprus Problem. Report 1*, Oslo: Peace Research Institute Oslo.

Cobain, Ian (2012), *Cruel Britannia: A Secret History of Torture*, London: Portobello Books.

Collins, Samuel Gerald, Durington, Matthew and Gill, Harjant (2017), "Multimodality: An invitation," *American Anthropologist*, 119:1, pp. 142–53.

Connor, Walker (1978), "A nation is a nation, is a state, is an ethnic group is a …," *Ethnic and Racial Studies*, 1:4, pp. 377–400.

Constandinos, Andreas (2012), *The Cyprus Crisis. Examining the Role of the British and American Governments During 1974*, Plymouth: University of Plymouth Press.

Constantinou, Costas M. and Papadakis, Yiannis (2002), "The Cypriot state(s) in situ. Cross-ethnic contact and the discourse of recognition," in Thomas Diez (ed.), *The European Union and the Cyprus Conflict: Modern Conflict, Postmodern Union*, Manchester: Manchester University Press, pp. 73–97.

Cooperman, Hilary (2018), "Listening through performance: Identity, embodiment, and arts-based research," in Moshoula Capous-Desyllas and Karen Morgaine (eds), *Creating Social Change through Creativity: Anti-Oppressive Arts-Based Research Methodologies*, Basingstoke: Palgrave Macmillan, pp. 19–35.

Cope, Bill and Kalantzis, Mary (2009), "'Multiliteracies': New literacies, new learning," *Pedagogies: An International Journal*, 4:3, pp. 1–30.

Council of the European Union (2006), *Council Regulation (EC) No 389/2006 of 27 February 2006 Establishing an Instrument of Financial Support for Encouraging the Economic Development of the Turkish Cypriot Community and Amending Council Regulation (EC) No 2667/2000 on the European Agency for Reconstruction*, Brussels: European Council, http://eur-lex.europa.eu/legal-content/EN/TXT/?uri=CELEX:32006R0389. Accessed 1 November 2020.

Crouzet, François (1973), *Le Conflit de Chypre 1946–1959* ('The conflict of Cyprus 1946–1959'), Bruxelles: Établissements Émile Bruylant.

Cvitanovic, Christopher, Hobday, Alistair J., van Kerkhoff, Lorrae, Wilson, Shaun K., Dobbs, Kirstin and Marshall, Nadine A. (2015), "Improving knowledge exchange among scientists and decisionmakers to facilitate the adaptive governance of marine resources: A review of knowledge and research needs," *Ocean & Coastal Management*, 112, pp. 25–35.

Cyprus 2015 Initiative (2011), *Solving the Cyprus Problem: Hopes and Fears*, Interpeace, https://www.undp.org/content/dam/cyprus/docs/ACT%20Publications/Civil%20Society/cyprus2015%20solving%20the%20cyprus%20problem%20en.pdf. Accessed 1 November 2020.

Dayıoğlu, Ali and Hatay, Mete (2015), "Cyprus," in Oliver Scharbrodt, Samim Akgönül, Ahmet Alibašic, Jørgen Nielsen and Egdunas Racius (eds), *Yearbook of Muslims in Europe*, volume 7, Leiden: Brill, pp. 157–73.

De Cillia, Rudolf, Reisigl, Martin and Wodak, Ruth (1999), "Discursive construction of national identities," *Discourse & Society*, 10:2, pp. 149–73.

De Cleen, Benjamin (2012), "The rhetoric of the Flemish populist radical right party Vlaams Blok/ Belang in a context of discursive struggle: A discourse-theoretical analysis," unpublished Ph.D. thesis, Brussels: Vrije Universiteit Brussel.

Dickens, Linda and Watkins, Karen (1999), "Action research: Rethinking Lewin," *Management Learning*, 30:2, pp. 127–40.

Dikomitis, Lisa (2012), *Cyprus and Its Places of Desire. Cultures of Displacement among Greek and Turkish Cypriot Refugees*, London: I. B. Tauris.

Doob, Leonard W. (1986), "Cypriot patriotism and nationalism," *Journal of Conflict Resolution*, 30:2, pp. 383–96.

Doudaki, Vaia, Boubouka, Angeliki and Tzalavras, Christos (2019), "Framing the Cypriot economic crisis: In the service of the neoliberal vision," *Journalism*, 20:2, pp. 349–68.

Downey, Anthony (2014), *Art and Politics Now*, London: Thames & Hudson.

Durrell, Lawrence (2012), *Bitter Lemons*, New York: Open Road Integrated Media.

Edensor, Tim (2002), *National Identity, Popular Culture and Everyday Life*, Oxford: Berg.

Efthymiou, Christos (2014), "Reflections on bi-communal relations in Cyprus," *openDemocracy*, https://www.opendemocracy.net/en/can-europe-make-it/reflections-on-bicommunal-relations-in-cyprus/. Accessed 1 November 2020.

Eisner, Elliot (2008), "Art and knowledge," in J. Gary Knowles and Ardra L. Cole (eds), *Handbook of the Arts in Qualitative Research*, London: Sage, pp. 3–12.

Elkins, James (ed.) (2007), *Visual Practices across the University*, Munich, Germany: Wilhelm Fink.

Ellis, Carolyn, Adams, Tony E. and Bochner, Arther P. (2010), "Autoethnography: An overview," *Forum: Qualitative Sozialforschung* ("Qualitative Social Research"), 12:1, http://www.qualitative-research.net/index.php/fqs/article/view/1589/3095. Accessed 1 November 2020.

Encyclopaedia Britannica (2014), *Britannica Book of the Year 2014*, Chicago: Author.

Errejón, Íñigo and Mouffe, Chantal (2016), *Podemos. In the Name of the People*, London: Lawrence & Wishart.

Eschle, Catherine and Maiguashca, Bice (2006), "Bridging the academic/activist divide: Feminist activism and the teaching of global politics," *Millennium: Journal of International Studies*, 35:1, pp. 119–37.

European Centre for Conflict Prevention (1999), *People Building Peace: 35 Inspiring Stories from Around the World*, The Hague: European Centre for Conflict Prevention.

European Commission (2012), *Closer to the European Union. EU Assistance to the Turkish Cypriot Community*, Brussels: European Commission.

Evangelista, Matthew (1999), *Unarmed Forces: The Transnational Movement to End the Cold War*, Ithaca: Cornell University Press.

Fahnestock, Jeanne (1986), "Accommodating science: The rhetorical life of scientific facts," *Written Communication*, 3:3, pp. 275–96.

Fals-Borda, Orlando and Rahman, Muhammad Anisur (1991), *Action and Knowledge: Breaking the Monopoly with Participative Action Research*, New York: Intermediate Technology/ Apex.

Faustmann, Hubert (2006), "Independence postponed: Cyprus 1959–1960," in Hubert Faustman and Nicos Peristianis (eds), *Britain in Cyprus: Colonialism and Post-Colonialism 1878–2006*, Mannheim and Möhnsee: Bibliopolis, pp. 413–29.

Faustmann, Hubert (2008), "The colonial legacy of division," in James Ker-Lindsay and Hubert Faustmann (eds), *The Government and Politics of Cyprus*, New York: Peter Lang, pp. 45–62.

Faustmann, Hubert and Ker-Lindsay, James (2008), "The origins and development of the Cyprus issue," in James Ker-Lindsay and Hubert Faustmann (eds), *The Government and Politics of Cyprus*, New York: Peter Lang, pp. 63–82.

Findlay, Ronald (1995), "Notes on the political economy of nationalism," in Albert Breton, Gianluggi Galeotti, Pierre Salmon and Ronald Wintrobe (eds), *Nationalism and Rationality*,

Cambridge, MA: Cambridge University Press, pp. 143–58.

Finley, Susan (2008), "Arts-based research," in J. Gary Knowles and Ardra L. Cole (eds), *Handbook of the Arts in Qualitative Research*, London: Sage, pp. 71–81.

Fisher, Ronald J. (2001), "Cyprus: The failure of mediation and the escalation of an identity-based conflict to an adversarial impasse," *Journal of Peace Research*, 38:3, pp. 307–26.

Ford, Brian J. (1992), *Images of Science: A History of Scientific Illustration*, London: British Library.

Foucher, Vincent (2011), "On the matter (and materiality) of the nation: Interpreting Casamance's unresolved separatist struggle," *Studies in Ethnicity and Nationalism*, 11:1, pp. 82–103.

Freeman, Matthew (2016), "Approaching knowledge exchange," in Matthew Freeman (ed.), *Industrial Approaches to Media: A Methodological Gateway to Industry Studies*, London: Palgrave Macmillan, pp. 153–74.

Gagnon, Michelle L. (2011), "Moving knowledge to action through dissemination and exchange," *Journal of Clinical Epidemiology*, 64, pp. 25–31.

Galatariotou, Catia (2012), "Truth, memory and the Cypriot journey towards a new past," in Rebecca Bryant and Yiannis Papadakis (eds), *Cyprus and the Politics of Memory: History, Community and Conflict*, London: I. B. Tauris, pp. 242–63.

Geertz, Clifford (1980), "Blurred genres: The refiguration of social thought," *American Scholar*, 4:2, pp. 165–79.

Geertz, Clifford (1993), *The Interpretation of Cultures: Selected Essays*, 2nd ed., London: Fontana.

Gentles, Ian (2007), "The iconography of revolution: England 1642–1649," in Ian Gentles, John Morrill and Blair Worden (eds), *Soldiers, Writers and Statesmen of the English Revolution*, Cambridge: Cambridge University Press, pp. 91–113.

Gibbs, Anna (2003), "Writing and the flesh of others," *Australian Feminist Studies*, 18:42, pp. 309–19.

Gibson, James J. (1979), *The Ecological Approach to Visual Perception*, New York: Psychology Press.

Giddens, Anthony (1985), *The Nation-State and Violence*, Cambridge: Polity Press.

Grady, John (1991), "The visual essay and sociology," *Visual Sociology*, 6:2, pp. 23–38.

Grady, John (1996), "The scope of visual sociology," *Visual Sociology*, 11:2, pp. 10–24.

Grivas-Dighenis, George (1964), *Guerrilla Warfare and EOKA's Struggle: A Politico-Military Study*, London: Longmans.

Gutberlet, Jutta, Jayme de Oliveira, Bruno and Tremblay, Crystal (2017), "Arts-based and participatory action research with recycling cooperatives," in Lonnie L. Rowell, Catherine D. Bruce, Joseph M. Shosh and Margaret M. Riel (eds), *The Palgrave International Handbook of Action Research*, New York: Palgrave Macmillan, pp. 699–715.

Güven-Lisaniler, Fatma and Rodríguez, Leopoldo (2002), "The social and economic impact of EU membership on northern Cyprus," in Thomas Diez (ed.), *The European Union and the Cyprus Conflict: Modern Conflict, Postmodern Union*, Manchester: Manchester University Press, pp. 181–202.

Haas, Gerrit (2017), *Fictocritical Strategies: Subverting Textual Practices of Meaning, Other, and Self-Formation*, Bielefeld, Germany: Transcript Verlag.

Hadjipavlou, Maria (2010), *Women and Change in Cyprus: Feminisms and Gender in Conflict*, London: I. B. Tauris.

Halbwachs, Maurice (1980), *The Collective Memory*, New York: Harper & Row Colophon Books.

Halbwachs, Maurice (1992), *On Collective Memory*, Chicago: University of Chicago Press.

Hall, Stuart (1996), "The question of cultural identity," in Stuart Hall, David Held, Don Hubert and Kenneth Thompson (eds), *Modernity: An Introduction to Modern Societies*, Oxford: Blackwell, pp. 595–634.

Hannay, David (2005), *Cyprus: The Search for a Solution*, London: I. B. Tauris.

Henderson, Lisa, Hogan, Mél, Christian, Aymar Jean and Erni, John M. (2018), "A dossier on making and doing," in Adrienne Shaw and D. Travers Scott (eds), *Interventions: Communication Research and Practice*, New York: Peter Lang, pp. 273–84.

Henn, Francis (2004), *A Business of Some Heat: The United Nations Force in Cyprus before and during the 1974 Turkish Invasion*, Barnsley: Pen & Sword.

Heraclides, Alexis and Alioğlu Çakmak, Gizem (eds) (2019), *Greece and Turkey in Conflict and Cooperation: From Europeanization to De-Europeanization*, London and New York: Routledge.

Herzfeld, Michael (2003), "Localism and the logic of nationalistic folklore: Cretan reflections," *Comparative Studies in Society and History*, 45:2, pp. 281–310.

Hockings, Paul (ed.) (1995a), *Principles of Visual Anthropology*, 2nd ed., New York: de Gruyter.

Hockings, Paul (1995b), "Conclusion: Ethnographic filming and anthropological theory," in Paul Hockings (ed.), *Principles of Visual Anthropology*, 2nd ed., New York: de Gruyter, pp. 507–29.

Holm, Gunilla (2008), "Visual research methods: Where are we and where are we going?," in Sharlene Nagy Hesse-Biber and Patricia Leavy (eds), *Handbook of Emergent Methods*, New York: Guilford, pp. 325–42.

Human Rights Watch (1999), *Landmine Monitor Report 1999: Toward a Mine-Free World*, New York: Human Rights Watch.

Hyvärinen, Matti and Muszynski, Lisa (eds) (2006), *Terror and the Arts. Artistic, Literary, and Political Interpretations of Violence from Dostoyevsky to Abu Ghraib*, Houndmills: Palgrave Macmillan.

Ioannou, Gregoris (2017), "Employment in crisis: Cyprus and the extension of precarity," in Carl-Ulrik Schierup and Martin Bak Jørgensen (eds), *Politics of Precarity: Migrant Conditions, Struggles and Experiences*, Leiden: Brill, pp. 138–59.

Ioannou, Gregoris (2020), *The Normalisation of Cyprus' Partition among Greek Cypriots, Political Economy and Political Culture in a Divided Society*, Cham, Switzerland: Springer.

Isachenko, Daria (2012), *The Making of Informal States: Statebuilding in Northern Cyprus and Transdniestria*, Basingstoke: Palgrave Macmillan.

Ivanič, Roz (1998), *Writing and Identity: The Discoursal Construction of Identity in Academic Writing*, Amsterdam, Netherlands: John Benjamins.

Jabri, Vivienne (1996), *Discourses on Violence: Conflict Analysis Reconsidered*, Manchester: Manchester University Press.

Jagodzinski, Jan and Wallin, Jason (2013), *Arts-Based Research: A Critique and a Proposal*, Rotterdam, The Netherlands: Sense Publishers.

Janesick, Valerie J. (2001), "Intuition and creativity: A pas de deux for qualitative researchers," *Qualitative Inquiry*, 7:5, pp. 531–40.

Jarldorn, Michele (2019), *Photovoice Handbook for Social Workers: Method, Practicalities and Possibilities for Social Change*, Basingstoke: Palgrave Macmillan.

Jarraud, Nicolas, Louise, Christopher and Filippou, Giorgos (2013), "The Cypriot civil society movement: A legitimate player in the peace process?," *Journal of Peacebuilding & Development*, 8:1, pp. 45–59.

Kadıoğlu, Ayşe (1998), "The paradox of Turkish nationalism and the construction of official identity," in Sylvia Kedourie (ed.), *Turkey: Identity, Democracy, Politics*, London: Frank Cass, pp. 177–93.

Kane, Anne (2000), "Narratives of nationalism: Constructing Irish national identity during the Land War, 1879–82," *National Identities*, 2:3, pp. 245–64.

Kang, Jin Woong (2012), "The disciplinary politics of antagonistic nationalism in militarized South and North Korea," *Nations and Nationalism*, 18:4, pp. 684–700.

Kansteiner, Wulf (2004), "Genealogy of a category mistake. A critical intellectual history of the cultural trauma metaphor," *Rethinking History*, 8:2, pp. 193–221.

Kara, Helen (2015), *Creative Research Methods in the Social Sciences: A Practical Guide*, Bristol: Polity Press.

Karaiskou, Vicky (2014), "Visual narrations in public space: Codifying memorials in Cyprus," *International Journal of Social, Political, and Community Agendas in the Arts*, 8, pp. 1–26.

Katsiaounis, Rolandos (1996), *Labour, Society and Politics in Cyprus during the Second Half of the Nineteenth Century*, Nicosia: Cyprus Research Center.

Katsourides, Yiannos (2014), *History of the Communist Party in Cyprus: Colonialism, Class and the Cypriot Left*, London: I. B. Tauris.

Kaygan, Harun (2012), "Material objects and everyday nationalism in design: The electric Turkish coffee maker, its design and consumption," unpublished Ph.D. thesis, University of Brighton.

Ker-Lindsay, James (2007), *Crisis and Conciliation: A Year of Rapprochement Between Greece and Turkey*, London: I. B. Tauris.

Khadka, Santosh and Lee, J. C. (eds) (2019), *Bridging the Multimodal Gap: From Theory to Practice*, Logan: Utah State University Press.

Kizilyürek, Niyazi (2003), *Milliyetcilik Kiskacinda Kibris ("Cyprus in the Stranglehold of Nationalism")*, Istanbul: Iletisim Yayinlari.

Kizilyürek, Niyazi (2005), "Modernity, nationalism, and the emergence of the ethnic conflict in Cyprus," in Giampiero Bellingeri and Matthias Kappler (eds), *Cipro Oggi*, Bologna: Casa editrice il Ponte, pp. 13–32.

Kizilyürek, Niyazi (2006), "The Turkish Cypriots from an Ottoman-Muslim community to a national community," in Hubert Faustman and Nicos Peristianis (eds), *Britain in Cyprus: Colonialism and Post-Colonialism 1878–2006*, Mannheim and Möhnsee: Bibliopolis, pp. 315–25.

Kizilyürek, Niyazi (2012), "Turkish-Cypriot left: A historical overview," in Nicos Trimikliniotis and Umut Bozkurt (eds), *Beyond a Divided Cyprus: A State and Society in Transformation*, Basingstoke: Palgrave Macmillan, pp. 169–84.

Klein, Julian (2017), "What is artistic research?," *Journal for Artistic Research*, 23 April, https://www.jar-online.net/what-artistic-research. Accessed 1 November 2020.

Kolev, Valery and Koulouri, Christina (2009), *The Balkan Wars: Workbook 3*, Thessaloniki: Center for Democracy and Reconciliation in Southeast Europe.

Koliopoulos, John S. and Veremis, Thanos M. (2010), *Modern Greece: A History Since 1821*, Malden: Wiley-Blackwell.

Kovras, Iosif (2012), "De-linkage processes and grassroots movements in transitional justice," *Cooperation and Conflict*, 47:1, pp. 88–105.

Kress, Gunther and van Leeuwen, Theo (2001), *Multimodal Discourse: The Modes and Media of Contemporary Communication*, London: Arnold.

Kristeva, Julia (1991), *Strangers to Ourselves*, Hemel Hempstead: Harvester/Wheatsheaf.

Kyriakides, Klearchos A. (2014), "The rule of law," in James Ker-Lindsay (ed.), *Resolving Cyprus: New Approaches to Conflict Resolution*, London: I. B. Tauris, pp. 158–69.

Lacher, Hannes and Kaymak, Erol (2005), "Transforming identities: Beyond the politics of non-settlement in North Cyprus," *Mediterranean Politics*, 10:2, pp. 147–66.

Laclau, Ernesto and Mouffe, Chantal (1985), *Hegemony and Socialist Strategy: Towards a Radical Democratic Politics*, London: Verso.

Lapum, Jennifer L. (2018), "Installation art: The voyage never ends," in Patricia Leavy (ed.), *Handbook of Arts-Based Research*, New York: Guilford, pp. 377–95.

Lauer, Claire (2012), "What's in a name? The anatomy of defining new/multi/modal/digital/media texts," *Kairos*, 17:1, http://kairos.technorhetoric.net/17.1/inventio/lauer/index.html. Accessed 1 November 2020.

Leavis, Frank R. (2013), *Two Cultures? The Significance of C. P. Snow*, Cambridge: Cambridge University Press.

Leavy, Patricia (2011), *Low-Fat Love*, Rotterdam, The Netherlands: Sense Publishers.

Leavy, Patricia (2015), *Method Meets Art: Arts-Based Research Practice*, 2nd ed., London: Guilford.

Lederach, John Paul (2003), *The Little Book of Conflict Transformation*, Intercourse, PA: Good Books.

Lederach, John Paul (2005), *The Moral Imagination. The Art and Soul of Building Peace*, Oxford: Oxford University Press.

Lemke, Jay (1998), "Multiplying meaning: Visual and verbal semiotics in scientific text," in James R. Martin and Robert Veel (eds), *Reading Science: Critical and Functional Perspectives on Discourses of Science*, London: Routledge, pp. 87–113.

Lewis, Jeff (2008), *Cultural Studies: The Basics*, 2nd ed., London: Sage.

Liebmann, Marian (1996), *Arts Approaches to Conflict*, London: Jessica Kingsley.

Life & Peace Institute (2014), *Participatory Action Research for Conflict Transformation: A Handbook Combining Inquiry, Dialogue and Collaboration*, Uppsala, Sweden: Life & Peace Institute.

Life & Peace Institute (2016), *Participatory Action Research (PAR) as a Tool for Transforming Conflict. A Case Study from South Central Somalia*, Uppsala, Sweden: Life & Peace Institute.

Literat, Ioana, Conover, Anna, Herbert-Wasson, Elizabeth, Page, Karen Kirsch, Riina-Ferrie, Joseph, Stephens, Rachael, Thanapornsangsuth, Sawaros and Vasudevan, Lalitha (2018), "Toward multimodal inquiry: Opportunities, challenges and implications of multimodality for research and scholarship," *Higher Education Research & Development*, 37:3, pp. 565–78.

Loizides, Neophytos G. (2007), "Ethnic nationalism and adaptation in Cyprus," *International Studies Perspectives*, 8, pp. 172–89.

Loveless, Natalie S. (2015), "Towards a manifesto on research-creation," *RACAR: Revue d'art Canadienne/Canadian Art Review*, 40:1, pp. 52–54.

Lutkewitte, Claire (2013), *Multimodal Composition: A Critical Sourcebook*, Boston, MA: Bedford/St. Martin's.

Lyotard, Jean-François (1984), *The Postmodern Condition: A Report on Knowledge*, Manchester: Manchester University Press.

Lytras, Eleni and Psaltis, Charis (2011), *Formerly Mixed Villages in Cyprus: Representations of the Past, Present and Future*, Nicosia: Association for Historical Dialogue and Research.

Mallinson, William (2005), *Cyprus: A Modern History*, London: I. B. Tauris.

Markides, Diana (2006), "Cyprus 1878–1925: Ambiguities and uncertainties," in Hubert Faustman and Nicos Peristianis (eds), *Britain in Cyprus: Colonialism and Post-Colonialism 1878–2006*, Mannheim and Möhnsee: Bibliopolis, pp. 19–33.

Markides, Diana (2019), *The Cyprus Tribute and Geopolitics in the Levant, 1875–1960*, Cham, Switzerland: Springer.

Matschke, Christina, Moskaliuk, Johannes and Cress, Ulrike (2012), "Knowledge exchange using Web 2.0 technologies in NGOs," *Journal of Knowledge Management*, 16:1, pp. 159–76.

Mavratsas, Caesar V. (1997), "The ideological contest between Greek-Cypriot nationalism and Cypriotism 1974–1995: Politics, social memory and identity," *Ethnic and Racial Studies*, 20:4, pp. 717–37.

McDonald, Maryon (1993), "The construction of difference: An anthropological approach to stereotypes," in Sharon Macdonald (ed.), *Inside European Identities: Ethnography in Western Europe*, Oxford: Berg, pp. 219–36.

McIntyre, Alice (2000), "Constructing meaning about violence, school, and community: Participatory action research with urban youth," *Urban Review*, 32:2, pp. 123–54.

McPherson, Tara (2009), "Introduction: Media studies and the digital humanities," *Cinema Journal*, 48:2, pp. 119–23.

Mead, Margaret (1995), "Visual anthropology in a discipline of words," in Paul Hockings (ed.), *Principles of Visual Anthropology*, 2nd ed., New York: de Gruyter, pp. 3–10.

Mesch, Claudia (2013), *Art and Politics: A Small History of Art for Social Change Since 1955*, London: I. B. Tauris.

Meyer, Morgan (2010), "The rise of the knowledge broker," *Science Communication*, 32:1, pp. 118–27.

Michael, Michális S. and Vural, Yücel (eds.) (2018), *Cyprus and the Roadmap for Peace: A Critical Interrogation of the Conflict*, Cheltenham, England: Edward Elgar.

Michael, Michalis Stavrou (2011), *Resolving the Cyprus Conflict*, Basingstoke: Palgrave Macmillan.

Mirbagheri, Farid (2010), *Historical Dictionary of Cyprus*, Lanham: Scarecrow Press.

Mitchell, Helen (2006), "Knowledge sharing: The value of story telling," *International Journal of Organisational Behaviour*, 9:5, pp. 632–41.

Mitchell, William J. T. (1994), *Picture Theory: Essays on Verbal and Visual Representation*, Chicago, IL: University of Chicago Press.

Moncaster, Alice, Hinds, Di, Cruickshank, Heather, Guthrie, Peter M., Crishna, Naeeda, Baker, Keith, Beckmann, Kate and Jowitt, Paul W. (2010), "Knowledge exchange between academia and industry," *Proceedings of the Institution of Civil Engineers – Engineering Sustainability*, 163:3, pp. 167–74.

Morag, Nadav (2004), "Cyprus and the clash of Greek and Turkish nationalisms," *Nationalism and Ethnic Politics*, 10:4, pp. 595–624.

Morgan, Tabitha (2010), *Sweet and Bitter Island: A History of the British in Cyprus*, London: I. B. Tauris.

Mouffe, Chantal (1996), "Deconstruction, pragmatism and the politics of democracy," in Simon Critchley and Chantal Mouffe (eds), *Deconstruction and Pragmatism*, London and New York: Routledge, pp. 1–12.

Mouffe, Chantal (1999), "Deliberative democracy or agonistic pluralism?," *Social Research*, 66:3, pp. 745–58.

Mouffe, Chantal (2005), *On the Political*, London: Routledge.

Mouffe, Chantal (2013a), *Agonistics: Thinking the World Politically*, London: Verso.

Mouffe, Chantal (2013b), "Politics and passions: The stakes of democracy," in James Martin (ed.), *Chantal Mouffe: Hegemony, Radical Democracy and the Political*, London: Routledge, pp. 181–90.

Müllerleile, Andreas (2014), "European studies and public engagement: A conceptual toolbox," *Journal of Contemporary European Research*, 10:4, pp. 505–17.

Murdock, Alex, Shariff, Razia and Wilding, Karl (2013), "Knowledge exchange between academia and the third sector," *Evidence & Policy*, 9:3, pp. 419–30.

Murray, Joddy (2009), *Non-Discursive Rhetoric: Image and Affect in Multimodal Composition*, Albany, NY: State University of New York Press.

Nadel-Klein, Jane (1991), "Reweaving the fringe: Localism, tradition, and representation in British ethnography," *American Ethnologist*, 18:3, pp. 500–17.

Navaro-Yashin, Yael (2012), *The Make-Believe Space: Affective Geography in a Postwar Polity*, Durham and London: Duke University Press.

Nevzat, Altay (2005), "Nationalism amongst the Turks of Cyprus: The First Wave," unpublished Ph.D. thesis, Oulu: University of Oulu.

Nome, Martin Austvoll (2013), "When do commitment problems not cause war? Turkey and Cyprus, 1964 versus 1974," *International Area Studies Review*, 16:1, pp. 50–73.

Norman, Don (1988), *The Design of Everyday Things*, New York: Basic Books.

Norval, Aletta J. (1996), *Deconstructing Apartheid Discourse*, London: Verso.

Özgür, Özdemir A. (1995), "In memory of Dr. Ihsan Ali," in Ihsan Ali Foundation (ed.), *In Memory of Dr. Ihsan Ali*, Nicosia: Ihsan Ali Foundation, pp. 5–6.

Özkirimli, Umut (2010), *Theories of Nationalism. A Critical Introduction*, 2nd ed., Basingstoke: Palgrave Macmillan.

Panayiotou, Andreas (2012), "Hegemony, permissible public discourse and lower class political culture," in Rebecca Bryant and Yiannis Papadakis (eds), *Cyprus and the Politics of Memory: History, Community and Conflict*, London: I. B. Tauris, pp. 71–93.

Papadakis, Yiannis (1997), "Pyla: A mixed borderline village under UN supervision in Cyprus," *International*

Journal on Minority and Human Rights, 4, pp. 353–72.

Papadakis, Yiannis (1998), "Greek Cypriot narratives of history and collective identity: Nationalism as a contested process," *American Ethnologist*, 25:2, pp. 149–65.

Papadakis, Yiannis (2005), *Echoes from the Dead Zone: Across the Cyprus Divide*, London and New York: I. B. Tauris.

Papadakis, Yiannis (2006), "Toward an anthropology of ethnic autism," in Yiannis Papadakis, Nicos Peristianis and Gisela Welz (eds), *Divided Cyprus: Modernity, History, and an Island in Conflict*, Bloomington: Indiana University Press, pp. 66–83.

Papallas, Andreas (2016), "Urban rapprochement tactics: Stitching divided Nicosia," unpublished M.Phil. thesis, Cambridge: University of Cambridge.

Papapolyviou, Petros (1997), *Η Κύπρος και οι Βαλκανικοί Πόλεμοι. Συμβολή στην Ιστορία του Κυπριακού Εθελοντισμού* ("Cyprus and the Balkan Wars. Contribution to the History of Cypriot Volunteering"), Nicosia: Cyprus Research Center.

Parla, Taha and Davison, Andrew (2004), *Corporatist Ideology in Kemalist Turkey: Progress or Order?*, Syracuse: Syracuse University Press.

Patrick, Richard A. (1976), *Political Geography and the Cyprus Conflict, 1963–1971*, Ontario: Department of Geography, University of Waterloo.

Pavlou, Pavlos (1993), "The semantic adaptation of Turkish loanwords in the Greek Cypriotic dialect," Irene Philippaki-Warburton, Katerina Nicolaidis, and Maria Sifianou (eds.), *Themes in Greek Linguistics: Papers from the First International Conference on Greek Linguistics, Reading, September 1993*, Amsterdam: John Benjamins, pp. 443–48.

Pink, Sarah (2004), "Introduction: Situating visual research," in Sarah Pink, László Kürti and Ana Isabel Afonso (eds), *Working Images: Visual Research and Representation in Ethnography*, London: Routledge, pp. 1–10.

Polat, Necati (2002), "Self-determination, violence, modernity. The case of the Turkish Cypriots," in Thomas Diez (ed.), *The European Union and the Cyprus Conflict: Modern Conflict, Postmodern Union*, Manchester: Manchester University Press, pp. 98–116.

Powell, Pegeen Reichert (ed.) (2020), *Writing Changes: Alphabetic Text and Multimodal Composition*, New York: Modern Language Association of America.

Press and Information Office for the Statistical Service (2015), *Cyprus in Figures, 2015 edition*, Nicosia: Press and Information Office.

Ragsdale, J. Donald and Brandau-Brown, Frances E. (2011), "Monuments and memorials: The synthesis of art and architecture," in J. Donald Ragsdale (ed.), *Compelling Form: Architecture as Visual Persuasion*, Newcastle upon Tyne: Cambridge Scholars, pp. 265–87.

Ram, Moriel (2015), "Colonial conquests and the politics of normalization: The case of the Golan Heights and Northern Cyprus," *Political Geography*, 47, pp. 21–32.

Reason, Peter and Bradbury, Hilary (2001), *Handbook of Action Research: Participative Inquiry and Practice*, London: Sage.

Reddaway, John (1986), *The British Connection with Cyprus since Independence*, Oxford: University Printing House.

Reid, Gwendolynne, Snead, Robin, Pettiway, Keon and Simoneaux, Brent (2016), "Multimodal communication in the university: Surveying faculty across disciplines," *Across the Disciplines: A Journal of Language, Learning and Academic Writing*, https://wac.colostate.edu/atd/articles/reidetal2016.cfm. Accessed 1 November 2020.

Richmond, Oliver P. (1998), *Mediating in Cyprus: The Cypriot Communities and the United Nations*, London: Routledge.

Richmond, Oliver P. (1999), "Ethno-nationalism, sovereignty and negotiating positions in the Cyprus conflict: Obstacles to a settlement," *Middle Eastern Studies*, 35:3, pp. 42–63.

Roudometof, Victor (2009), "Le Christianisme Orthodoxe au Sein de la République de Chypre: Développement

Institutionnel et Attitudes Religieuses" ("Orthodox Christianity in the Republic of Cyprus: Institutional development and religious attitudes"), *Social Compass*, 56:1, pp. 60–68.

Routledge, Paul (1996), "The third space as critical engagement," *Antipode*, 28:4, pp. 399–419.

Saldaña, Johnny (2011), *Ethnotheatre: Research from Page to Stage*, Walnut Creek, CA: Left Coast.

Saldaña, Johnny (ed.) (2005), *Ethnodrama: An Anthology of Reality Theatre*, Walnut Creek, CA: AltaMira.

Sant Cassia, Paul (2005), *Bodies of Evidence: Burial, Memory and the Recovery of Missing Persons in Cyprus*, New York: Berghahn Books.

Schiele, Bernard, Claessens, Michel and Shi, Shunke (2012), "Introduction," in Bernard Schiele, Michel Claessens and Shunke Shi (eds), *Science Communication in the World: Practices, Theories and Trends*, Dordrecht: Springer, pp. xxiii–xxv.

Scott, Julie (2013), "'Properly playing': Casinos, blackjack and cultural intimacy in Cyprus," in Rebecca Cassidy, Andrea Pisac and Claire Loussouarn (eds), *Qualitative Research in Gambling: Exploring the Production and Consumption of Risk*, London: Routledge, pp. 125–39.

Segal, Joes (2016), *Art and Politics: Between Purity and Propaganda*, Amsterdam: Amsterdam University Press.

Selfe, Cynthia (ed.) (2007), *Multimodal Composition: Resources for Teachers*, Cresskill, NJ: Hampton Press.

Shipka, Jody (2011), *Toward a Composition Made Whole*, Pittsburgh, PA: University of Pittsburgh Press.

Silverman, David (2006), *Interpreting Qualitative Data: Methods for Analyzing Talk, Text and Interaction*, 3rd ed., London: Sage.

Sinclair, Tom (2006), "Ihsan Ali: A historian's view," in Ihsan Ali Foundation (ed.), *Dr. Ihsan Ali's Life and Deeds*, Nicosia: Ihsan Ali Foundation, pp. 14–18.

Sinner, Anita (2014), "Flight of the 'artademics': Scholarly gentrification and conceptual+art discourses," *Visual Arts Research*, 40:1, pp. 124–26.

Smith, Anthony D. (1995), *Nations and Nationalism in a Global Era*, Cambridge: Polity Press.

Smith, Anthony D. (1998), *Nationalism and Modernism: A Critical Survey of Recent Theories of Nations and Nationalism*, London: Routledge.

Snow, Charles P. (1998), *The Two Cultures*, Cambridge: Cambridge University Press.

Soulioti, Stella (2006), *Fettered Independence: Cyprus, 1878–1964. Volume One: The Narrative*, Minnesota: University of Minnesota.

Spryridakis, Constantinos (1974), *A Brief History of Cyprus*, Nicosia: Zavallis.

Stearns, Monteagle (1992), *Entangled Allies: U.S. Policy Toward Greece, Turkey, and Cyprus*, New York: Council on Foreign Relations.

Stefanidis, Ioannis D. (1999), *Isle of Discord. Nationalism, Imperialism and the Making of the Cyprus Problem*, New York: New York University Press.

Sztompka, Piotr (2000), "Cultural trauma: The other face of social change," *European Journal of Social Theory*, 3, pp. 449–66.

Takayoshi, Pamela and Selfe, Cynthia (2007), "Thinking about multimodality," in Cynthia Selfe (ed.), *Multimodal Composition: Resources for Teachers*, Cresskill, NJ: Hampton Press, pp. 1–12.

Talmon, Stefan (2001), "The Cyprus question before the European Court of Justice," *European Journal of International Law*, 4, pp. 727–50.

Tesser, Lynn (2013), *Ethnic Cleansing and the European Union: An Interdisciplinary Approach to Security, Memory and Ethnography*, Basingstoke: Palgrave Macmillan.

Themistocleous, Christiana (2015), "Digital code-switching between Cypriot and standard Greek: Performance and identity play online," *International Journal of Bilingualism*, 19:3, pp. 282–97.

Thorndike–Breeze, Rebecca, Block, Aaron and Brown, Kara Mae (2019), "Entering the multiverse: Using comics to experiment with multimodality, multigenres and multiliteracies," in Santosh Khadka and J. C. Lee (eds), *Bridging the Multimodal Gap: From*

Theory to Practice, Logan, UT: Utah State University Press, pp. 159–81.

Trench, Brian and Bucchi, Massimiano (2010), "Science communication: An emerging discipline," *Journal of Science Communication*, 9:3, https://doi.org/10.22323/2.09030303. Accessed 1 November 2020.

Triga, Vasiliki, Mendez, Fernando and Djouvas, Constantinos (2019), "Post-crisis political normalisation? The 2018 presidential elections in the Republic of Cyprus," *South European Society and Politics*, 24:1, pp. 103–27.

Trimikliniotis, Nicos (2012), "The Cyprus problem and the imperial games in the hydrocarbon era: From a 'place of arms' to an energy player?," in Nicos Trimikliniotis and Umut Bozkurt (eds), *Beyond a Divided Cyprus: A State and Society in Transformation*, Basingstoke: Palgrave Macmillan, pp. 23–46.

Tringides, Orestis (2013), "The role of mass media in the settlement of the Cyprus problem," in Mensur Akgün (ed.), *Managing Intractable Conflicts: Lessons from Moldova and Cyprus*, Istanbul: GPoT, pp. 39–48.

TRNC (1987), *North Cyprus Almanack*, London: Rustem & Brother.

Trudgill, Peter and Schreier, Daniel (2006), "Griechenland und Zypern" ("Greece and Cyprus"), in Ulrich Ammon, Norbert Dittmar, Klaus J. Mattheier and Peter Trudgill (eds), *Soziolinguistik: Ein internationals Handbuch zur Wissenschaft von Sprache und Gesellschaft* ("Sociolinguistics: An International Handbook of the Science of Language and Society"), second completely revised and extended edition, Volume 3, Berlin: Walter de Gruyter, pp. 1881–88.

Tyler, Stephen A. (1986), "Post-modern ethnography: From document of the occult to occult document," in James Clifford and George E. Marcus (eds), *Writing Culture: The Poetics and Politics of Ethnography*, Berkeley, CA: University of California Press, pp. 122–40.

Tziarras, Zēnōnas (2019), *The New Geopolitics of the Eastern Mediterranean: Trilateral Partnerships and Regional Security*, Nicosia: PRIO Cyprus Centre.

Ungerleider, John (1999), "My country is cut in two: Music and poetry build bi-communal peace," *People Building Peace*, The Hague: European Centre for Conflict Prevention, http://artonconflict.blogspot.fi/2011/03/music-and-poetry-build-bi-communal.html. Accessed 1 November 2020.

UNICEF (2015), *Knowledge Exchange Toolbox: Group Methods for Sharing, Discovery and Co-Creation*, New York: UNICEF.

Uslu, Nasuh (2003), *The Cyprus Question as an Issue of Turkish Foreign Policy and Turkish-American Relations, 1959–2003*, New York: Nova.

van den Berghe, Pierre (2001), "Sociobiological theory of nationalism," in Athena S. Leoussi (ed.), *Encyclopedia of Nationalism*, New Brunswick, Canada: Transaction, pp. 273–79.

Varnava, Andrekos (2009), *British Imperialism in Cyprus, 1878–1915*, Manchester: Manchester University Press.

Volkan, Vamik (1979), *Cyprus: War and Adaption*, Charlottesville: University of Virginia Press.

Vural, Yücel and Rustemli, Ahmet (2006), "Identity fluctuations in the Turkish Cypriot community," *Mediterranean Politics*, 11:3, pp. 329–48.

Wallensteen, Peter (2009), "The strengths and limits of academic diplomacy: The case of Bougainville," in Karin Aggestam and Magnus Jerneck (eds), *Diplomacy in Theory and Practice*, Malmö, Sweden: Liber, pp. 258–81.

Weber, Max (1991), *From Max Weber: Essays in Sociology*, New York: Psychology Press.

Wodiczko, Krzysztof (2012), *The Abolition of War*, London: Black Dog.

Wodiczko, Krzysztof (2014), "The transformative avant-garde," *Third Text*, 28:2, pp. 111–22.

Wysocki, Rick, Udelson, Jon, Ray, Caitlin E., Newman, Jessica S. B., Matravers, Laura Sceniak, Kumari, Ashanka, Gordon, Layne M. P., Scott, Khirsten L., Day, Michelle, Baumann, Michael, Alvarez, Sara P. and DeVoss, Dànielle Nicole (2019), "On multimodality: A manifesto," in Santosh Khadka and J. C. Lee (eds),

Bridging the Multimodal Gap: From Theory to Practice, Logan, UT: Utah State University Press, pp. 17–29.

Yakinthou, Christalla (2009), "Consociational democracy and Cyprus: The house that Annan built?," in Andrekos Varnava and Hubert Faustmann (eds), *Reunifying Cyprus. The Annan Plan and Beyond*, London: I. B. Tauris, pp. 25–39.

Yeşilada, Birol (2009), "Islam and the Turkish Cypriots," *Social Compass*, 56:1, pp. 49–59.

Yin, Robert K. (1994), *Case Study Research: Design and Methods*, Beverly Hills, CA: Sage.

Zembylas, Michalinos (2015), *Emotion and Traumatic Conflict: Reclaiming Healing in Education*, Oxford: Oxford University Press.

Zembylas, Michalinos, Charalambous, Constadina and Charalambous, Panayiota (2016), *Peace Education in a Conflict-Affected Society*, Cambridge: Cambridge University Press.

Žižek, Slavoj (1993), *Tarrying with the Negative: Kant, Hegel, and the Critique of Ideology*, Durham and London: Duke University Press.